KNOTS
AND THEIR UNTYING

KNOTS
AND THEIR UNTYING

Essays on Psychological Dilemmas

Ann Belford Ulanov

Spring Journal Books

Publications in Jungian Psychology
www.springjournalandbooks.com

Published by:
Spring Journal, Inc.
New Orleans, Louisiana, USA
Website: www.springjournalandbooks.com

Cover image by Barry Ulanov.

Editorial and production assistance:
Drummond Books, drummondbooks@gmail.com
Cover design, typography, and layout:
Northern Graphic Design & Publishing
info@ncarto.com

Text printed on acid-free paper

Library of Congress Cataloging-in-Publication Data Pending

DEDICATION

In gratitude to my students of forty-seven years—all the knots we worked on together!

ACKNOWLEDGEMENTS

My warm thanks to Siobhan Drummond for her great skills and her graciousness as copy editor, and to Nancy Cater for her graciousness as publisher.

CONTENTS

INTRODUCTION

K nots are human problems that vex us. They appear insoluble. We stub our toe on them, stumble over them every time we try to force a solution. Hence they can make us lose heart, even lead to despair. They are knots of mourning when we lose someone we love, or experience a grave loss of part of ourselves, or misplace a precious object that bears to us the "freshness of instinct"—that life is alive, good, evoking gladness (see the sketch by that name in Matisse 1983, 101). Mourning demands our careful untying of every knot of connection to what we lost. Then we must feel all the way down the experience of this loss, how much this other meant to us, and bear the full weight of the lost lived tie to the other. Then, slowly, we must tie up the threads of loss and of our connection to this other into our present life. Doing one or two knots this way makes us feel immensely better, gives us fresh energy. Until we realize there are many such knots in this connection, maybe thousands, demanding our attention.

The knots I write of here demand the same patient suffering and work. They present entanglements with our complexes that open to human problems, not ours alone. Hence they are not solvable with a fix-it approach. But they do yield to an untangling, a sorting, putting the parts in each of their places. An analysand's dream comes to mind: she sees from above an open box with compartments; her task is to put things in their due place. I was reminded of the Zohar's notion of goodness: everything is in its rightful place. We see the knot in its larger setting as part of a whole picture, without which the picture is not complete.

Knots are terrible, and we can break our fingernails trying to loosen them. They are our very own, peculiar to our personality and our time in social and cultural history, expressing what remains unresolved, fractious, painful. But they can also function like handholds and footholds composing, we discover, the ladder for our descent into what is undeveloped in us and requires our attention. We are not just dropped flailing into chaos, or if we are, we find something to grasp that punctuates our fall, orienting us in our suffering. Knots of trouble that recur or persist can also function as handholds to pull ourselves up. Placing our feet on a familiar entanglement gives us purchase to come up for air, see the wider picture, and recognize that we have traversed this descent and ascent before. Instead of compulsive repetition we see that we return each time to work still another strand free, or we go back to find something we missed, necessary to what is revealing itself as our path which we must claim.

In this way the string of knots we encounter becomes our ladder, a small version of Jacob's, our means of traversing between human and divine, below and above. Our particular knots form a ladder down to the taproot whose life energy is blocked and back up with new vision and out into the world. Working on each knot we are lowered into dark confusion and loss, into new energies that can spurt fire! Or we struggle in terrifying blankness of nowhere and nothing, going neither up nor down but stuck in place. But right there we see how the *aqua gratia* springs up from this hole of hell and humiliation we have landed in, becoming visible for all and multiplying in others' lives, however it has irrigated our own.

I invite you to read the essays in any order you choose. Each is located in a specific time and place in relation to the people to whom I was speaking. They mark as well authors with whom I was in conversation and the analysands' clinical materials that captured my attention at the time. The essays are presented here in their original form and do not reflect what I have developed since their dates of composition. Even though written separately over a span of years, themes emerge that tie them together, principally of knots that trouble us.

The essays are divided into four sections. The first addresses the sufferings such knots inflict, and the first essay I wrote especially for this volume. It speaks to the anguish of being forgotten and the rage such anguish inspires to express and to counteract being ignored. But this knot here, at the beginning, does not get untied, nor is it even considered, so nothing is learned from its event. It is important to note that this can happen. The second essay deals with the horrors of trauma that threaten to obliterate our very existence as a subject in our own right which can tie us up tight for years. Pathways, both psychological and spiritual, emerge through this agony. These themes of suffering and their release reappear in the penultimate essay. It may surprise the reader that the third essay is included under the topic of suffering. But it belongs here, I believe, for individuation is a lifelong process confronting us with dangerous tasks as well as boons of happiness.

The second section focuses on knots that occur in our bodies, often forgotten or downplayed in matters psychic, which will not work as our body is our self in definite form and place and time. Whatever illuminations or darkenings come our way, they come in embodied forms. They can shock like lightning and point to the source of such sudden flashes. The fourth essay takes up the body-based illuminations and numinous events within our literal physical existence as well as subtle body experiences and body transformed. I give particular emphasis in this essay to the feminine body and symbol. The fifth essay addresses our inferior function and takes seriously that it really is inferior, bringing the whole unconscious with it. Its knots take the forms of crises, panics, limitations, yet they can also yield radically new energies and gifts so valuable Jung calls them the treasure hard to attain. The sixth essay addresses a knotty problem that turns up in analysis when eros ignites for the analytical couple. Instead of the customary focus on the analysand's transference, I ask about eros in the analyst that influences what can and cannot come up in the analytical work

The third section looks behind the scenes to the knots found there that inform and bedevil work with psyche. The seventh essay explores what knots of personal problems and potentials of psyche form the analyst's vocation. The eighth essay speaks to painful knots in analytical societies, splitting them into opposing factions with seemingly insurmountable loss of cordiality, forestalling lively discussion of differences on theoretical points. Underlying the knot are questions of when such splits are repudiation and when they are differentiation and whether they are always both. I take up the discoveries we make in such splits and what might be our contribution as analysts to the splits between nations, tribes, religions, and political parties. The ninth essay muses on a knot that is never untied and should not be: the paradox of the Many and the One, belonging together, informing each other. Yet pulling out the strands of each lays bare psychological issues and insights into the whole they symbolize.

The final section raises pivotal issues in the intertwining of psyche, spirituality, and religion. The tenth essay dares to ask about a spiritual subject, recognized as beyond as well as in and through psyche. Depth psychology is increasingly caught up in what heals and the ineffable source of such liberation, even using religious vocabulary to describe its effects on us, yet shying away from the referent. The eleventh essay takes up a religious problem and uses psyche to see our way into untying the knot when forgiveness for violence inflicted does not happen. The twelfth essay focuses on the analytical experience of the powerful symbolism connected with the ancient and contemporary city of Jerusalem. Thought to represent the *axis mundi*, it symbolizes the space in between heaven and earth, where we wrestle with all our knots and their untying, building our relation between human and divine.

Ann Belford Ulanov
Woodbury, Connecticut, and New York City, 2013

SUFFERINGS

THE 13ᵀᴴ FAIRY

This first paper deals with a knot that does not get untied and shows us how such entanglements can go on existing in us for years, sometimes a lifetime. The result is a life half lived or a suspended life. Time passing may inexplicably lead to a sudden clearing when we are able to take up our life again, but in this predicament we are helpless to bring about any change. Endurance counts but consciousness does not intercede, an omission that underlines how precious consciousness is. It can make the difference between living as if asleep and waking up to full use and participation in being alive.

The Story

We are all familiar with the fairy tale "Sleeping Beauty." It tells of a king and queen yearning for a child, a wish that is not fulfilled for a long time. Then a frog appears in the queen's bath foretelling the arrival of a child. A beautiful daughter is born. Overjoyed, the king orders a magnificent celebration. In this version of the tale, the king has only twelve golden plates, and so he invites twelve fairy godmothers (called Wise Women) as honored guests who will bestow their generous blessings on this new daughter (Grimm 2011, 172). But at the dinner something terrible happens. The 13th fairy swoops in, furious at being forgotten, insulted at being left out, and curses the child, saying she will prick her finger on a spindle on her fifteenth birthday and die. Everyone is horrified. Fortunately the twelfth fairy godmother has yet to give her blessing, and she softens the curse, saying the daughter will not die but fall asleep for a hundred years.

The king orders all spindles in the kingdom burned, but on the day of the princess's fifteenth birthday, both parents are oddly absent from the palace. Wandering alone through its many rooms, the daughter discovers a small locked chamber high up in the tower. Turning the key in the door, it springs open, and there she finds an old woman spinning flax. She asks what is that gaily turning thing and takes the spindle in her hand. It pricks her finger, and she falls into a deathless sleep, taking the whole palace and everyone and everything in it with her—the horses in their stables, the dogs barking, the courtiers, the food cooking, the fire blazing. The curse is fulfilled.

A hedge of briars grows up around the palace, concealing it. When princes come to the castle to rescue the maiden, they are impaled on the thorns and die. Finally a prince decides he too will risk death and try to penetrate the briar hedge. Just then the hundred years are up. The thorns part, roses bloom; he reaches the castle, the princess awakes as he bends to kiss her, and with her the whole castle revives and returns to living. The wedding of the new royal couple is celebrated, and all live happily ever after.

My focus here is specifically on the 13th fairy godmother and on all that she implies about our psyche and its tasks. As von Franz indicates, this tale of godmothers, whom she likens to goddesses, belongs to the larger theme of the disappearing goddess, but this daughter has a dozen fairy godmothers present to give their blessings (von Franz 1972, 20). Nonetheless, the girl does not escape the revenge of the humiliated 13th fairy godmother, and though not killed on her fifteenth birthday, the girl falls asleep for a century and the 13th fairy disappears once again. What is happening here?

A Personal Level

Responding to the fairy tale on a personal level, we can understand the 13th fairy to represent a part of psyche fallen out of both individual and collective consciousness. No one remembers her or thinks to invite her to the festive dinner. She personifies the plight of vanishing as the deep hurt and outrage of the forgotten one, the one not noticed, the one ignored, the one not respected enough to be considered for an invitation, or welcomed when she blows in. The number of gold plates in the table setting takes precedence over her existence. There are not enough plates; hence she is excluded.

No sisterly relationship between her and the other godmothers exists, nor do the king and queen, representing the reigning conscious attitude, give adequate respect for her sphere of existence. No thought of how she might feel at being set aside occurs. The value of her presence is subsumed under proper protocol: her admittance would disarrange the appearance of the table to honor the remarkable birth of this child, ending a long period of barrenness and unfulfilled desire for new life. The new arrives as specifically feminine and celebrated by the whole community, and persona; how it looks, trumps proper acknowledgment of the 13th fairy's existence along with the other fairy godmothers.

Our persona is a complex formed around how we see ourselves in others' eyes, how we see we are seen by the public. Persona comprises a larger notion than is operating in this tale. Here it shrinks to our public mask, the right table decoration according to collective conscious standards. Conventionality reigns. But at its best, persona is how we see ourselves being seen by others. This includes awareness of the value of conventional mores and decorum, but it also makes space for us to try on different and varying images of how we desire to be seen by others and to see ourselves. We imagine assuming this role or that role, compare what we expect with how others actually respond to how we appear to them. Persona embraces an interior space for our experimentation and extends intersubjective space between us and others for flexible adaptation. In this tale persona contracts to what the king and queen, symbolizing the ruling attitude, identify with as collectively required, a conventional ideal.

What is left out? The 13th fairy! She storms in—furious, vengeful, ready to aim her wrath at the king and queen's offense. She is ready to kill. If we understand the goddess-godmother to represent archetypal content pertaining to feminine wisdom that can become a core of a personal complex as well as represent a living element in the collective unconscious, we can understand the 13th fairy to personify a natural psychic pattern of behavior that is omitted because forgotten. The king and queen are not portrayed as intentionally hurting her, let alone engaging in active sadism. Rather, they seem captive to a stereotypical ideal about what is proper and just do not think about what or whom conventionality excludes. But the 13th fairy, outraged at being so carelessly disregarded, acts as if they had intentionally scorned her, rejected her worth, and she wants them to pay. She is murderous and displays all the lethal and cursing intents of the hag figure, living on the borders of society, cooking up plots and potions to punish anyone who disrespects her (Ulanov and Ulanov 1987, chap. 4). She shows the opposite pole of the loving godmothers who bestow all the positive blessings on the child. The 13th fairy shows the negative pole of the feminine—ruthless, destructive, sinister.

Her rage knows no check; it prompts her to destroy the new feminine, and with cunning, because it is not this instant the child must die, but fifteen years from now, after the child becomes known and loved in a relation full of cherished moments that then can only be mourned. The forgotten godmother inflicts the pain of loss as payment for the loss of her, for not being held in their minds. Even further, the experience of the loss of her is not recognized. No apologies are given her nor is room made for her place at the table. So we find loss of experience of loss piled on top of losing her by forgetting her. Nothing is mourned or welcomed again because this godmother is not remembered. And has she forgotten herself? Where has she been and where does she retreat to, disappearing once again? All we see is her wrath.

Beneath this fury lies the 13th fairy's deeply hurt feelings. But what shows is vengeance. She wants the king and queen to suffer deep hurt just as she has, to experience unbearable loss, and for the kingdom to lose its new feminine life represented by the miraculously born little girl. The 13th fairy I take to represent on a personal level an abyss of hurt feelings for not being loved. But that experience of loss is itself lost, buried under fury and revenge. This makes for a knot not yet untied.

When this pattern becomes our personal complex our ego is easily overwhelmed. It is hard to reach the agony that drives the surface destructiveness. What shows are recriminations, reproaches, accusations against others who have behaved thoughtlessly, unkindly, dismissively. The wish for love and the heartbreak for not receiving it, the loss of not continuing to exist in others' minds, is hidden, maybe even from the 13th fairy herself. For lurking in the reproach is a secret appeal for love mixed in with a deep wound at being treated in an unloving way, indeed, not noticed, not counted as worth attention. Von Franz surmises that evil springs from not dealing with such an abyss of pain (von Franz 1972, 27). We are susceptible to this kind of hurt from being overlooked, not treated with respectful attention. For women, it is just here that animus opinions and right rules jump in, armored arguing and rigid positions are taken up which breed destructiveness toward others and attack against self. What is not reached and must be personally felt is the actual injury to feeling that fuels the complex on a personal level with all its flagrant raging.

That the 13th fairy utters her curse and disappears again for fifteen years indicates how long such a problem can lie dormant in us. She reappears in the more human form of an old woman spinning flax, which is an improvement on spewing curses. It indicates that even erupting in angry accusations begins to humanize archetypal force. Each time an archetypal affect or behavior enters human dimensions, even if negative, it promotes transformation of the impersonal toward personal and interpersonal relatedness. For the next time she turns up it is now not as a magical fairy godmother but as a human being, albeit malign in intent and only to effect her foretold curse through the spindle. And the hex, the evil spell, though softened from death to sleep, goes on for a century! Nothing changes the problem, let alone transforms or heals it. Time spent imprisoned eventually runs out, and then girl and castle come to life. She and the prince marry and will be the new king and queen, that is, a new attitude will reign in the kingdom, but without having dealt with the original 13th fairy problem.

For any change to happen to the complex and to those held captive to such pain, we must trace back through the fury to the personal loss of not being remembered and to forgetting our self. We must recover the lost experience of that loss of love or, even worse, the loss of love never found in the first place. Vulnerability to such personal wounds of this deep sort is heightened if we already suffered mismatch, neglect, or outright negativity in our early mothering relationship. The experience of being seen, welcomed, received with gladness and attentive loving usually has not happened or not happened enough. So there is a hole where some living tissue should be growing. The slight of being excluded from the dinner party falls right into that hole.

On the personal level of the complex, we must trace the roots and extending threads from that earlier abyss to the present. Both our looking into the injury and into the lack of connection with a principal other shifts such suffering toward healing.

A Collective Level

The fairy tale addresses a collective level, too, for the 13th fairy represents something that drops out of collective consciousness, that is, an archetypal pattern of psyche, not only one's personal experience of lack but a pattern of lack in shared existence. She who goes unheeded inflicts oblivion on the whole castle; all become mindless, held fast for a long time in dreamless sleep, sleep that knocks all living out of commission.

If we think of the 13th fairy as portraying a goddess as well as personifying a human pattern, and as if she wants to become more human, as she does in her second appearance as an old woman spinning flax in a forgotten room, then what might it mean that she is not invited, indeed is forgotten altogether? Maybe she has forgotten herself, been gone for so long she does not come to mind when others gather. Is she a pattern of disconnecting or failing to connect, so to speak, with what she desires and aims for? Then she would only notice those inner impulses when someone else ignores them. Desire arrives via accusation: you did not think of me! Or, she may represent bad things that just fall on us, bad luck; we did not cause them, rather they are an impersonal blow delivered upon us out of nowhere, changing our lives. If we do not deal with it, it consumes us, crushes us. Or, she might represent a theme of resentment, spite, misery, or grudge-holding, a vindictive mood that just arrives seemingly out of the blue and takes us over. That the child is female and that the girl is put to sleep by the 13th fairy at an age when pubescent sexuality awakens suggests that a whole chunk of feminine sexuality and its relation to destructiveness falls out of collective awareness as a revenge for the Wise Woman being disregarded.

I suggest that our task is to invite all these possibilities to the table and register which ones click, which ones provoke our own response of "aha, that's it." What I see running through all these possibilities is a failure to respond to and reflect on patterns of the feminine in the human psyche. I say feminine because the new form of renewing life comes as female, and it is fairy godmothers bestowing blessings and the neglected godmother who exerts an evil spell. We must meet and respond to the feminine form of hurt feelings and vengeful reprisal—a primitive eye-for-an-eye retaliation. She makes herself known in the tale by destroying a joyous event, threatening death. (I have witnessed occasions in group life, for example, where the feminine can get into collective discourse only by making a mess—eruptions of hurt feelings, long-harbored grudges bursting out in public accusations of being treated with disrespect, wrecking any attempt at conversation together about what has happened between the longtime members of the group.)

The feminine, symbolizing a mode of being embodied in the female figure of the 13th fairy in this tale, is not recognized or respected in her own right nor as a way of being in the world honored in the collective gathering. The forgotten one is forgotten, treated as disposable. With gratitude for many changes toward recognizing the precious value of the feminine, I maintain it is still far from enough. Evidence? To take but one example, the horrific gang rape and murder of the young student in India (in New Delhi in December 2012). Enormous outrage rose up from Indian society in response, with many reports of how common is the occurrence of rape and sexual molestation of women and how often their complaints brought to police and those in authority are disregarded. Quick passage of a new law under which rape automatically brings a penal sentence of twenty years astonished many. But the dismissive attitude toward the feminine generally and as embodied in actual females was recognized as continuous.

We can understand forgetting the 13th fairy as the neglect of fundamental recognition of being in female form. A feminine mode of being belongs to all of us qua human (Ulanov 1971, chap. 9). Disregarding an organ of the psyche is as dangerous as neglecting of one of the body's organs and the negative consequences that result. The bill will be presented and payment must be made. Our psychological health necessitates the functioning of our total psyche—instinctively, emotionally, spiritually. In the fairy tale, the 13th fairy is female, a goddess maybe, but symbolized by a person. So what falls out of awareness is recognition of this particular constellation of affect, behavior, and imagery the 13th fairy embodies, as well as consciousness of our responses to her. And behind her are the archetypal resonances of fate, or nemesis, suggesting we must see our personal life in relation to ineluctable passages of time and align with them lest we wake up too late.

The theme throughout the story, I suggest, is the absence of a meeting between ego and this psychic pattern the 13th fairy symbolizes. Careless disregard of her disappearing, reappearing, and disappearing again with all its penalties suggests we fall out of tune with the contents she enacts. Moreover the conscious attitude, symbolized by king and queen, disappears just when we should show up: the parents go missing the fateful day of spindle pricking.

The Spindle

The spindle is the means of inflicting deathless sleep wherein consciousness, both personal and collective, is just blotted out. Because we do not remember the 13th fairy, nor does she herself seem to remember her presence until it is ignored by the collective, we lose not only the hurt she represents but also her pattern of existence and consciousness. It is erased. Everyone falls asleep. Initially, she arrives to inflict a curse. Then she disappears again for a decade and half.

That the curse will be effected when the girl is fifteen suggests also lapsing into disregard of sexuality, as age fifteen is within the transition to puberty, waking up sexually to becoming a woman. In the tale the feminine is allowed in its child form, its girl form, but is consigned to oblivion when sexual desire and adult womanhood begin. The feminine is not to be recognized consciously in its forming power for human society and civilization. Keep her as a child or with the children as their mother, not as a power and potency in herself. For at that juncture sleep falls upon her, she who would bring the new to everyone in the kingdom, a recognition of renewing feminine form and, as it plays out, a new reigning attitude when this feminine joins with the masculine represented by the prince. Instead she falls victim to Hypnos, brother to Thanatos. Here we can look into those states where we as women or feminine aspects of human being get stuck between life and death and do not cross over into conscious living in society. Instead, we fall under a hypnotic spell that renders us immobilized to claim the power, sexuality, and wisdom that belong to us.

An example illustrates this: a woman able and effective in her job and circle of society, but unable to own her various accomplishments as real, feels herself more like a helpless child who does not know her strengths, does not take title to them. Her dream says outright: "Three times I do not claim my feet under me." Note that she has feet; she just does not take charge of them, depend on their support, and thus achieve her own standpoint.

A clue to this pattern of neglect can be gleaned from the 13th fairy's use of the spindle as her weapon of choice. Its "regularly turning motion" gives energy and directs the thread for the weaving, thus representing an "unchanging lawfulness, inexorable fate" (*Herder Symbol Dictionary*, 179), "revolutions of the universe," "of weaving destiny" (Cooper 1982, 156). The spindle directs the flax for weaving, hence symbolizing both a human activity and the turning activity of the cosmos.

Such images of the spindle are archetypal and associated with a feminine capacity to weave an atmosphere of trust and confidence around oneself and with others. On a lunar level such spinning calls to mind a picture of the three Fates weaving destiny through past, present, and future and of birth, life, and death. Symbolically, such weaving brings together different elements, suggesting creating an ambience that engenders both support and growth. Examples are reveries around one's unborn child, hoped-for projects like a new painting or social event, our desire for spiritual fulfillment, peaceful relations, even for justice. This creative aspect of feminine power is being ignored in the fairy tale and falls into its negative version— plotting revenge for being forgotten. Spinning also associates to witches as well as to the wise old woman, for example, the hag who can be both a wise woman manqué and a source of great sagacity (Ulanov and Ulanov 1987, chap. 5).

Flax is the material being woven by the old woman. In its positive associations, flax is used for royal or priestly cloth (see Ulanov 1993a, 39–41). Its being spun also calls up female sexuality intertwining emotional mood, physical impulse, and spiritual longing for union. But in this tale, an old woman, alone, hiding out in a locked room, spins flax with the turning spindle to carry out her revenge. Granted she is in more human form and relating, albeit negatively, to the girl, but the intent is destruction.

Failure to attend this pattern of psyche that instead falls out of consciousness exacts a kind of eye-for-an-eye justice, making the other fall out of consciousness too and with her the whole world. Loss of subjectivity takes with it the world of intersubjectivity. Literalism replaces imaginative weaving of atmosphere. You did this to me, I will do this to you; you must suffer the same. Coarse equations of this equals that, this is nothing but, replace subtlety of attitude that spins into life the reality of the intangible, the enlivening invisible emotional atmosphere that makes learning and relating possible.

The 13th fairy uses the spindle to catch the girl's attention and to deliver the poison. Its phallic shape within the weaving activity can be taken to represent a feminine kind of penetrating, going back and forth as it revolves around, making thread available for weaving together a whole fabric (von Franz 1972, 42). But here the spindle becomes a pricking weapon to plunge the girl into a long trance of nonliving. This sleep happens to women where whole chunks of their lives fall out of consciousness into oblivion. One analysand in her sixties said, "I have lived as a child my whole life, never stepping into my own full self!" Another woman in her fifties, growing frantic with the limit of years left to her to live before death, felt she had woken up to a kind of living she had never known, as if breaking out of a cocoon or a deep sleep.

The 13th fairy is captive to spinning for negative purposes. The rich notion of weaving atmosphere of tone and depth in a relationship or in her working life or in her family falls instead into vindictive scheming, plotting revenge. Clinically I have seen a woman caught in such a web of persecutory fantasies that circle around a deep, as yet to be fully acknowledged, hurt. Obsessive thoughts spin her around, with annihilating blows to her sense of self delivered by others and by her self. Repeated semiconscious assumptions level her fate, declaring: I assumed I could never find a mate; you disrespect me; I cannot stand on my own; my existence is a mistake. These rigid opinions of her own and her acute suffering of others' assumptions about her prick her into sleep to escape the pain. She just vanishes. She is kidnapped. Imaginative possibilities of being someone or creating something are snuffed out. The 13th fairy is awake, not asleep like the girl, but awake to rage and plot. This can be the beginning of living, but it is a very hard life to endure. It initiates a sense of self in asserting: you have not annihilated me; I do exist.

On a collective level payment must be made for this injury inflicted, and the payment is everyone falling asleep, life stopped, everything rendered into suspension. Nothing happens for a long time. Growth is blotted out.

Result

The result is a tale where the task does not get done, the knot stays tied. The problem is not solved; the curse just wears out, and life resumes without any reflection on what happened, without redemption of the 13th fairy seemingly cursed to noninclusion. If we take her to represent a complex of our own, it is one that stays unworked through, suspended between the unconscious and consciousness, without the benefit of our interceding for some release and resolution. This is hard to bear.

We all suffer this plight to some degree, and it touches an archetypal theme of human grief and regret, enlisted into confession of sin—of things we have done that we ought not to have done, of things we have not done that we ought to have done. We have done them against ourselves, and against others, and against God, that entire pattern of living that makes up the wholeness of the whole. In these instances we have been held captive as if in the hundred years long sleep, surely better than death but also like a life sentence without parole. In such situations that fall upon us, what we can do is wait with a sense that that is all we can do and give devoted attention to the *materia* (the stuff) we find our selves in, within and without, without being overwhelmed by it nor maniacally denying it.

Such a tale reminds us vividly of the preciousness of consciousness with its interceding role to reflect upon what is happening, to take note of the surround that is not ready for transformation (see Ulanov 1998; Ulanov and Ulanov 1975, chap. 11). We may live in a war zone and first must survive; or in a place of famine, either literally or spiritually, and must look out for crumbs; or we may be situated in a world of seasons, hence alert to tiny seedlings of greenness that may appear. Things exist before our knowing about them, hence the preciousness of the unconscious—it goes on and from it the new may emerge. The sorrow surrounding the 13th fairy is her aloneness, that she disappears into forgottenness, only to repeat her swooping in at a future time, then vanishing again.

I return to my theme in this tale: there is no meeting between personal subjectivity and archetypal psyche. They suffer each other. No ego and Self assembly occurs. Without that, little or nothing happens. The human ego sense of I-ness is receiver, responder, the vessel in which *materia* gets transformed (Jung 2009, 252 n211). We provide the hut in which the operation can occur, and hence we are changed; but the transformed exceeds ego dimensions and hence is symbolized by the most exalted figures, like Christ on the cross or in the mass, or in alchemy by the element of supreme value, the *lapis* stone, the *aqua permanens*, or in tales like Psyche becoming half goddess. She achieves her tasks by failing to do the last one of handing over to Aphrodite the precious beauty ointment, because Psyche longs to be beautiful for her beloved Eros. We participate in the transforming of what gets transformed and are essential in that participation to the transforming happening, but it happens. We house it.

In this tale the figure of the 13th fairy displays what comes to pass for us when invaded and gripped by archetypal force. We become possessed. The girl remains cursed until she wakes up a century later. She represents our getting stuck in an in-between place where we are not alive or dead, not in heaven or on earth, not conscious and not entirely unconscious either, just arrested, not living. Life passes us by. The social order is not redeemed. No change of attitude toward the feminine happens. No one learns anything. What would facilitate learning?

Our human subjectivity is possible only in relation to external reality, to an other, an object, to otherness. It is that kind of intercourse, mutual joining and seeing, that does not ensue in the tale or for the 13th fairy. The girl and all the kingdom do not come into fuller conscious living nor does the archetypal content symbolized by the 13th fairy; it remains unconscious, coming and going, exploding and withdrawing, and nothing happens to change it.

I think of an analysand whose task is a common one we all know something about. Early in her life, she fell into absorption in her mother's psyche, her mother's subjectivity in dealing with the overwhelming emotions of immigration to a place with a different language and culture, including the hard loss of a dying child, nursing a husband through serious surgeries, and raising all the other children during the dying and death of their small brother. My patient loved and hated her mother. She came to see that she could become subsumed in her mother's emotions, losing space for her own. In efforts to extricate herself she used her spiritual discipline to rise above these conflicts and to surrender herself in devotion to her God. The infinite was going to rescue her from the finite. Her entire analysis was taken in the opposite direction of going down into the matrix of her body experience, her desires and angers, to free her feelings for living in the world. She reached her own alive life separate from her mother's and still loving this parent. Her spiritual discipline enlarged to embody the infinite in her here-and-now finite everyday life.

Our service to truth is to live it into the world, to deal with our particular problem and not disappear into self-attack, nor to fall captive to blaming the other. We feel both our mistakes and the actual hurt dealt us by another, without too much denial of either. We see truth emerging here and now, an unknown we do not invent but receive, a surprise, wondrous, called grace in religious traditions.

Our service to the whole, in alchemical terms, reaching moments of *rubedo*—bringing insight into living—grows in our human capacity to open to the force of the archetypal and sustain our personal feeling connections to self and others and to the influx of the new, to participate in these incarnations. In this tale, the 13th fairy is a blast of elemental feminine justice, not tempered by human concerns or limits. She would wipe out the offending parties by stealing from them what they cherish most—a child bringing the new, evoking love and protection. The beginning of including this archetypal force is the 13th fairy saying, I do too exist, thus symbolizing the needed human response to annihilating trauma. Aggressive assertion needs to enter the ego, be felt and used against forces that would kill, obliterate, or at best postpone living.

At the second appearance of the 13th fairy what is needed is to wake up from the hypnoid state she inflicts. Our service to the whole is to reach human subjectivity, our response. Unlike animals ruled by instinct or an archetypal reflex, we have the elbow room to choose forms of expression to check an onslaught of instinctive fury and then look into it, protect our self against it, and engage curiosity to learn to domesticate this energy so flagrantly exploding. Personal response makes something of what is happening, reflects and lives through an experience with an other, and thus begins a meeting that may evolve into instances of incarnation of the new. In this tale it does not happen, but we can reflect on what needs to happen and thus spy the knot calling for untying.

The 13th fairy's emotional protest against being ignored humanizes her into an old woman and the possibility not yet realized of weaving a human path between possession by archetypal energy and rigid identification with its force that issues in fanaticism. I am struck that thinkers—that is, in Jung's typology, persons who display thinking as their dominant function, including Jung—attribute the potential to check onslaughts of destructiveness (in this tale expressed as vengeance and a retaliatory justice) by recourse to a binding feeling attitude. We must let our feeling function evolve and slowly build up a moral compass, to experience affective connection to others and to events. Jung says, in the Red Book, that as a man he partakes of all the heinous deeds of mankind, and we also must deal with violence inside ourselves instead of taking it out on others (Jung 2009, 239). We must sacrifice our dominant function, here thinking, to let our "incapacity," here feeling, develop (ibid., 240). Only thus can personal values grow, values that check rampant destructiveness from exploding into the world and that also rescue us from disappearing into collective values and into the collective unconscious.

I also ask, how do other dominant psychic functions find the way to check destructiveness? We share the pattern of each of us having recourse to develop our inferior function ("incapacity" in the Red Book). Enlivening questions appear: What would help a person with the dominant function of sensation? Would a hint of possibility (of intuition beginning to develop) begin to check eruptions of rage? Would recourse to developing the sensate function to perceive what is, to see the facts of a situation, begin for the person with dominant intuition to check accusatory tones, to detach hurtful action from motive to do harm, suggesting instead the limits of the other? Would a person with dominant feeling get a glimpse of logical connection of thinking that sets in broader system the other's wounding behavior toward us, flowing from their own complex that holds them captive? This musing is for another paper. But the fate of the 13th fairy, a fate that does not change, raises afresh the question of what is the source of checks on our destructiveness.

2

Transforming Trauma
Psychological and Spiritual Pathways

Trauma ties us in knots, ties us up so tight we fear we will never get free. As one woman put it, "I can't turn off the obsessive buzzing thoughts going round and round in my head." The untying, if it comes, emerges from our psyche persisting toward emancipation, toward release from emotional confinement within what hurt us. Spiritually, untying, if it happens, moves to center stage our experience of being addressed, even rescued, by what we find to be the source of life and brings a new task of how we live in this new relationship.

To speak of pathways to healing, whether psychological or spiritual, evokes in our awareness the source of healing. That reality we speak of is not abstract and distant, but near. It is what the thirteenth-century mystic Marguerite Porete named "Farnearness" (Babinsky 1993, 155). This reality is not content we can present or even talk about as though it were an object we can examine. This reality is the subject, present, here before us, out of which we came, and which will be here after this day is over and long after we are over. We are speaking of the subject who is forever, what orthodox Christians call "of the ages to the ages." This subject, present here and now, will affect us, shape us, touch us, wound us, as though we were speaking of our lover, our beloved friend, our mysterious other, our sheltering mother, our providing father. It is an intimate, personal conversation we are to be having about the source of pathways to healing, through the psyche, through the spirit. My focus is the nexus point, the juncture, the hookup between the personal, the mortal, the here and now, and the transcendent, the All, the Vast, the Source without Source as Porete put it (ibid., 46–47).

But in the event of trauma, both individual and collective, our spiritual object, whatever we name it, which we experienced as constant, as abiding, as trustworthy, as there, is called into radical question: How could God let this traumatic event with its destructive aftermath happen? Whether we speak of God theologically as true, fact, being, or reality itself or psychologically of how the sacred affects us, mirrors us, trauma pushes us right to the borderline, the frontier between these two approaches. Trauma raises the theological question of whether there is a sacred object, a spiritual zone. We may lose access to it entirely. Or we may reject it outright, because if a God does exist and this terrible event can happen, then, with Ivan in *The Brothers Karamazov*, we refuse this God. Trauma raises the psychological question of whether the self as we know it in ourselves and with our neighbor can survive.

Although we distinguish between psychological and spiritual pathways—and necessarily so in order to discuss different routes to healing—in living, psyche and spirit intertwine. It is only with the advent of depth psychology as a discipline that interdisciplinary conversation can happen with the age-old tradition of spirituality already established. I will draw on both strands of psyche and spirit and their inevitable congress.

Trauma

At the beginning of the new century and new millennium, trauma has become a focus of attention. For Americans, the attacks of 9/11 brought us closer to what citizens of other countries have already been suffering. And our soldiers have known trauma since the beginning of war.

When trauma occurs, whether it is a distinct event or cumulative over time, it is as though a shock goes through us (Khan 1963). We are stunned, even paralyzed. We know dimly but decisively that this is the unmaking of us. We feel that our circuits are blown; we are fatally infected; our chest shot open; our roots dug up, left lying about. As if electric current buzzes through us, we cannot think; we cannot comprehend that what is happening is happening. We disavow what we experience as we experience it. How can I, a person, be treated like an object of no consequence, disposable, there for another's use, no longer a subject in my own right? No longer counting, and no one accountable? How can a whole neighborhood disappear under water, burn to the ground, fall into an earthquake's crevasse, what was thriving now gone? How can a whole town turn into nothing but rubble, with rockets or bombs or suicide devices blowing up the place in time and space we called ours, as if we are no more than blips on a radar screen? How can there now be No-thing—no connection, no one stopping this, no one acknowledging this violence—where before there was something—a caring, a meaning, a universe which held all of us? Presence transmogrifies into shocked absence.

Trauma inflicts shock and wounds us with an experience we cannot assimilate. This produces anxiety of terrific intensity, but it is not attached anywhere. We know what happened, but we cannot take it in. Trauma, then, remains something that assaults us and then encapsulates us. The trauma goes on happening to us, but separated off, dissociated. Within that encapsulation we suffer terribly.

First among effects of trauma is deep hurt. We feel discarded like a piece of garbage, a throwaway; we do not matter or count and are made to feel we are not significant enough to give an accounting to. Rather, we are told that these things happen, you are one of many, it could be worse, get over it, others have suffered more. We are made to feel ashamed of our suffering, as if we are crazy or, especially, as if we are making a mountain out of a molehill.

Hurt is met with denial: it never took place, I didn't do it, I do not remember any such thing occurring, you imagined it, it wasn't so bad. Insult is piled on top of injury. The first blow of trauma is something terrible that happened to us. The second blow of trauma is that it is denied, minimized, deflected. When we protest, howl, weep, there is no one there to hear and recognize what transpired.

In response to thus being hurt, blanked out, told to move on, rage erupts that feels destructive. We may be told by our spiritual traditions: forgive, let it go, pray for your enemy, practice mindfulness. In fact, the rage is in exact proportion to the deep hurt that has been inflicted and is a compensatory step toward healing. It is an instinctive thrust of energy to push out the dent in our sense of self which the blow of trauma inflicted. Rage asserts that we are a person who matters, we have agency, we are worth listening to as we speak of this event. But rage is archaic, not civilized; it appears in fantastic images of what we would do to the other who so hurt us or to ourselves and makes us and others feel afraid. Rage is also exhausting, making us feel crazy; it can spill over into action, and then others label us crazy. Obsessive thoughts spin around in our minds in an effort to speak the truth of what happened, not just to retaliate. We are obsessed with the truth that has been denied.

Waves of hurt and rage act like an undertow that pulls us far from common ground with others. We feel we are far away from communal understanding and can fall into abysmal confusion, as if pulled under the waves, not knowing which way is up or back. Maybe we are exaggerating, not remembering accurately, or off the deep end, but we want to throw a truth bomb at the other's denials and pretense that nothing happened. A dream captures this confusion: a woman dreams that a man in love with her pushes her through the water to the other side and through a door so she will not die. She is furious, locked out, stranded, or is she locked in, protected from being drowned? He pushes her through the water and locks the door. She asks in her dream, Is she locked out of the water or is she rescued from it? Is she locked on the other side, he thinking he is helping her? Yet she can hear in the dream the click of the lock as the door closes upon her.

Captivity to hurt, denial, rage, and abysmal confusion delivers us into radical self-doubt, afraid we are slipping out of sanity, falling through the holes of being, or abandoned in outer space, to cite various people's descriptions. We feel we are drifting away from the community of others, as if our lifeline is fraying or will be completely severed.

Whatever resources we depended on in the past—our capacity to reason, a commonsense style of action, a determination to fight, a belief in an ethical or religious guideline—does not help us now. It proves ineffective. We feel we are in danger: this could kill us. Yet simultaneously something impels us to seek our way through this suffering. We are both the lost sheep and the shepherd who must find the sheep and bring them home.

Personal traumas are all our own, while collective traumas become real in our personal experience of them: the hell of war in the specific buddy blown to pieces, now a body part before our eyes; sexual trauma in the specific person we loved and depended upon who put their fingers into us, touching as if we were part of them at their disposal, committing sexual theft; crime in the specific other who terrorized us on the street to take from us what was our own, the money we worked for, the dignity we grew; emotional abuse in the specific other whom we loved in intimacy but who now keeps out of range and denies that they do so, destroying our trust in our perceptions; enemy attacks in the specific violence of our neighbor's husband beheaded and broadcast on television; injustice in our specific poverty that constructs us as the abject in the world, dismissible. Large and petty, instant and cumulative, trauma unmakes the self, junks our center of initiative and connection. Trauma breaks the spirit into bits. If there is a God in this universe of sudden intrusion of the unthinkable, the unbearable, it is the God who forsakes us.

Personal trauma takes place in a collective context. The dregs to which poverty assigns us occur in a society where other economic classes enjoy enough, even plenty. In Brazil, to rise economically affects one's racial persona, thereby exhibiting the trauma of racism: "money makes things white" (Boechat and Pantoja 2007). The violation of the body in sexual predation occurs in a family that does not see or hear it, and there appears to be no one to whom the traumatized can protest. The shooter of the wife in the blue coat, seated in the back of St. James Church in South Africa when gunmen broke in, tells the shocked husband, who cannot yet grieve in tears, that her murder did not have to do with her, that it was the situation in South Africa: "we had to take guns to open the ears of those not prepared to listen" (Krog 2007).

Psychologically trauma renders the self no longer a subject seen by other subjects nor by one's own eyes, but instead a heap, a discard. The psychological consequences of trauma destruct us so that at very best we are left in a reactive position, no longer an agent. We feel rendered invisible, inaudible, to our self and to the other(s) who injured us. And trauma lives on in us; it is not consigned to the past but repeats endlessly in the present (see Symington 2001, 107). We become coconspirators with the one who traumatized us by repeating to ourselves the attitudes of intrusion and dismissal that the other once imposed upon us. Like a squirrel caught in a bird feeder, we circle round and round the wound left in us, unable to break free of it and unable to resolve it. Our obsessive thoughts seem to be a sign of craziness to us, crowding out the life offered to us now. Yet such ruminations may be the one frail tree branch to hold onto instead of plunging over the edge or committing assault. Though our numb dissociation may make us no fun to be with or our preoccupation with pain may make others dread spending time with us, this morbid narcissism is the one thread keeping us in life.

Cumulative trauma is no better, though it may initially appear so because no definitive appalling event occurred. Like the drip drip of water torture where the drops steadily obliterate the same spot, the tiny events of cumulative trauma over time repeatedly strike the center of our subjectness, our connectedness to self and others and to spiritual source, wearing it away, with no protection against radical self-doubt.

Spiritually, trauma ejects us from a universe of meaning. No longer held in being, we exist in the realm of the No-thing. The Vast and the All are now a void; emptiness as loss pervades, not as fertile beginning. Where there had been a containing coherence and, even if dim, a sense of the author of such wholeness, now there are fragments, bits and pieces strewn here and there, like disjointed body parts, shards of thoughts, shreds of feelings. No firm foothold can be found to support us, no kinship to sustain us. We have misplaced or lost entirely the capacity for belief (Winnicott 1963, 93). Randomness reigns: anything can happen, because it already has. Our moral imagination has been infiltrated by the traumatic event and by the other person refusing to recognize us as a fellow sufferer, another animal, a sister citizen in the community of human beings.

Our sense of heaven and earth hanging together, of transcendent and mundane joining in a purpose that infuses our existence, has been vitiated by the stunning shock of trauma. If there is a god, we cannot find it; if there is mindfulness, we cannot reach it; if there is love, we have been exiled from it.

The consequences of trauma are legion. We can understand better the demons begging Christ not to send them into outer darkness but into the Gadarene swine which, thus possessed, rush to destruction over the cliff. Trauma is not quiet. Even though dissociated from daily living, trauma is not passive but ferocious in its vortex of swirling preoccupation, rushing toward the cliff and, once over, pulling us into the sea. We are adrift in the unconscious, pushed this way and that by currents of unbearable hurt and bubbling rage, compelled to protest, to strike back and assert that we, too, have impact, we are not a throwaway. But these rageful impulses take us over the cliff, as they did Lisa Nowak, the astronaut who wrecked her career (after all the money our country invested to train her to high levels of skill), her marriage, and her motherhood by driving all night hundreds of miles to strike at a rival astronaut for a third astronaut's affections, he who had forsaken her for this other woman. Looking on from the sidelines, when she was arrested in the airport while stalking the other woman, we can say that she was crazy, caught in the grip of an archetype, captured by the temptation of anger, committing the sin of concupiscence—that she was foolish to destroy her life. But looked at as her traumatic response to the loss of this relationship, the rage that prompted action was better than the despair that threatened to kill her. But how to relate to this rage, to act in an effective way with it?

Destructiveness must be included in our pathway to healing. If not, the traumatic event and our suffering of it is split off, dissociated, becoming a dead place in us that undermines any subsequent belief we have in living. And any time we attempt intimacy—with a child or a mate, with an idea, a cause, a spiritual object, poetry, or painting—this dead place comes to the fore. The lost sheep presents itself and the rest of the group, the rest of the personality, cannot function without including this disowned part.

Immigrants, legal or illegal, often have fled from terror in their home countries, where a torturer or a whole social system wants to destroy humans in their wholeness. Unable to solve this, only able flee it, the trauma is dissociated and conscripts the person into being its accomplice. The immigrant fears abandonment for having abandoned good objects in the home country, suffers narcissistic shame and sadness for escaping, and cannot find roots in the new country. He or she thus feels shunned and will ask, "Do I smell?" as if that would explain the feeling of not being accepted in the new society (Langendorf 2007).

Similarly, citizens who need to belong to a family or racial, sexual, or class group may feel forced to deny chunks of their experience in order to fit in. Their desire to belong conflicts with the group's ethos of who can be included and what must be rejected. For example, Anatole Broyard, a black author passing for white in order to succeed professionally, found that, cut off from his roots, his talent had been hollowed out (Layton 2004, 4). A boy may feel cursed by his homosexual nature and try to closet it or even kill it by killing himself; a woman may deny and subvert her own power, her own authority, lest she be shunned by those she wants to love her, and on and on.

One of the most profound consequences of trauma that empties out both psychological and spiritual meaning, I believe, is abysmal confusion. The traumatized part of us disappears as if into thick polluted fog, and we cannot read the signs accurately: Did it really happen or did I make too much out of it? Others suffered this, too, or suffered more, so why am I so grievously upset? Am I just puffing myself up to be important? Am I avoiding the real tasks of life? Or am I going mad, that I cannot make sense of what happened to me, and I cannot be quit of it and move on?

Questions abound and distress intensifies. No vision endures of what could hold us together. Collective trauma—holocaust, forced starvation, rape camps—horrifies. We cannot cast a net of meaning over such events; they are too big, too horrible; their victims retreat into decades of silence, maybe even to their graves. Current film documentaries of World War II, in which soldiers who were there in the midst of it are interviewed, may for the first time, to the full surprise of their family members, speak of the horrors that bombarded them as soldiers. Words are found to speak of the traumas that now find their way into human discourse. This is the beginning of healing.

Pathways to Healing

Healing also has profound effects as deep and lasting as trauma. Healing undoes the encapsulation caused by trauma. Healing opens the wound, and our blood flows. Healing reenlists our subjectivity, inspires our agency to look into what happened to us, revives the hope that our experience of destructiveness can find its necessary place.

Chief among the ingredients of healing is recognition: to know again what took place. To find that we need to be recognized. That means dependence on an other who wants to know what happened and listens intently as we struggle to speak of what is unspeakable. Recognition defeats denial. The other gifted with recognition may be an analyst, a spiritual mentor, a teacher, a chaplain, a priest, a wise one. Or the other may be a poet, a composer, an artist with paint or stone, a tradition that offers us the speech of lamentation, words of rescue that stir gratitude.

Refinding precious pieces of self that were lost, stolen, wrecked, abandoned, or walled off breaks the captivity of trauma, transforming it into emotional memory. The trauma becomes part of us instead of us being frozen within it. The emotional memory, even with all its sadness for what was suffered and was locked up and paralyzed, replaces the trauma in thought and sometimes in deed. The psyche will press to get that piece of glass out of our flesh; it will keep thumping on the door to liberate us from what holds us hostage. Being recognized by another and recognizing with another builds up space to reach the self that was before the trauma. What was stuck begins to move in fluid warm-blooded consciousness, holding in awareness the self wounded in trauma, the self looking into trauma, the self living beyond trauma.

In the process of recognizing the self held captive, destructiveness finds its appropriate place. We cannot dodge it, but we can find out where it belongs. Our psychological task is recovering ability, ableness, after the destructive wallop of trauma. From the new land of recognition in which archaic rage transforms into aggressive energy, we feel our dependence on another who brought respect to the trauma that threatened to annihilate us. Captivity to trauma changes to emotional memory of all that happened to us, individually or as a group, and we house it. Synchronistic events bring home what the healing of trauma instigates—for example, a phrase in a dream turns up in a public event. One man heard his very own words describing what was lost to him in trauma—"the color of his loving"—turn up in sermon on Easter Sunday. The space made by warm-blooded consciousness, grown in mutual recognition, begins to exceed personal boundaries, opening to shared kinship of things human.

Our spiritual task is to allow the question, What is the source of the miracle of recognition? Where does it come from? Who is the other who recognizes us? Here we open to the vastness of human experience— the Buddha mind, the God who bestows love on us first, unconditional love that does not give up on us (Martyn 2007, 69, 74). In the Christian tradition this love enters into our suffering, patiently endorsing the goodness of who we are.

In the Christian tradition, the *catena aurea,* the golden chain, refers to commentaries on texts in scripture that link together across cultures and historical eras, made up of different authors' responses to the text and to others' readings of the texts. It is like a jazz riff in sacred words, each crafting a link in a long chain of response to all of us being recognized. Each of us has in our own histories golden moments where something broke through and we felt held in a source beyond ourselves. Such a link bestows on us recognition of our priceless unique subjectivity participating in the larger whole.

Over decades of clinical work and teaching psyche and spirit in a graduate school of religion, I have gained the insight that healing happens in the nexus, the connecting point between personal and universal, psyche and spirit, individual and collective. Jung talks about this space as the *coniunctio,* the conjoining of opposites wherein each finds fulfillment in relation to the other, symbolized by the marriage of the king and the queen or the linking of the sun and moon, a mystery that transpires in the dark of the moon, that is, outside ego consciousness. Winnicott speaks of this nexus point as a space of transitions where self and symbol are found and created in play (Winnicott 1971a, chap. 1). Contemporary analysts speak of this locus of healing as the third, constructed between the one and the two of analyst and analysand (Ulanov 2007a). The pathways to healing will be different for each of us, but I am able to say something about what we share in common and point out the intertwining of psyche and spirit. In living, they are mixed with each other, each a pathway to the other, mutually enlivening.

Healing Is Cumulative

Healing is cumulative. We can distinguish cumulative trauma from sudden trauma, but the pathway to healing is always cumulative, even if a decisive breakthrough or conversion has occurred, because trauma always brings flashbacks that hurl us once again to square one. We are returned to that first shock, that shattering of self, that splintering of meaning, ejected from our own center with the thread that linked us to the center of reality snipped, however we formulate that link—belief in God, devotion to the arts, service to neighbor. We are thrown right back to being immersed in doing violence to ourselves that mimics the violence done to us in the trauma.

Hope can be lost in these repeated returns, these iterations of square oneness. But the nature of healing is layer by layer, dream by dream, giving in to dependence on an other again and again, a sliver of insight and then another. We put down layers of a new way of being and forge new links back to the self we were before the trauma, just as a painter applies layers of pigment to build up a painting that gives the artist's particular vision of and attitude toward the reality depicted. In this process of return and forging the new, strata of meaning accumulate, a new skin for the self is grown, taking time and taking space, as befits our finitude. We might have a whirlwind of definitive insight, true enlightenment, samadhi, touching the *lapis*, knowing the resurrection, and then need years to actualize it in work and love and living.

I think of an analysand raised in a home that grew shabby around the mental illness of her mother, her father leaving, and their poverty increasing. As a late teenager, she galvanized her girl-self to become a model by studying fashion magazines, obtaining photographs of herself, working little modeling jobs, and building a portfolio to bring to interviews she persisted in getting. This was her dream, her ambition, the self she believed in and gave all her stamina to create. She had gained enough success by age nineteen to launch a next step toward a big modeling agency. Then her father returned home. He looked at his daughter's modeling only through his own lens, his own assumptions, ignorant of what modeling could be. He scorned her portfolio as prostitution. Yelling in anger, he called her a whore, "throwing the portfolio across the room and tearing up the magazines in which I appeared. It was no good; I was evil." She was a source of shame to him, the cause of her mother's depression, and he threw her out. He did not recognize what this was for her and did not see the energy she devoted to creating this opportunity of income for the whole family. He imposed his split view of woman—whore or homemaker— on his daughter's teenage self striving for a self-supporting place in the world. His rage and repudiation crushed her and broke her confidence. She destroyed her portfolio and became a slut in her own eyes, going off on her own by living with different men who supported her. Faith in her ambition was killed because she never could accept the various men's offers to set her up in movies or business or to write scripts. "I gave up modeling and got a food disorder." She became, she felt, her father's version of herself, and it took many years to slowly unpeel this traumatized self, to risk again living her own self. Now in her fifties, this healing still accumulates.

A decisive shift occurs at some point, but even that needs building up, consolidating, daring to let our whole weight depend on it, outgrowing the trauma and finding a symbol that continues to grow. At the heart of this growing is being recognized and recognizing something given which, if we can receive it and work it and submit to its working us, creates the new.

The Necessity of Ego Response and the Emergence of Others

Healing demands our participation; it is offered more often than not, but we need eyes to see and ears to hear its advent. By ego response I mean willingness, a building up of readiness to take what is given without prior assumptions. In that we are like a child, but with consciousness; we have an openness to see what is there and what is not there. This quality is what makes children so moving to us: children are still so transparent. We can see through to an originating process going on in them, when, for example, seated next to us to hear a story read, the child's arm and body weight lean on us, the reader, giving total concentration to looking and hearing the tale unfold as we turn the pages. In healing from trauma we must give this kind of attention. This is paradoxical, not intellectual, understanding, and paradoxical "does more justice to the unknowable . . . and reflects a higher level of intellect . . . by not forcibly representing the unknowable as known" (Jung 1954c, par. 417). I have worked with people whose brain tumors knocked out their intellect who found ways to this open quality of response that yielded a pathway to healing (Ulanov 1994; Ulanov 1996b, 176).

This childlike willingness includes "the consciousness of a mature adult," and this is where destructive energies, aggressive energies, must be part of healing (Jung 1954c, par. 417). From a psychological side, the psyche is ruthless in pressing us, again and again, to heal trauma, to include all our parts. Jung calls this process of becoming all of our unique self individuation and sees it as the most insistent of instincts. Flashbacks to square one of trauma make us feel so helplessly stuck, tethered like a horse with one leg hobbled, still held fast to old obliterations of self and other that happened years ago. Yet our struggle to free ourselves also reveals the persistence of psyche to break through the blockage, to loop in the missing part, to move us on to fuller work and love. If we try merely to get past the trauma, to get over it, we may succeed but at the cost of turning down the volume of our living, or amputating our sexuality, or stifling our aggression. Injury to our being a subject of agency and connection is worse than rape and cannibalism, worse than losing an eye (Winnicott 1963, 187; Sacks 1985, 34).

Aggression, even to the point of deconstructing whatever stability we have achieved, figures into healing. Destructiveness appears as rage at what happened to us, to our body, to our buddy, to our country, and it must be suffered, not denied, not acted out on oneself or on others. Its energy, linked to the trauma-self, also reasserts subjectivity, the me-ness that exists and is precious. Destructive energy slowly transforms into stamina to take the strain, to go down again to the bottom of emptiness to bring up pieces missing from our wholeness.

Spirit also employs aggression; it ruthlessly digs up the secrets of the heart and even the secrets of God (see Ulanov 2007b, chaps. 3 and 5). It brings a sword, not only peace, insisting that we take up our cross in order to follow Jesus's call. The thirteenth-century Buddhist Dōgen says a beginner may instantly experience enlightenment, but the beginner does not know that and must take years of reading sutras and practicing meditation to secure what was at first lavishly bestowed. The Spirit is there for the taking, but we are all thumbs and ignorance and must work to see, to hear, to receive, to take. That is where aggressive energies are necessary. Like the child with the story, we must give our full self to the fullness given us in order to take it.

In addition, the destructive patterns we engaged to protect us from trauma must be dismantled. This requires aggression and risk. I think of Ronald Fairbairn's symptom of urinary retention when away from home, mirroring his father's phobia of dreading having to urinate on the floor in a moving train with no bathroom available and in front of women accompanying him (Sutherland 1989, 70–71). Wrapped up in the sentry Fairbairn calls the antilibidinal ego, which attacks the libidinal ego wanting to invest in life and which restricts the central ego's effective functioning, is Fairbairn's inability to be pissed off—to let his aggressive reactions rip, flow out of him— and to experience his own destructiveness in this body form (Dobbs 2007, 180). Instead of dreading humiliation, he would have felt release, convention be damned. Mindful of other passengers, he would have been sorry but not annihilated.

Each of our vexing symptoms holds the riddle of the whole trauma. We need aggression to unlock their secrets and risk dismantling them in order to put ourselves in the position to face the loss, the injury of the original trauma that we keep repeating in the present. To experience repetition of trauma symptoms as persistence of grace, given through psyche larger than ego consciousness or through the Spirit itself liberating us, changes the vexing symptom into a communication from this source, however we name it (Barry Ulanov, personal communication). The destructiveness that was conscripted to protect us against anticipated abandonment is freed up to plow the very earth of us, aerating our entrenched structures, engineering us to face again the unbearable and respond in new ways.

Using our aggression to meet the destructiveness of trauma is the work of consciousness. What does mature consciousness bring? A soft light that sees how the parts are related in the whole psyche, a sliver of light shining on the hobbled foot we could not get free. Consciousness perceives what the rope is, how we tied that foot, now doing to ourselves what was done to us. We see the split-off dissociation of annihilation and its constant underlying threat to present functioning; we see our projection of its cause and solution onto someone else, some other group to fix, and we can see that we are the one who now violates this injured part as it was violated in the trauma. It is ours to hold and heal and cherish. We take it back, receive it, notice it, reach for it, empathize with the traumatized one who is our self. We give to it what was never given. We love it.

This shift of focus from the other, whom we held responsible, to us, who now has the ability to respond, makes room for others in the present. They are not stand-ins for the abusing object of the past but emerge as others external to us as subjects in their own right in the present. We see their particularity now that they are relieved of being surrogate objects from our past. As Augustine says, love and let the other be what they will. That freedom makes social space that fosters communication in place of domination by our own or others' projections.

Consciousness that inserts itself into the dumb suffering of trauma also redeems our sense of being damaged, made crazy by trauma we have suffered. When trauma occurs, ordinary boundaries of behavior are breached, even torn open, leaving gaping holes. Our response creates a range of symptoms that also transgress cultural civility. Obsessive thoughts, rageful fantasies, weeping as if autonomously, discovering tears flowing down our cheeks, staring mindlessly, waking up to hours of bleak insomnia, terrifying dreams, and even extreme actions like the astronaut attacking her rival in a Florida airport. One feels psychotic and helpless, damaged and ashamed, afraid these symptoms may break out in public. For consciousness to shed light on the rope that binds us to these behaviors and emotions not only introduces more freedom from them; it yields insight into their meaning. That redeems us from just being crazy or damaged goods, a broken object. Weeping or obsession or rage are protests, standing up for the self that felt it was being annihilated and could not bear the psychic and spiritual pain. Understanding pays the ransom, buys back meaning from frightening feelings of breaking down, and one may reach compassion for oneself.

One learns the personal language of one's own subjectivity. The woman whose young modeling career was wrecked came to the question, What if my job in life is to forgive my father? And she did! And her mother was diagnosed and given medicine for her schizophrenia, her young sister was sent to live with an aunt, and she gave her father a job in her restaurant. She found trauma's place in the whole of her.

The particularity of each person's language of their own subjectness reveals a danger to the much touted rush to globalization in our contemporary media. People want their diversity; they want their food, linked to the particular soil that grows the hot peppers or the blueberries, not the mass-produced food; they want the myths and songs and customs peculiar to living close to mountains or the sea or the canyons of skyscrapers. Though promising valuable improvement of economic conditions for many, globalization also produces new winners and losers—those who would establish a Western lifestyle for all versus those who see their rootedness in the cosmos enabled by their specific geographical location. How to keep our own spiritual and psychological language and enter shared discourse with others? This is a matter of translation.

Translation

Psychological and spiritual work mean translating the idiom of our particular experience of the unconscious and of God into language we can understand and with which we can converse with what shows itself and tell others about it (see Bollas 1991, 9–10). Annunciations are grand, but the whir of unfurling angel wings must be transmuted into human terms. Jung's method says as much when he posits his experience of the unconscious as tumultuous affects. With concerted attention, affects can be bundled into images that, with further meditation, can be translated into words. This is true of any psychological method, although Jung is distinct, I suggest, in leaving space for the objective psyche to make itself known with as little imposition of our theory as possible on the wholeness of its nature (see Bright 1997, 615; see also Ulanov and Ulanov 1975, 66; Ulanov 2007b, chap. 8).

Spiritually, it is the same in that the transcendent comes to earth, or mindfulness replaces monkey mind, indicating a direction to take toward what is beyond all mind, toward what is numinous. Contact with the numinous, with the Holy, heals. That contact is the nexus point. To live it we must work it, render it into psychic images, ethical guidelines, verbal expression, all of which make up symbolic discourse through which we arrive and arrive again at that assembly where the divine, the All, bestows on us its presence, and we in turn make it present to ourselves and to each other through acts of translation.

Our psychoanalytical theories are translations of autobiographical experiences from which we have gleaned insights into shared language about our psyche as humans. Similarly, our religious rituals and texts spring from revelatory experiences; we go on working to translate the ineffable into effable forms. Marguerite Porete reaches this translation of her unique experience of God in her description of living from "a country of peace" beneath, I suggest, the conflictual unconscious of Freud or the unconscious as tumultuous affects of Jung.

Pathways to healing trauma follow the same route and, again, show aggression as well as discovery. Turning to face the loss and the impact of injury, perceiving with a new sliver of consciousness how we reenact trauma of the past on ourselves in the present, redeems the madness in our symptoms that express our being traumatized. Symptom translates into symbol. We give full attention to what new images arise from the psyche and what events of the numinous we begin to notice. Here is where psyche and spirit intertwine for often we experience the new image as numinous, as a gift. Its idiosyncratic idiom convinces us that we did not invent this image; it is new, and our job is to take it.

Sticking thus to our original speech, our primary speech voiced in conversations with ourselves and in our prayers, we resist any other discourse imposed on us from the trauma, from a theory, from a forced religion (see Ulanov and Ulanov 1982). Our aggression destroys any other framework, resists it in a feat of social action, in our justice of including the forgotten, marginalized, repressed voice that was all but crushed in us by trauma. We are not a whore, the father's version of our self; we are our own self, thus linking back to the girl-self's ambition and creativity, still alive to be lived now in different forms.

Examples of this original speech abound. Testimony of atrocity in South Africa's Truth and Reconciliation Commission springs into vivid life through such primal language. A woman said she stood there, her hair aflame and her chest a furnace, not that she burned. A man said a red butterfly appeared on his wife's chest, not that she had been shot (Gobodo-Madikizela 2007). An analysand describes the first barest hint of a new symbol for the No-thing space into which trauma has tossed her: the No-thing space takes on a green furze, a faintest greenness on the ends of tree branches before they come into bud; the analyst replies, a beginning of a beginning. I think of Louis Armstrong orphaned and later able to create a song called "God Bless the Child That's Got His Own" and of Winnicott's patient who kept bringing her young daughter to the clinic as a way of expressing her own desperation for treatment as she suffered horrific images that expressed her abandonment to an orphanage. With Winnicott she reached back to an image of before the orphanage, of being taken to it in "the memory of her own good mummy" just enough to quiet the images of rats biting her (Winnicott 1971b, 341).

These images, these protosymbols, spring from our indigenous soil. Paying attention to them forges space in the thicket of our dense reactions to trauma. Working to translate them into language we can share with others makes space with others as separate subjects who voice their own idioms. For in translating our primary speech we accept that it is only our argot, not universal. We recognize the limits of our dialect and that allows us to recognize the speech of others. In this nexus of personal and collective, our translations construct a social space to conduct cross-cultural, interreligious dialogues.

There always endure, however, untranslatable experiences of psyche and spirit. We remain vulnerable and untranslatable. Collective trauma such as murder by holocaust or by necklacing, forced marches, starvation, or gulags can never be given adequate reparation, and personal traumatic shattering of our center and our connection to the center of reality leaves a scar on our psyche. How to draw on resources of our culture, our personal connections to others and to life itself, so that our having suffered trauma might translate us into an interlocutor between death and resurrection, pathology and becoming better than well? If we find those translations, then our suffering is not wasted but contributes to social congress a language that transcends wounds, that presides over death-dealing experiences.

Shift to the Primary Real

In this translating work, we are being translated. A shift occurs from past trauma to the self being created now, an ongoing act of creation in which we participate. A shift occurs from ego consciousness down to the elemental level outside ego yet including it. Jung calls this the Self, and Erich Neumann calls it the ego-Self axis. I would add that it is also a shift to the reality to which the Self and the ego-Self axis make a bridge: reality beyond our theories and beyond our ability to translate them into words.

We name this All, this Vast, differently—God, Buddha nature, pleroma—as we thread our particular individual and cultural experiences through the eye of its needle. With my focus on the nexus of personal and universal, individual and collective, human and transcendent, I think names are of great importance as they become the argot through which we advance into fuller conversation. You can't talk to an abstraction, but you can talk to Jesus or Buddha or Mohammed, or to the One who is Shepherd in the shadow of death (Psalm 23).

The shift takes place in the dark, outside consciousness, and is always making ready through all the things I have mentioned: cumulative movements toward healing, ego responsiveness, aggression, paradoxical understanding, recognizing the other as other and even our self as also other. We become aware that the shift has happened by events so surprising we know we did not invent them. They happened; they came from some other source, giving evidence through synchronicity that we live within the interconnected whole of reality. We live (more often) in Tao.

For example, we link up to the self we were before trauma smashed us. That self is not lost forever but translated now into a new grammar so fundamental it includes new verbs capable of being spoken now in an ongoing creating. Our psyche presses us to individuate; the Spirit presses us toward abundant life. We must get all the sheep together, the lost one being found, and this new one just showing up, this new sense of being created now, not recovering but creating in relation to a source beyond what we know and name, for example, the God beyond the archetypal god. We feel more freedom in this process and moments of astonishing joy. We allow for meaning to be made.

This self that goes on being created includes others. In clinical work the other is the analyst, and we are freer to allow our aggression within the relationship, facing the fears of abandonment and destruction. We risk accepting that the analyst knows things we do not know and can provide things we want to receive. The other may not be an analyst but rather a religious figure, an animal, a cultural object found in the arts, or a psychic other from active imagination or a dream. In each case we give sustained attention to this other and allow the full weight of our dependency to take us down to this elemental level. There we inquire who authored this other subject that recognizes me as subject? Who sent me this dream at this time? We open to a mystery that is beyond our need for known order and meaning. In this opening we discover that even the core of our self is a mystery. We reach an existential knowing without prior cognitive insight, a knowing before we can explain.

A most startling example of living from this added depth comes from the extraordinary venture of the Truth and Reconciliation Commission in South Africa, in which some participants leaped into forgiveness. Forgiveness is a grace; it falls upon us, and we then give it if we can receive it. By the perpetrator of trauma telling the victim's relatives the story of the violence he did, in cases of authentic remorse, he shows how his actions destroyed his own humanity by making the victim invisible and making himself invisible, too, by destroying his own conscience. In telling what he did, he faces his own destruction. Translating the violence into words witnesses to his own lost subjectivity and the subjectivity of the victim and recognizes them once again. The encounter between perpetrator and the victim's relatives begins to unravel the trauma. Hearers of the story are drawn into their own pain, replicating the reciprocal witnessing occurring between perpetrator and victim's relatives. The language may draw on cultural forms, as it did in one instance of parental language: the perpetrator asked, "Forgive me, my parents." The mother whose son the perpetrator murdered said he was the same age today as her son would have been had he lived. She responded, "I forgive you, my son; go well" (Gobodo-Madikizela 2007). The madness that unspeakable, untranslated trauma incites is met by untranslatable forgiveness that is beyond comprehension.

We cannot keep happiness out forever.

———————

This essay was a presentation for the Coming Home Project, serving Iraq and Afghanistan veterans and their families and caregivers, April 11–12, 2008, San Francisco, California.

THE PERILS OF INDIVIDUATION

I ndividuation as our most "costly task" to discover "you have the
secret of your particular pattern" is itself a great big knot that if
taken up occupies us all our lives long (Jung 1988, 1401; see
also Jung 1943, par. 24). As we untie one strand and then another,
the mystery at the center of our self emerges more clearly, but as a
mystery, never explained or resolved. As we work on ourselves we
discover that such work affects others near us and even others we do
not know directly. Like a runner of a root our soul links up with lives
of others that bloom or wilt, influenced by what we do or fail to do.

Possibilities and Perils

Jung's hypothesis of individuation—that each of us grows toward
becoming a whole person—is a wonderful idea. We can look at
ourselves, and other people too, from this perspective of growth and
not just in terms of problems and pathology. But it is also a perilous
idea, for wholeness means entire, intact, complete, an assemblage of
all that belongs to us, not leaving anything out. That means we will

be ushered into the chancy, the unsafe, even the unsayable, let alone the unbearable. It means we must include what menaces us, causes alarm, and leaves us feeling a radical vulnerability. Perilous means going into the dark, the slime, the ghosts, as well as into the blinding light that leaves us parched and panting for the waters of life, all dried up and afraid. Perilous means coming to bear more because our path is linked to the world's, and coming to ourselves means coming into the world and the world coming into us. The world means the other— the other groups in our neighborhood and country, the other religions, the other classes, our siblings, even our enemies. We might even say individuation is a process that takes place in that liminal space between conscious and unconscious.

Jung's notion of individuation is one of his most compelling ideas; it grants dignity to each one of us, that we are involved in "the process by which a person becomes a psychological 'in-dividual,' that is, a separate, indivisible unity or 'whole'" (Jung 1939b, par. 490). And again, "individuation means becoming. . . . a single, homogenous being"; "in so far as 'individuality' embraces our innermost, last, and incomparable uniqueness, it also implies becoming one's own self" (Jung 1928, par. 266; Jung 1963, 383). It implies a prior adaptation to collective norms, for, as Jung says, "if a plant is to unfold its specific nature to the full, it must first be able to grow in the soil in which it is planted" (Jung 1923, par. 760). We are dependent on the soil in which we are planted, on this family, not an ideal one, this town, nation, and culture, this time in history. We see, then, that we are in something which we did not create but with which we can align. We are dependent on the place where and persons to whom we are born, and our particular uniqueness affects the whole world near and far.

But individuation also means differentiating a standpoint and consciousness; it is not opposed to collective norms but is "differently oriented" (Jung 1923, par. 761). Becoming our unique self does not mean separation from others or society for "individuation does not shut one out from the world, but gathers the world to oneself" (Jung 1954b, par. 432). Thus our particular journey means the whole world's journey, too, as it shows itself in our particular problems and possibilities.

Rooted in the place into which we are born, we develop a conscious sense of I (ego) in relation to others and grow toward a wholeness of personality. Yet unfolding our unique self also means relating to the unconscious, and that opens uncertainty right in the middle of us, for "the concept of the unconscious *posits nothing*, it designates only my *unknowing*" (from a letter dated February 8, 1946; Jung 1992, 411). Our conscious knowing dwells with unknowing. That flings the door wide, doesn't it, to "the wondrous and terrible boon of original experience" (Jung 1954a, par. 19). Who knows what or who will come in, or go out, or go into exile? Can we stand this uncertainty, ambiguity, possibility that grows into something? Instead of calm proceeding, we now see individuation as risky, introducing a gap between what we know and have confidence we will come to know and the unknowing that lives within us as well as around us in the world. There is the certainty of what we take for granted and the uncertainty of anything that can happen instantaneously—a flood like Katrina, a car accident, a diagnosis, a shattering of confidence, a rape, the wondrous birth of a child, the miracle of falling in love, an eruption of laughter at what's seriously funny in life, the grace of forgiveness. In addition, the unexpected marvelous or hazardous may appear from another point of view within us, in a nightmare, a vision of basic goodness, a dream character stealing our car, a monstrous violence arising in our chest.

What is going on here? What is this urge to wholeness aiming toward, so ruthless, with unconscious thrusting into consciousness, matter into spirit and spirit into matter? Spirit matters. This experience recalls Jung's notion of psychoid as an "aura that surrounds consciousness" and "presents relatively autonomous 'images,' including the manifold God-images, which whenever they appear are called 'God' by naive people and, because of their numinosity . . . are taken to be such" (Jung 1955–56, par. 786). An example of the mixture of spirit and matter is illustrated in the 2007–2009 economic recession in the United States. Money is matter, we thought, material stuff, gain. But it is also psyche. Once we no longer trust money, once we no longer believe it stands for something, means something, it does not exist; it vanishes, poof! We will not lend it, spend it, exchange it, circulate it. In Iceland, whose government went bankrupt, it was reported that a man took all his money from the bank; for him, only cash he could touch was real. He hid it in his house, but then paranoid fears beset him that he would be robbed—by tourists or American gangsters who would come in planes to besiege his house, to get his dough.

Jung studied this gap between known and unknown in terms of ego and Self. Ego is what we are conscious of; it has a history of development, dependence on and relation to others, location in neighborhood, methods of reflection and inquiry. Self is a postulated ordering capacity in the psyche, to make a whole of it, conscious and unconscious, around a center, accepting that "however much we may make conscious there will always exist an indeterminate and indeterminable amount of unconscious material which belongs to the totality of the self" (Jung 1963, 386). Where ego consciousness feels located in history, Self feels of the ages. The transformation of this gap between them into a space of conversation has occupied me in much of my work, and this paper extends that focus once again.

Right away, we sense the danger of individuation. It means feeling this gap between two centers within, one we know and one we posit and for which we have images—derivatives turning up in our behavior or emotions. Examples are numerous. Think of those times when we feel there is something we must be doing with our life but do not know what it is. But we go forward with only a hint of definition, as if carried by a current or saying yes to a mere nudge. Or we say no and later regret this refusal. I have seen this demand from within put even to the most elderly. A woman in her nineties says she is ready to die, does not want to live now as a burden to herself and to others. She is ready to go, but she lives. The unvoiced question is, What is asked of her to be doing and being before she dies? And who is doing the asking? Her ego does not get to decide everything but must listen for the other point of view. Our own process of becoming who we are is framed by forces, usually beyond our control, of when we are born and when we die. Another woman in her nineties tried to commit suicide (because she, too, felt life was a burden) but did not succeed because she was physically too frail to accomplish it. She came for analysis, and we talked over the suicide attempt. She dreamed a powerful dream. She was viewing again her friend the painter Orazco's collection, and there was a blank space on the wall. What is to be put here, she asks? The dream answers that it is to be her painting, and it is not finished. She must finish it so it can be hung with the others. Some part of her says no to her wish to die; there is life to be lived, for her self-expression and for others, as the painting is to be hung in a gallery open to the public. People need to see what we have discovered and made of our experience, for their own use and to sustain human culture which recognizes such living (Ulanov 1986b, 65).

The symbolic concept of the Self as an archetypal image of an ordering, centering urge to fill out and make whole is just that, a drive, with all its forcefulness. We are in its grip. We may ride it like a horse if we learn how to relate to it, but it has its life, too, and can run away with us. This push, this impulse to life, prevails upon us, moves us. Jung says, "as soon as you deal with the self as an experience . . . wild things come up, because you are confronted with mountains of obscurity; it is just like being actually in the jungle in the midst of an excited herd of elephants" (Jung 1988, 416). Jung calls it a daimon that had its will with him; even his creative impulses cost him dear (Jung 1963, 356, also 337, 344; see also Jung 1988, 58, 61, 75, 653, 661–662, 667, 680).

Often a neurosis hides this urge to individuate (Jung 1948b, par. 518). Perceiving in our problems a potent conversation struggling to be heard between our ego—our ordinary I-ness—and this other center we imagine organized by the Self—which would enlarge us to be all we could be right up to the end of our days—is immensely helpful in looking into our distress. For then there is something to be heard, not just a former functioning to be regained. I was startled to hear myself say to a young woman, "Thank God for this bulimia; it rescued you from a life of diminishment" (despite the damage to her teeth and many sessions with the dentist). She said, "The model of, am I making progress [meaning to achieve a normative goal set by her experience of her family and mores of her class] keeps me on the treadmill."

Becoming whole, then, that sounds so wonderful—who wouldn't want to be whole in a whole world—also brings uncertainty, wildness, looking into our suffering rather than rising above it. Like water, the life in us that wants to be lived "always seeks the deepest place" (Jung 1988, 508). Individuation means submitting to that water of life filling up all the cracks, the fault lines, the depressions and sharp cutting edges in our self. No wonder we would rather do anything than "accept ourselves in our particular concreteness. That is the thing of which we are most afraid" (ibid., 87).

The deepest place includes every bit of ourselves and our ties with each other: "the existence of an individual implies: his needs, his tasks, his duties, his responsibilities, etc. Individuation does not isolate, it connects" (from a letter dated July 2, 1948; Jung 1992, 504). "You proceed beyond the ego to ever-widening horizons. . . . You integrate your animal, your parents, all the people you love" (from a letter dated January 25, 1954; Jung 1976, 146). We become ever more conscious of the web of connection to each other that holds us in being. Individuation is a knot that will not be all tied up; it remains untied, open to a task that is our self.

Yet individuation also means accepting what we want to reject and that we must accept it for the sake of the world: "The purpose of individuation is that every part of the individual must be integrated, also the criminal part; otherwise it is left by itself and works evil" (Jung 1988, 469). If we do not face it, it lives beyond the control and moderating effects of our own ego and of the collective consciousness we share with others. Left to roam free, it contaminates or attacks others, even our children or innocents for whom we feel compassion, who were just bystanders and end up paying the price we avoided. We do not get away with it despite the cost others have paid in our stead. We must pay too: "The humiliation allotted to each of us is implicit in his character. If he seeks wholeness seriously, he will step unawares into the hole destined for him, and out of this darkness the light will rise" (from a letter dated January 5, 1952; Jung 1976, 352).

Becoming more whole, then, brings a sense of being found out, turned out, all the parts and needs, the desires and frights turned up to be counted and fitted into the sense of self, even reaching to what is criminal in ourselves. We need not think up the bad in us; it is the hole we step in, the humiliation that is peculiarly ours. We can all this moment think of such humiliations, as a child, as a woman, a man, a parent, a citizen. That, too, must be loved into the living whole, lest we damage our neighbor, and lest our neighbors damage us with their unlived parts.

Symptoms and the Claim of Wholeness

Even more arresting is the discovery that one of our troublesome symptoms springs from a claim of our wholeness. This does not make the symptom any less vexing, interrupting our functioning and drawing the criticism of others. But it does redeem it: we see the symptom has kept something alive that belongs to us. Several examples come to mind. A man discovered that hiding within what he called his perversions was a small boy self who had not found nor expressed his own aggressiveness. Recognizing this part of himself loosened the hold of his repetitive masochistic acts (Ulanov 1996b, chap. 3). He counted connecting with this small boy the second great accomplishment of his life, after finding and marrying his wife.

A woman discovered that her rising panic and flooding emotions of helplessness, which interrupted her capacity to function and angered her children and colleagues, was a part of herself she had turned away from as a very small girl who was helpless in response to not being recognized or loved for herself. She built up a life for herself but never included the girl, who was not noticed, remembered, or searched for. Her adult eruptions into helplessness, she discovered, were the spaces where this small girl part had taken up residence, stayed alive, and pressed her claim to be integrated. The small girl part was authentic helplessness whose claim was levied by her growing wholeness. Another woman, who was married young to a workaholic and sexually inhibited man, discovered, only at a friend's suggestion, masturbation as a help in the sexual desert this young couple seemed to inhabit. She felt she was violating her relation to God and promised to desist, but did not; she then felt bad, that she was bad. Yet she discovered that in that space her sexuality maintained its aliveness.

In each of these examples, the person was introduced to moral ambiguity. What they thought was bad—perversion, helplessness, singular sexual gratification—turned out to reveal what was good and a necessary part of them—aggressiveness, a child's dependence, sexual desire. Wholeness pressed its claim upon them, making them see differently even if that was unsettling. They saw the goodness of what was left out and that it was not to be gotten rid of as bad. We are thus ushered into questions about the uncertainty of our categories of good and bad.

Awareness of our task of including everything that belongs to us tempers our spiritual ambitions and our mere curiosity. When unconscious contents step over into consciousness, our moral burden increases, "because the unconscious contents transform themselves into your individual tasks and duties as soon as they become conscious" (from a letter dated April 10, 1954; Jung 1976, 172). Hence becoming conscious of the process of individuation going on within brings a life-and-death seriousness: "The attainment of wholeness requires one to stake one's whole being. Nothing less will do . . . no easier conditions, no substitutes, no compromises" (Jung 1939a, par. 906).

Individuation is perilous—bringing awareness of a ruthless urge, a dependence, an uncertainty, the world's suffering, our moral obligation toward all the parts—past, present, and yet to come. And it has no decisive outcome. We are always on the journey and never arrive at the promised completion. Jung says of himself, "with all my experience of nearly eight decades I must admit I have found no rounded answer to myself. I am just as much in doubt about myself as before" (from a letter dated April 6, 1954; Jung 1976, 163). We live on this path always moving toward completeness, ever arriving. In this consists our psyche's resilience and our surprise of hope.

Summons

I want to explore some of the parts that come, bidden and unbidden, in the process of individuation. Individuation is a natural process, augmented by our conscious participation. We can feel it as an urge toward an unknown goal, a sense that there is something we must be doing in this life, as if there were a river running through us and we are only barely able to discern its direction or its source but keenly know the force of its current. Such an awareness can embolden us to leave a relationship, a job, a family business, or a belief system and venture into unknown waters, uncertain but also with hints and inklings that support this great risk taking. We will bet on our own desire and move to another city, dare to engage in a relationship, commit to what a dream told us. We can feel this urge as ruthless, pushing us, pulling us, insisting that we go with the current even if we do not know where it is heading. We know only that it is our current, in which we will find our own self. The great thing is to recognize this current, acknowledge its presence, pay it close attention, observe our relation to it.

We feel its paradoxical presence. We feel this is our self, not anyone else's, authentic. This summons is to us and about us and only ours to answer. Yet this summons comes upon us like a stranger, some urge that we did not invent or even invite, which feels like an other, an it, issuing from another place that is in us but not of us. It addresses us, and we are left with the door flung wide: Who authors this? For what aim? Paradox permeates us like a light rain—this is all about my own self at my deepest core, to do with answers to what am I doing on this earth, what am I to fulfill. Yet the sense of otherness convinces: an other presence is involved, one we barely discern but sense through animal whiskers, the soft padding sound of a foot on the earth. Through the mist around us we begin to see that this other is transforming into a shape, that our job is to assist in its coming into being.

The negative versions are more frightening. If we do not reach toward a rocklike solidity, we may do it negatively through becoming petrified. If we do not eat the juice of life, then, like Tantalus, we may feel tortured by an unquenchable longing for fruits forever out of reach. If we do not carry our burden, we may, like Sisyphus, feel condemned ever to push the rock up the hill only to have it roll down again. The body can play a central part. If we cannot get into the rightful current, the body may push us there. There we know we must get out of the house, but we put it off, cannot see how to get free of our responsibilities for the ill one in the house. One woman said she felt she lived under a rock pressing down on her, as if in suspended animation, all but crushed. But she put off finding time to herself to look into what was blocking her, preventing her from taking up her own creative life and the specific work she wanted to do. Then, as if the body takes over, we shift instantly from caregiver to needing care given to us. We fall ill, and our illness takes us out of those responsibilities to the other, finally to tend to the increasingly depressive weight on our souls. The surprise is that what we feared was an either/or choice of giving care to oneself or the other turns out to be a capacity to combine responses to both.

The body has its own life, as mysterious as the psyche's, so we cannot reduce physical illness to psychic attitude. But the body is joined to the psyche, and what we cannot carry psychically is often pushed over to the body's burden, like a faithful animal laden with our responsibility. I have seen radical surgery somehow connected to being unable to get free of unconsciously driven behavior or a condition that lasts half a century until consciousness intervenes (see Ulanov 2001a for a detailed example). I have seen a body problem with joints too loose to hold the body securely together related to a lifelong defense of holding one's breath as a way of leaving a painful, chronic situation of not being held as a child in a loving family.

The urge to individuation is the most ruthless of our instincts; it will out, one way or another. Sometimes it is through our children, who get all the force of what we have not lived and should have lived because we could have. Then the children must fight through our problems to reach their own problems, which will yield paths for their own lives. They lose a lot of years trying to resolve their parents' problems instead.

To find our own voice we may have to kill a murderous inner critic and take that energy to learn the discipline to attend, adhere, go through the gate. We may have to ask, in the midst of wreckage of groups we love, what is emerging from the splitting into opposed factions in our country.

Collapse

Another way decisive individuation announces itself is through collapse, especially after achieving a lot of stable growth and fulfillment. Looked at from our ego's point of view, this can be devastating, threatening our trust in our self. Looked at from the centering function we call the Self, we see we can afford this eruption now precisely because of the growth and stability achieved. We can afford to retrieve the missing pieces, the lost ones we had to put aside at an earlier time in order to survive. The urge toward individuation means taking a person as a whole, not just those fragments we choose to make up a wholeness that we design. We are faced with what the whole is when we take all of ourselves. Thus here, in collapse and going back to pick up what was put aside, split off, lost, or never lived in the first place, is to reach for all of it.

Here I lump suffering such as that caused by trauma, with all its catastrophic effects of splitting up parts of ourselves, and living as though suspended in half light, as when mourning what we lived and lost because of death, illness, poverty, or war. Or we may need to mourn what we never lived, what was not available to be lived because it was absent in the setting in which we lived. Heartache, sorrow, self-doubt, and anxiety about being annihilated all come into play here. One woman could hardly distinguish which part it was when she fell under an avalanche of sadness, weeping, feeling isolated, taking to her bed in misery, and unable to function. She could list the traumas that happened to her and her family, and we differentiated and looked into each one (they included killing, maiming, denial and restraint, and affection withheld). But the overall sorrow did not lessen, but became more distinct, a sorrow for the human condition—hers, her family's, the planet's. If she ignored the sorrow, tried to move on, get a grip, rise above it, her body would fall ill and force her to break down and go back to bed. She was flooded with archetypal emotion joined to her own feelings about personal wounds.

What is being worked here? Collapse is terrible to experience, but it also can mean a radical shift of orientation, to perceive and respond from a new location. It brings discovery of a new task: the necessity of maintaining a connection to the point of origin, what we experience as the source and aim of life, however we experience it and name it. Collapse looked at from the ego perspective makes us feel we are back again to square one, back to go without collecting two hundred dollars. Fusion of archetypal affect and personal feelings can overwhelm us and drag us out to sea. From this point of view, we must hear and explore each personal feeling and differentiate it from archetypal underpinning, so my sorrow is mine and not tears of blood for all the suffering in the world. An unguessed privilege of finitude is its limitation. Then we can hold on to the good even in the face of the bad.

Collapse looked at from the Self perspective transforms the gap of loss into a searching conversation with what is emerging, the task that is our very own. In this woman's case her job was how to bear inevitable presence of suffering (she could hardly stand to listen to the daily news) and subscribe to deep hope about the world; how to trust the good and its thriving when there was so much wrong in the world. For her it meant taking seriously her lifelong religious experience and giving it "ever-deepening concentration," as Jung put it. Jung stated that, for him as for the mystics, "the innermost self of every man and animal, of plants and crystals, is God, but infinitely diminished and approximated to his ultimate individual form" (from a letter dated August 3, 1953; Jung 1976, 120).

Her undertaking, then, was to make room for God in her individual form. How do we house the eternal in our finite lives? How can we pay attention to the All and Vast in our particular daily life? How can we give close observation to the individuation process going on within us in the midst of our jobs, children, the upcoming election? This language made sense to her, drawing on her religious experience of making a space and place in her heart for Jesus to abide. This may have been the secret of her individuation, her path to her own new stability and to contributing to the rest of us.

The proof is always in the pudding. She prayed for a relative with whom there was friction and even hate, who made her feel ever minimized, dismissed, not worth engaging, of no importance. She prayed "that the love of God proceed me into life, that I receive and give love without feeling so vulnerable, and that when I am angry and judging others that God blesses them and they feel his love and being cared for." Whatever the strife between them, over the course of a year it melted away and friendliness grew up, simply to be accepted, even if not fully understood. Here is resilience of the psyche, and hope a gift of the soul.

This example illustrates the path we all find in individuation: we are relocated to new country, surprised by its appearance, surprised that something grows up and claims us as we struggle to claim all of ourselves. We need to make space—a magic square or whatever our dream or imaginative symbol for it—where we house what we call God, the point of origin. It takes up residence in our small but decisive struggle to include all the parts of ourselves. In our labor to find our lost sheep and bring them home, new sheep turn up that we did not know about. And the community of sheep needs these lost ones and the new ones to function. The whole group needs the parts of each person; we need others in order to grow more whole, and to grow into a community that differentiates from the collective mass. We do not individuate alone: "we only become ourselves with people and for people. . . . Being an individual is always a link in a chain" (Jung 1988, 102). Thus our individual selves, even though small, enliven the whole. Our relationships with each other bring oxygen to the whole garden; we bring God or whatever we call the source of the whole, to each other. Therein lies our hope.

We may settle instead for a life of self-imposed limitation. One man said his emotional life reached from A to B; that he was like a marble rolling around in the universe. Another example comes from two different analysands, unknown to each other, both men highly educated and successful in their professions, one dogged by severe isolation from other people, the other dogged by massive phobias that strongly restricted his relationships. As little boys each believed that when he was not around his family spoke another language to each other that he did not know and that they kept secret from him. What a poignant image of feeling one does not belong: my family shares a closeness, the very grammar of communication of which I am ignorant and from which I am excluded by their secrecy. To compensate for this feeling of being shut out, the first man worked to be in control, in charge, to the point of paranoid fear. As he put it, "Anything I want is not going to happen." He could not acknowledge his dependency, not even on our long work in analysis. The second man found his very body kept him apart. His germ phobia made him afraid his children would make him sick, afraid his body would sabotage him with a disease, and hence he avoided medical checkups; fear of flying isolated him from his friends and made him unable to see his colleagues at meetings.

To include left-out parts in individuation means mourning for what was not there—not just what was there and lost, but what was never there and should have been, a primary safety, feeling loved and protected, with an easy back and forth connecting to family members. In the transference this lack shows up in our very hard work to establish connection. In the one man's case he used his formidable intelligence to lecture me, judging me a dope with a force that attacked my ability to think and feel. In the other man's case, he talked nonstop, and I could not get a word in edgewise and felt frustrated and useless. In both relationships, I could tell when more linking between us grew by feeling, in the first man's case, that I too existed as a person with elbow room to imagine, to have thoughts arrive—a loosening of the former straightjacket. In the second man's case, the pace of the talk eased a bit, admitting a silence now and then, as if space were opening up for words between us back and forth.

To mourn for what we did not have and should have had is deeply sorrowful. It is sad for everybody. Nobody is the bad guy, the scapegoat; it is what we all missed and never enjoyed. The man who lectured me was studying his roots in Judaism and arrived at a deeply felt interpretation of Yom Kippur. He said, "That is the day I mourn the opportunities of the last year I did not take, what should have been lived and was not, and they went missing, wasted." Here we glimpse a meaning of original sin: we are born into societies afflicted with prejudices of all kinds that stain our own orientation to life. In the groups to which we belong, we can feel the weight of painful histories that burden us with a legacy of misunderstandings, restricting our recognition of one another and our free communication. We are born into complexes that trouble our family members for generations and blight the possibility of living our own lives with full colors. Space shrinks.

The image of full colors comes from another analysand, a woman who described what was taken from her in a trauma of sexual interference when she was a girl. "I lost the full colors of my loving," she said, "my sexuality split off from my loving, my loving having no easy firm connection to my sexuality after that." She had worked very hard to get back her sexuality and with success. But she had never mourned the sorrow the split inflicted, mourned all the hard work the split necessitated. And here she was now, an older person, having to go back to lament the loss of a simple wholeness of her girl-self that had been split apart. She could see that her entire family suffered this blight; otherwise this trauma never would have occurred. "All of us were caught," she said, "in not living fully. We missed a lot."

Central to original sin is how we hurt each other when our dependency is not met, or is manipulated for the other's use, or is exploited sadistically. An illustration of how violent can be the effects of misusing another's dependency came my way via email. A person wrote to me about having lost connection to her orienting vision (what

I might call a God-image) of the eternal river, feeling it had been stolen from her by the abandonment of her former lover, who had been her analyst. I was struck that this was already a situation of harm and undoing, instigating rage as part of her recovery. "What to do?" her letter asked. I responded by saying that the river is eternal, so it had not gone out of existence nor out of her reach. She must ask it directly what she must do to come close to it again, or if not that, then what? And wait on its response. I added that if she felt another had stolen her access to this river, then a new access might mean that she must steal it back. My point is that we cannot individuate alone, but only with and in relation to other people. We depend on each other and cannot be without each other. We live as part of a whole webbed connection among us and within us, and we need each other to come right in the end. Even our dreams, says Jung, happen in the spaces between us (from a letter dated September 29, 1934; Jung 1992, 171).

This odyssey of looking for the missing parts is likened to a night sea journey, a dark night of the soul in which every solution we had created proves no longer effective. Stripped of resources and reference points, we feel lost, even frightened. What is asked of us, what are we readying for, that we must now gather in all these missing parts of us that we once defended ourselves against in order to survive? We split off those parts because the violence of them endangered our keeping alive, or because to feel the depth of the abandonment would have killed us, or because persisting in our own way upset Mother or Father and threatened our vital tie to them, on which depended our well-being (Atwood and Stolorow 1992, 368).

An Example

One analysand said that, for as long as she could remember, her mother would say to her, "Do not tell me, I do not want to be upset." Not until she was in her fifties and told her mother she was in analysis did her mother tell her that she had wanted to get some help, but her husband forbade her, and when she was at the end of her rope, the mother would go sit on the floor in her dark closet and close the door. For the daughter, it was different. Unlived parts of her came to hunt her down. No closet, no removing herself from upset was possible.

Tears bubbled up in her eyes and fell down her face. Crying came of its own; she could not stop the tears, and she could not understand them either and that was the most alarming. She had no words to represent what the tears were saying, no way to communicate it, even to herself. Finally, sentences came, but they were seemingly so abstract her husband and children were tempted to seek a clinical name for her state. She said, "I have been struggling two and half years. I feel lost with myself; I don't know where to put myself in the world. I do not know how to place myself in reality; I do not know what I need to know."

The lost parts hunted her down, disrupting her persona (that is, how she saw herself appearing to others) and making it impossible for her to go out in public. Often the only way the lost part can find us is through the back door, breaking down our usual way of conducting ourselves, disrupting our functioning, pressing for attention. From an ego point of view, this disruption is alarming; we feel we are losing our grip on reality. In the case above, others who loved the woman thought she was breaking down and wanted her to take medicine, pull herself together, get over it. I could understand them thinking that, but I was not at all sure. I was struck by something breaking through, saying, "Recognize me." Each time the tears cascaded, we stopped and asked, What emotion now overcomes you? A sorting through began. With attentiveness, she slowly began to put words to specific feelings, and a picture developed of years of remaining like a child who, like Sleeping Beauty, had now awakened.

Her individuation process was not hers alone, not singular, but occasioned each member of her family to face their own unvoiced serious upset, and in each case this caused an upheaval of big proportions. I was struck all over again by the web of our connections with each other. Despite her husband's strong attempts to say the problem was hers, some kind of depression or worse, it became immediately clear that he too had lived as if asleep, cocooned within repeated complexes. When she awoke, his insularity was challenged, as was her son's and daughter's. Individuation means the world comes to us, we involve the world, the immediate world of family and friends, but also the larger one of our cultural setting and beyond.

Recognition

Recognition is our key to locked-up, split-off life, to the fragmented parts dispersed into symptoms, to the knot of suffering that fuels our awakening. One of the many things that so impresses me about the psyche's resilience is its insistence that all its feelers be included, all its legs, all its feathers. It repeats and repeats and repeats, trying to gain admittance for the parts of us that belong to us yet remain unintegrated.

Looked at from the ego perspective, this is the symptom that we never get over, the one that continues to interrupt our functioning and annoy those around us. Our list of weird habits and troublesome symptoms—like having to make perfect order in the cabinets, or being too spent to get off the couch, or erupting in rage and awful attacks on someone we love and denying it afterward—these things repeat until a door in us opens. Sometimes, with practice, we learn how to open the door or a new joy flings it open. But the passage to openness always means feeling psychic pain, and we must build up stamina and the hope, based on experience, that the pain is not the end point. It leads somewhere we desire to go, to dwell. Hope, then, is not a bleak hanging on but juiced with desire for a fuller life, a life of gladness, gaiety, meaning, and contributing to others. Looked at from the Self perspective, we see wholeness presses us to claim what we left out and to claim that we are claimed.

Hope is an odd thing because it ushers in the world. By its nature, hope is relational. What we hope for extends to others, too. Through art and literature, we can see where the lost parts of the world are shoved. Did we send them to the segregated neighborhoods? To the prisons? To the mental hospitals? To the captivity of drugs, whether illicit or prescribed? To ghosts or vampires, the distant life of aliens from outer space, or into the characters in computer games (Doninger 2007, 252)? All those pieces of us and of our societies stay alive in these cultural spaces that house our repressed, split-off parts. Yet the arts also bring us the resilience of human creativity that opens our hope. The single line of a Matisse drawing, where he has cut away everything inessential to reveal there is this line to depend on, displays a lifeline that quickens us into our aliveness. The vicious words about women in a rap song speak of rage against lost dependence, dependency not met, fear of no control, and savage assertion of taking control over the tender, painful, abandoned parts of the male self. The reenergizing of our political vision in the 2008 presidential election in the United States bespoke new hope in the process, whichever candidate we favored, hope that our response would make a difference and that our new elected government could make a good change in the world.

Recognition of our lost parts, recognition of who hurt us and whom we hurt, recognition of those hints, subtle clues, inklings, pointers, prods, intimations, odd dreams, even jolts pointing to which path to take, attunes us to the resilience of our psyche, and of the psyche operating between and among us. From such recognition springs communication. Once we can talk to ourselves and each other, or make pictures, or have sense impressions that we can relate to, then that awful gap of confusion, self-doubt, lostness begins to transform into a space of conversation. Like electricity or telephone lines, or even the invisible Internet connections and radio waves, a beginning, a reaching, a humming forth and back commences. We impart, pass on, announce, transmit, make known; and we receive, take in, meet, acquire, accept. The world we create buzzes with aliveness between our consciousness and unconscious figures of dream or active imagination, with painful symptoms or clarifying insights. We speak to each other and as groups back and forth, able to hear through the obstacles to join in a common, limited purpose and leave to hope the next time we talk to get further. We confess we pray all along, even if we do not know there is a God or what we would call the Holy, and are able to wait in a listening silence, ready now in response to what comes or to what we discover preceded our efforts to sit still and is already there, waiting for us.

This recognition and the communication it engenders is, I suggest, the nexus point between personal, social, and transcendent. God must come into the here and now in order for us to experience God's reality there beyond us. Suffering in the here and now can only be borne if we find meaning in its connection to purpose that is real. We enter a paradoxical space where we author this conversation that is already authoring us. It is as if we tuned into a wavelength already existing, new and surprising to us but present all along, just not real and alive until we pull it into our own words, images, and body feelings.

Added as well is another dimension of knowledge. Could this be the mystical? We recognize a knowledge that is not communicable in the terms we have at our disposal, no words, barely an image. The body feels it, but how and where? It is through recognition of nonrepresentational knowledge that we apprehend but do not comprehend. Our words about such experience slip and slide, as T. S. Eliot says. Its presence bursts our images like a painting going off the canvas into the frame. Lovers sometimes in the ecstasy of their lovemaking feel it touching them and, as if exhausted by joy, joke that this will kill them. Having experience of such moments impresses us deeply with the resilience of the psyche. We sense this even in the abyss of confusion and self-doubt, like the woman crying incessantly, looking as if she is breaking down but instead breaking through to a wellspring of experiencing life as she comes awake. That means her feeling anger, sadness at the loss of decades of experience, the excitement of naming what is happening to her, fervor and determination to stay awake and live in a bigger space. A plenitude of life can break through to us; we need a witness as a companion to the validity of what is happening in order to have hope to receive all that would be given us.

Primitive, crude, destructive urges appear in us, as do advanced spiritual perceptions of who or what lies at the heart of all of life, legacies of culture and civilization, lines of poetry, elegant mathematical formulas, perfected knowledge of how to cook the lamb chop to just the right degree of rareness. All these things go together, the most base and the most exalted; that is what makes the spiritual real not just an idea or ideal that is quickly overrun by savagery or acute suffering.

Recognition of this other part of the psyche—this other person, part of the world, intimation of the Holy—enlarges our sense of life within us and around us. We grow a capacity to be conscious of our consciousness as an organ of seeing the Self process at its center and the whole surround. The Self is not an actor behind the scenes, a fixed content now revealed. It is process, relationship, which we catch in images, like a bigger bowl in which we sit, a larger sea that feeds and is fed by our small brooks and rivers. We recognize our own experience of something beyond us yet relating to us; we make analogies, images, symbols to represent it to ourselves. As one woman said, "God is like the wind in the heavens."

Something happens to us, and we are involved in creating it. This changes what we want. As Jung said, even approaching eighty he was still a puzzle to himself, full of doubts, not a clear individuated whole. We shift our desire from a goal to be reached to recognizing the creating going on now, the *creatio continua,* those moments of the *nunc stans,* the eternal now, where we know that all that is, is now, an entire, complete moment. This sort of moment shows chronological time of past, present, future, which we grasp under the principle of causality, intersecting with synchronistic phenomena that bespeak qualitative time, the "eternal presence" of a single creative act (von Franz 1974, 12, 194; see also Jung 1952b, pars. 965–966). Successive time, successive experience, intersects with simultaneity, the experience of all togetherness.

Such synchronistic moments give us hope at a deep level, for though we do not create those events, we participate in them. Our participation is necessary for such moments to be registered. Our subjective witness of such synchronicities is intrinsic to them. Our subjective wonder and deep impression of meaning forms part of the objective coincidence of noncausally related events. Without our subjective response, the objective coincidence goes unincarnated in human experience. The coincidences do not get noticed if we do not register our awe at their meaning for us, a meaningfulness that ushers us into the whole surround, the whole of life transcending us and into which we fit as a necessary part. Our hope is grounded in something that endures even when we falter.

To deal with what comes across from unconscious to conscious—this lump of stuff, crude, monstrous—is to engage in the human task of transforming primordial matter and being transformed by it. We each have stuff to work on as our job, so that the primordial matter—God, it, what we believe in, belong to—can take shape, be accessible to live through, in, and between us as its threshing floor, its vessel. We fit into the wholeness of individuation like a piece of a puzzle's whole picture. We do not become whole. We find our place in the wholeness being constructed.

Precisely here we experience our unique individuation process linked to the world, indeed gathering the world into itself. Through such synchronistic moments that happen in every individuation process, I believe, we not only see the surrounding totality and that we belong to it, what Jung calls the *unus mundus*, but also that our contribution is necessary for the whole to be whole. It matters; we matter. Hope is the capacity to find, more than it is the object found. In one of those remarkable paradoxes, to feel our capacity to find endorses our confidence that we are found, that we have a place in the complete scheme of things and help build up its wholeness. Our efforts to integrate our lost parts, to withstand a radical change of orientation in accepting new parts, brings our human-centered approach in line with the greater nonhuman-centered cosmos.

Our singular identity thins, opens to the surround, all parts of us included. For example, even our criminal parts—the one that cheats on the SAT tests to get into the good college but then feels like a fake when there, or our murderous part that would kill what we fear, or the part that dumps on our relative all the rage we do not process but export, polluting another's life with our undigested toxicity—are faced when we feel the click of synchronicity. The coinciding opposites become an unimaginable complexity and may, as in the Zohar, move toward conjunction where goodness puts each part in its place.

Jung, using the alchemist Dorn's stages, investigates our human individuation process in relation to the whole world that transcends our human perspective. In the first stage of *unio mentalis* we extend our consciousness in uniting soul and spirit by withdrawing our projections, discovering our shadows, and in that sense overcoming the body (Jung 1955–56, pars. 694–696). We gain knowledge of the Self beyond the ego, the Self indistinguishable from image of God (ibid., par. 711). In the second stage we reunite this conjunction of soul and spirit with the body again, that is, we realize our greater consciousness of our ego-Self connection in our actual living. Insights should be made real. Our consciousness (spirit), differentiated by self-knowledge, unites with the soul previously abstracted from unconscious contents (ibid., par. 736). What we usually think of as the final stage, the stage of living aligned with Self images, approximating a completion of our individuation process, in fact is only the second stage, not the end point, but now ready for uniting with the world. In the third stage, we reach beyond our personal and even our shared human perspective, to see our place in and contribution beyond what's human to the whole of the cosmos. Our human spirit-soul-body unites with the *unus mundus*, "not the world of multiplicity as we see it but with the potential world, the eternal Ground of all empirical being, just as the self is the ground and origin of the individual personality past, present, and future" (ibid., par. 760). Here the human personal and interpersonal individuated approach links with the suprapersonal, the "individual tao with the universal tao" (ibid., par. 762).

This linking is not a fusion of individual and totality but a mystical union with the underlying oneness of life. On this fundamental wholeness our hope depends; it is the rock on which we rely when all else fails. Symbols of the center and the source of this wholeness include the *caelum*, the *lapis* stone, the Christ. The *caelum* corresponds to the incorruptible original stuff of the world, God's obedient instrument, God in matter, matter in God, psyche in matter, matter in psyche.

On this psycho-physical wholeness of the whole depends our hope and resilience in our own individuation process that we engage and share with one another.

———————

This essay was originally presented at Jung on the Hudson in Rhinebeck, New York, July 2008. A revised version was presented to the Jungian Psychotherapy Association in Seattle, Washington, in October 2008, and another expanded version to the Jung Society and Pittsburgh Theological Seminary, Pittsburgh, Pennsylvania, March 28–29, 2009.

BODY AND PSYCHE

4

How Much Lightning Can We Stand?
Our Bodies: Bound and Transformed

K nots in our bodies can tie up our emotions, and knots in our emotions can tie up our bodies. There is no way to leave out our bodies when we take up the subject of knots and their untying. We live in our bodies; our life is here and now in the body of the world and the body of our psyche. Bodies bring dependence, especially on women and on what we imagine is the feminine matrix of being which feeds us into life. So concrete in suffering an illness and so unnoticed when in the bloom of health, our actual body presents mysterious knots that may never get untied and may instead need only to be remarked, beheld. The mystery of the brain and the mystery of the soul as embodied—of what sustains the body politic, mystical body, subtle body, resurrection body—stay mysterious and become even more so the more we work to untie their inner forces. It helps to stick first to our actual body in which we have all the out-of-body experiences.

The question, How much lightning can we stand? signals the shift that occurs when the analysand and analyst succeed in doing psychoanalytical work. Attention moves from a focus on the conscious problem that brings us to treatment, which we hope to resolve, to a look into the unconscious depths that may have caused it. A seam opens, a fault line, and reveals our inchoate desire to be alive before we die, to find and create our own self in relation to others and to whatever we call the One we believe in, or do not.

This shift decenters us from conscious knowing and gives way to what Jung calls "inner dialogue with someone unseen. It may be God . . . or with [ourself], or with [our] good angel . . . a living relationship to the answering voice of the 'other' in ourselves, i.e., the unconscious" (Jung 1944, par. 390). The clinical task shifts from how can we be safe and secure to how can we receive all that is given us to become and give all that is asked from us (Ulanov 2007b, 16; see also Ulanov 2001a, 140). At that juncture, explosions of light happen; energy like electricity kindles, and psyche touches spirit.

Opening to the unconscious is not a solipsistic venture, but a relational one. The isolation imposed by our problem opens to the unknown in ourselves, in others, and to otherness itself. We become destabilized from our wish for a God who defines all certainties and our containment within them to glimpse a God who is with us, but never completely graspable, ever to be discovered. The mystery of our self with its evolving subjectivity meets mystery at the core of reality. Like the vision of thirteenth-century Hadewijch of Brabant, we find abyss of soul meeting abyss of God, and also that connection between Rebecca and the Lord "as one inexpressible being speaking to another" (Ulanov 1998, 198; Zornberg 2009, 226).

Physical Body

The lightning flashes of such encounters are always body-based. We live in our bodies; they locate us. Body means limit, form, concreteness, realization in time and space, history, a network of interconnected or broken relationship to both social and nonhuman environments. Body means living in this whole world, including the unseen, large reality in which our world exists. We are bound in our body, and our body is also the place in which transformation happens, or fails to.

Bound can mean stuck, fixed, helpless, as well as consolidated in time and place, coherent. Our body is a container in which things can be realized, come into being, secured into livingness and sustaining change. Think of the great range of experiences our body evokes, especially in relation to women and symbolism of the feminine. We never leave our body until we are left by it in death. Woman's body and mysteries of birth are associated with mortality, as Otto Rank described so long ago, stating that as long as man held himself to be born of the clan totem, he could claim immortality. But once he acknowledged his birth as being from woman, he fell into humanness with a beginning and an end (Rank 1941, 202–234).

The mystery of being born from a woman's body strikes all of us as strange, astonishing; yet for anyone who has been pregnant and experienced her body as food by blood and milk for an other, the strangeness is in our bodies. We are the womb where aliveness begins. In beholding the child coming forth as someone where before there was no one, we feel metaphysical shock on a literal plane, the transpersonal in the particular shape, sounds, skin, toes, and fingers of this utterly new being. We know the All in the singular. Those of us who give birth in other ways, in teaching, for example, recognize the mysterious embodiment of truths, from the flesh of our insights to the flesh of insight in students or, for example, in creating new patterns of the coming to be, whether a new recipe or scientific hypothesis.

We can feel the before-birth of body—those fugitive fantasies, wisps of ideas, and body hints that exist before language, before symbol. Children are close to this and create myths to describe this body-speech. My sister imagined seven men on roller skates whizzing around inside her body to take in food, make skin or fingernails, grow her hair. Psychoanalysis daily returns to this before-birth place in hovering over unconscious experiences that are not yet formulated but nonetheless real, that take form through the relationship between analysand and analyst, not as clear, finished conclusions but as wish, dream image, body sensation (Stern 1983). Ricoeur asks how the unconscious exists in the world and answers from his phenomenological perspective: "its mode of being is that of the body, which is neither ego nor a thing in the world" (Ricoeur 1970, 382).

We speak of the unconscious realm as matrix, the feminine encompassing of the yet-not-yet that exists before language, before symbol, which we contact through reverie, according to Bion (1970, 31, 125). Jung, from his researches in alchemy, calls this *imaginatio*, that "creative imagination . . . the real Ground of the psyche, the only immediate reality" (from a letter dated January 10, 1929; Jung 1992, 60). Through the unconscious we create what we find, as Winnicott explores in transitional space where opposites of external-internal coexist in illusion of union (1971a, chap. 1). We never ask a child, Where did your bear George come from? You made him up, didn't you? Or did you buy him in a store? We would not impose dualistic thinking on the child's emerging symbol, although, alas, we do question people's God-images, even telling them their pictures of God come from their class, or gender, or ethnicity, or sexual orientation. Psychoanalysis encourages us instead to listen in on these remarkable experiences of union of self and otherness that give birth to the numinous where we catch our image of God.

For all the majesty of birth, bringing forth life from the female body, there is the horror of it, too—the death mother who can pull you back into oblivion, bound by guilt, which Marion Woodman researched (Sieff 2009). The world of womb is made abject, its humanity repudiated as nonhuman according to Kristeva and this is further replicated in abjection of women into the sex trade, indentured servitude, reduced to labor-producing or child-producing commodities, or restricting them to maternity through discrimination in pay and lack of promotion in jobs (1995, 118, 122). Envy of women's creative power is hidden in such practices. She is lauded in the arts as the carrier of beauty in her body but restricted in access to become herself the originator of art. In Melanie Klein's blunt language of the unconscious, a woman cannot be allowed to have a penis as well as a vagina, inseminating good things in the world as well as creating out of her body (Klein 1957, chap. 11). The violence against women for daring to be doubly potent was shown recently in Guinea, Africa, where soldiers fell upon demonstrators rallying for women's rights in a stadium. Stripping off the women's clothing, gang-raping them, shooting guns or stabbing knives into their vaginas, the soldiers shouted, "You belong at home!" (National Public Radio news report, October 20, 2009).

Woman's body is seen as the material, the matter with which we create symbols of what matters, yet this ground is also seen as falling away, breaking up. We lose our ego, slip into unconsciousness, give way to lunacy and vagaries that must be protected against by fundamentalist boundaries: forbidding girls education, voting rights, control of property, access to courts of justice. A girl of eleven, the news reported, who had acid thrown in her face by a Taliban member to thwart her going to school, said from hospital, "As soon as my injuries heal enough, I return to school."

We can never reduce our physical life to our psychology. Our body has distinct existence and vocabulary, its organ dialect—witness the psalmist saying we pray from our bowels, the sweat of our palms, the longing of our hearts. Nor can we reduce psyche to body. Brain research reveals the site of our dreaming and locates different emotions but does not tell us what our dreams mean or the relational truth of what we feel (Fairfield 2002, 71, 79ff). Medical research probes the history of disease, borrowing political speech sometimes to describe the renegade cell that infiltrates healthy organs. Disguised as a liver cell, this thug cell refuses to join the community of liver cells, instead intent on colonizing the whole organ for its own aggrandizement in cancer. Illness and its pain can overcome us, isolate us, and kill us.

The body's distinct life and death is conscripted into sacred rituals of spiritual meaning where, for example, we create the baptismal font as another womb through which we are born into spirit and life in community. The Eucharist employs images of being fed, reaching all the way down to cannibalism to make real the eternal giving of love through this "precious body and blood," "this bread of heaven" (*Book of Common Prayer* 1944, 339).

The body commands our respect and devoted care. But the body bound can also mean the body stuck, transfixed to roles imposed on it by the psyche. By this I mean the situation, of which there are a multitude of examples, where we cannot bear something in our consciousness, and so it is loaded onto our body, which like the good beast carries our burden for us (Ulanov 2001a). A deep hunger for our own agency is rerouted onto food. In anorexia, denying our need to be fed by others lest we feel our helplessness to be in charge of our lives, we try to master hunger, a project doomed to failure because it is an instinct of our animal life. It is like starving a tiger. The ten pounds or forty pounds for which we mercilessly attack our selves conceals the power struggle over who is in charge of this body—our will? Instinct? Mother? Fashion idol? We would not treat our pet the way we treat our body, attacking its shape, submitting it to surgery to change it instead of enjoying the interplay of its rest and exertions, its sexual capacities, colors, textures, and pleasures such as dressing up in silk.

Worse still are examples of taking out on our own or someone else's body aggressive energies that threaten us from within. We project destructiveness into spousal abuse or toward elders or, worse still, a small child. Addictions to drink, drugs, pornography, or sex detour bodily and psychic energies. The messages from the hidden center of these compelling behaviors bypass consciousness and repeat over and over, so we feel entrapped in body. We miss the body's beautiful conjugation with psyche in life's journey, so that with tender regard we together accept that from dust we come and to dust we return.

Even soul is symbolized as being embodied, not abstract but housed in the flesh, capable of being lost, waiting for our homecoming. The soul, often imaged as feminine as opposed to the masculine symbols for God, thus thrums with erotic tension. Such imagining of soul and God coming together includes deep pleasure and allows someone as spiritually supple as John of the Cross to change his gender to go out to his beloved Christ in the darkest of dark nights. In such profound body and soul passion we can imagine a funeral homily beginning with words from the Song of Songs, "Arise, my love, my fair one /And come away; / For now winter is past, / The rain is over and gone" (Song of Songs 2:10–11).

Surprisingly, the body shows generosity in the bane of its being trapped in repetitious compulsion. Like a good dog, it keeps nudging us through our symptoms, barking at us through repeated migraines, respiratory infections, or vexatious allergies or behaviors such as losing things, going in the wrong direction, or having wrong words jump out of our mouths at the wrong moments. The body is speaking our story of distress, offering it to our consciousness if we have ears to hear and eyes to see (Ulanov 2001a). And in its dreaming the body tells us secrets kept even from ourselves.

The body carries what the psyche neglects which can infect those we love. A mother who devoted her life to her four daughters and the needs and desires of her husband reached a point in her life where she took to her bed. She no longer cooked, cleaned, arranged schedules. The conscious reason was that she did not feel well, though tests turned up no physical maladies. In her bed, she turned to her own life, writing and drawing pictures, but always under the cover of feeling too exhausted to get up.

Her eldest daughter, now in her fifties, inherited this pattern of orbiting around her husband and struggled to liberate herself, with some success. But on returning home from visiting to help her mother, her body fell into a stupor of sleep; she slept away hours, days, on the living room couch. The intercession of consciousness, fostered by our work in analysis, introduced space between her and this compulsive sleeping. Like her mother, she felt she could not continue this orbiting pattern around her husband as if she were a satellite to a superior planet, yet to break free seemed impossible. The sleeping obliterated the conflict while protesting it. In this kind of bodily knowing, space is made for imagining energy for something else to emerge. She came to see that sleeping for hours on the couch like her mother was an indication of her fight against that pattern of being a satellite at best. The body acted out the psychic message that needed to be heard: she was not available to revolve completely around her husband's needs. But she also was sleeping away her own life.

A dream heralded a change. She dreamed that her mother at the last minute put her into a play about the life of a woman now seventy. "There is no way I can learn all the lines," she says in the dream, "so I close my mouth and do not say anything; I will imagine the whole story of this stranger's life and then I will ad lib from that." Contrary to fitting herself into a prescribed role, something she felt she had done her entire life, she improvised out of her understanding who this woman was. Not until the end of the dream did she

> realize the woman is me; though I do not know her, she depends
> on me, I am preparing to play a woman I don't know. Then I
> realize she is me: a stranger in me I do not know, and I thought
> of an artist [she is a painter] saying you reach something you
> don't know and it is life-changing. It is time for me to admit
> the stranger and speak from there. But I am afraid, and it
> can fade. I think my life has not been a negotiated life but
> designed for me. I do not feel I had permission or power to
> influence my life; it never occurred to me it could be another
> way for me, nor for anyone.

The alternative to oblivion of sleeping is to face conflict and the
fear it arouses and to acquire the power to carry that fear and slowly
change her life.

Body also means vulnerability to destructiveness. Psychological
trauma violently separates psyche from body. Whether sudden or
cumulative, whatever its source—in war or violence at home, in forced
starvation or withholding emotional food, in torture or emotional
abuse, in rape camps or rape from a family member, in genocide
or untamed aggressiveness in our neighborhood, where an other
projectively identifies our self as her or his target—the repeated
theme in trauma is erasure of our subjectivity, denying it, and then
denying that denial.

To go out of existence, even for a few seconds, leaves a gap. We
have gone away from ourselves and cannot get back. A hole is left in
our memory. We are then compelled to repeat this shock to try to
witness what happened, to resurrect our life as a subject from this
eradication. We need to see this rupturing gap, take in our bodily
knowledge that is also now psychic conscious knowledge, not knowing
about it but participating in it, testifying for and with this lost part
of our self. This testimony to what happened "*begets* the truth in the
very process of speaking" (Zornberg 2009, xii).

Whether individual or social, trauma arises from conscious or
unconscious refusal to recognize the other as a subject in his or her
own right, erasing the other. We experience destructiveness (both
without and within). Any body of knowledge must include
consciousness of it, any body politic or mystical body of Christ
must include it. Destructiveness runs like a theme through our
body life. We experience it in self-attack against our body,

criticizing the pounds we cannot lose, the habits of sluggishness or emotional envy we cannot rid ourselves of, attacking even the rage we feel when treated as a nonperson by an insurance company that denies our claim as if we do not matter.

Only with connection to our constructive capacity, what Kleinians call relationship to the good object (the object in which we experience goodness displayed), can we bear interpretations of our destructiveness. Yet we must bear it, for destructiveness is part of us and goes to make up the whole of us. If we do not address our destructiveness, we risk the danger of staying victim, and if we do not address the context of our destructiveness, we risk the danger of feeling totally responsible. Then we succumb to a ruthless superego capable of "cannibalistic appropriation of all that is good," including "appreciative love" (Brenman 2006, 97, 102). Stripping self and others of our capacity to love, we are left in a loveless world whose desperate bleakness shows itself in savage criminal acts.

The very fact of physical illness previews or conducts us to final destruction of our body in death. How to bear it? How to align with forces of healing to return to full life, and, when they reach their limit, how to partner our body so that together we make our way to the end, echoing Winnicott's prayer, "May I be alive when I die!" (Winnicott 1978, 19)? Physical pain can overcome our subjectivity so that all we can do is seek the relief of unconsciousness through medicine, diving beneath the waves of suffering to drift and dream toward whichever final outcome is ours—to return to daily life, which we may resist, or to be conducted to the frontier.

The effects of our body's decline on our psyche are huge, prompting creation of myths, religions, and rituals that testify to human intervention in the forces of life and death and contribute an essential ingredient that makes for aliveness over against mere survival. How to harness this energy, to see the secret connection between the monstrous and our symbols of highest spiritual meaning? South African poet Antjie Krog finds the power of imagination that transforms rage against the hot flashes of menopause—that rehearsal for death—into shocking lines of poetry: "But one day you . . . / feel this enormous crucible destroying your last juiciness . . . / burning like a warrior you rise—

a figurehead of fire—you grab death like a runt and plough its nose / right through your fleeced and drybaked cunt" (Krog 2006, 17). Wallace Stevens asserts imagination's power to impose meaning on reality: "It was she not the sea we heard." Here the sea is reality and the singer a girl who sang words: "For she was the maker of the song she sang / . . . And when she sang, the sea, / Whatever self it had, became the self / That was her song, for she was the maker" (Stevens 1935, 57).

The Subtle Body

How do we become makers of meaning, gathering destructive and creative energies into our imaginative living? Jung, borrowing an ancient term from alchemy, the subtle body, describes a zone of living in which symbolic meaning is as vivid as the quotidian. This symbolic sight perceives that body and psyche are two sides of the same reality. Matter and psyche make up the whole. Living our subtle body, we awaken to synchronistic happenings. Coincidences of noncausally related events occur which we experience with intense subjective meaning; they convince us we live in an interconnected world that displays signs of its wholeness and our particular place in it. A woman sending off her first book manuscript with hopes for its publication hesitated and pulled back. To bolster her courage, she pulled up a memo she had saved on her computer from her advisor from two years before in response to another moment of hesitation and doubt. The advisor's words directed her to what she believed in and bolstered her confidence in her writing. The date of that old memo was the same day of the same month. It felt like a sign, in New Testament sense, and unlocked her faith to go forward into the unknown.

A clinical example of symbolic seeing is found in the symptom of bulimia, stuffing oneself with food only to disavow its digestion by throwing it up. The problem exists in the body and holds the psyche in its addicting grasp. Something is not being fed; the bulimic consumes food as if starving and heaves it up as if it is a false way of life. The symptom shows the struggle with trying to exert control while being controlled. The food is shown to be a false solution to what is hungering within. This symptom, a conscious problem, is an urgent communication from the unconscious, told in body behavior and spiritual symbols. The subtle body that lives between the body and the psyche receives these messages.

Where do we find language for spirit lived into body that becomes like banisters of stone on which we lean to guide our way toward death? How do we craft or discover symbols of durable spiritual meaning that will survive emergency trips to the hospital? This is the work that comes into the analyst's office, where body and soul, psyche and spirit hover, intermingle, block and release each other into wholehearted living. A depression crushes our body, robbing speech, flattening silence into vacancies, depriving the body of food and sleep. What transforms this depression? Like the "unplummable spot" of every dream, that Freud calls its "navel, that point of contact with the unknown," if treatment works, we descend from knowing to unknowing to hear what this body and spirit are speaking through this depression (Freud 1900, 111). Our theories deconstruct as we are ushered toward what the psyche shows us. What complex has taken over and what primordial image lies at its center summoning us to recognize and relate to it?

The subtle body idea is neighborly to the "glorified body," the "resurrection body" in Christianity. The alchemists for seventeen centuries included some of the best minds and many ardent religious believers; their efforts to transform base material into gold are best understood psychologically as aiming for the wholeness of personality and its union with the potential wholeness of creation (Jung 1955–56, pars. 760–763 and par. 238; see also Ulanov and Ulanov 1991, 146–148). The subtle body exists in that intermediate realm between matter and psyche, partly physical and partly spiritual, and manifests in physical as well as mental forms that emerge as concrete and symbolic. Its reality "can only be expressed by the symbol," which Jung describes as "neither abstract nor concrete, neither rational nor irrational, neither real nor unreal. It is always both" (Jung 1944, par. 400).

We can catch the subtle body in Winnicott's exploration of transitional space where the baby senses its emerging I-ness in finding and creating symbols of its union with its mothering one as separation between them occurs. We find a transitional object as a real object existing external to us in material form, like a special teddy bear or blanket. We also create this precious object as a symbol by imagining the smell and texture of the blanket connecting us to a soothing source or qualities of personality of the bear. Thus the transitional object and the space in which it dwells are both objective and subjective, surpassing the distinctions between inner and outer, real and imagined, matter and psyche.

For alchemists, imagination aims to wrest gold from base metal, but the gold was spirit, a spiritualization of matter, including our bodies and all of nature and the material world to be joined in the redeeming action of spirit culminating in creation of the everlasting water, precious stone, or miraculous medicine. In clinical practice, the subtle body is seen when the shift occurs that enlightens the unconscious in relation to consciousness. It appears in the intermediate realm of projection between patient and therapist, where both perceive complexes, impulses, and imagery operating between them, bringing them together or interfering with their relationship. For example, is anger coming from the patient or from the analyst? Do they toss it back and forth? Do they see they are both at that moment caught in anger itself that bids their attention? Are its energies present? Does each in their separate ways face anger, and do they face it between them, and do they face it together, as if pondering the human problem of what to do with this emotion that could be freeing and could be destructive? How shall this energy be related to, understood, transformed into livingness? In such imaginative seeing, both persons are changed and healing happens— the exiled anger returns to find a home, the broken place knits into a larger whole, the wound receives mercy.

Body Transformed

By looking into the physical body and the subtle body, we can look into the transformed body. For transformation happens in the body to which we are bound, in the space and time and history in which we are living. Transformation is like being ushered into new land, a new place of living. It is not the densification of literalizing, nor an ethereal rising above, but a symbolic seeing of new country and a crossing into a new livingness. Thus we are not wed to concrete settlements, nor are we like disembodied angels who do not live anywhere. We are human persons, together and individually, who relate to something infinite when bounded to the finite self we are. The lightning flash transmutes into contemplative gaze. Fully in our subjectivity, in our lives with all their history, flaws, and capacities good and bad, we register the presence of something objective, and we register it with trembling. The trembling is body recognition of what has happened.

Where do we see it? In the figure of Mary, who withstands the lightning and is not destroyed but is a portal, the point of intersection, through which the All and the Vast enters our existence as incarnate body. We see it when the smallest version of such incarnation takes place in us, so that, with Paul, we say it is not I but Christ who lives in me. We register something there in the midst of our body-self changing all our living—objective presence in our subjective self. Rebecca's prayer was followed by her pregnancy; Mary's pregnancy was followed by her prayer—the Magnificat.

Mary, seen symbolically, is heralded as Virgin and as Mother. As Virgin she symbolizes being intact in body, that is, her specific form, place, and time, and intact in spirit not determined by human culture, man-made laws and customs. She bodies forth feminine as sui generis, not as equal to masculine, not as an essentialism to be slapped onto actual women, but displaying a capacity of housing the infinite within the finite, awakening, pondering, suffering, praising its otherness all her days, coming to be intercessor for all the rest of us. She houses the lightning without being destroyed.

As madonna with babe at her breast she is at once nurturer of the new that comes as a helpless infant dependent on relationship to survive and thrive. Yet she is not privileged as mother over all those who accompany Jesus. Have we idolized maternity and missed the astounding role of Mary as mother of revolution, bringing into the world the One who ends all religions? The story that begins in the garden ends in the city where there are no sacred versus profane places, but the radiating presence of the Holy, the ungraspable, unimaginable who wipes tears from our eyes.

In clinical work, when transformation happens we discover the new enters in an inconspicuous form, distant lightning at best, a scintilla, a spark that needs shelter and attention to survive. We sense

with our body antennae, our whiskers, that something other is on
the scene, accompanied by the disturbing question, Has it always
been so, and only now we come to see it, to be aware of it? The
other usually arrives in a remote corner of the person's psyche, a
neglected place, a Gilead that promises no balm, a stable with its
muck. But the psyche, like the base metal of alchemists, brings the
prima materia, the unconscious body, reaching for consciousness,
like the dream of the woman cast in a play by her mother who
discovers she can improvise her performance, create it instead of
fitting into prescribed lines. She discovers that she is embodying
the stranger who is herself.

How to grasp in our tininess that the ungraspable has flashed into
our awareness? The event in our own psyche intimates a still larger
reality that makes us ask, What do we then believe in or about reality?
The spiritual, named or unnamed, enters the psychological. This is
not a hearing about otherness but immediate experience of its arrival
or of its having been there all along. The impact of the
incomprehensible decenters us at least and at best summons us to
fleshify it, make it real in our limits of time and space without
substituting our reification for its reality. But the ungraspable is just
that, beyond our reach, beyond our understanding, moving us to
multiple forms for its expression. The other, whether sighted in our
dream or in our religious devotion, shows itself as ever provisional, ever
unfolding, never fixed once and for all. Who is this stranger who is
myself, my analysand may well ask, and then experiment to find forms
for expressing this stranger in daily living and in her art. She speaks of
entering her studio and not knowing how to proceed. With this new
announcement, the old way of painting is destroyed, shown up as
gravely limited, without a strong voice.

No wonder all of us resist the entrance of the new! Seen from
its vantage point, what went before seems to us inadequate now,
off the mark. Thus destructiveness finds a creative place, as showing
the limits of our smaller perspective, as we open to a larger view
initiated by something we never thought before, never saw before.
How to accommodate it without being demolished? From a clinical
point of view, we may be directed to see that our neurotic problem
boils up not as indication of our underlying pathology but as our

resistance to announcement of the new. Unlike Mary, we may say to the muscular rustle of angel wings, "Go away!" Jung puts it pithily: we can walk to our fate or get dragged there by a neurosis (Jung 1933a).

The shadow of a lightning illumination is destructiveness of the way we did things before we saw this new otherness. Taking courage from Mary's adamantine intent to give birth, destructiveness, like a wild animal, may get tamed instead of acted out on self and others. Can this otherness become "absorbed into a personal ritual" (Zornberg 2009, 232)?

Not only is the past shown up now in its limitations, the new itself, even the God behind the new if we are believers, shows itself as ever incomplete in its realization, ever unfurling, never final as secured in fixed form. It may be dependable but not finished, nor exhausted in its expressions. The infinite shows itself as infinite possibilities uncontained in our conscious narrative of its coming and of our reception. Unconscious murmurs, amplifications, counter-narratives, analogous images, and unguessed thoughts break down platitudes of knowledge we have taken for granted and insert openness to the not yet disclosed God.

Are we then set loose, unmoored? No. We are ushered into generative interplay of known and unknown, of found and improvised, created and discovered, a relationship composed of self as unfolding and provisional as is its other. We know this partner, ungraspable, unoriginated, the mystics say, through the beloved's perfumed scent after leaving the room or as the polar bear shows from the frozen shards that break only after its tonnage daintily traverses the ice in its forward-moving torque.

The Incarnate

This arrival of otherness, whether in our own small psyche with its dreams, its body nudges, its new thoughts, or in the revelations of transcendent meaning, includes the subtle body's symbolic mode and exceeds it. Here understanding crosses over into changed behavior. Once unconscious content becomes conscious, we are enjoined to take ethical responsibility for it; it does not go back to unconsciousness except through defenses of repression or dissociation that cause psychic disturbance. We can fall ill if we commit such perjury. Once the leopard appears, we cannot pretend we do not know about it. But the finding and endorsing of ethical action is a repeated process. Again and again our efforts fall to pieces, and we start over. The woman who dreamed of the stranger who was herself said, even as she experienced this insight, "I can see it, and it's disappearing fast; a glimpse, but only that. I peek at it because I am afraid."

Our efforts to ground the new in our living fixes it, embodies it, not in stuckness but in the fluidity of living. The incarnate body includes the physical and the subtle body, by bringing into living one of the infinite possibilities of becoming. The All and the Vast comes into the particular and the tiny, which nonetheless is everything to us. It is our embodied life in this time and place, including our flaws, so that even what we achieve and contribute to the group shows marks of our limitations and mistakes. No matter. That is still our offering. But to happen at all, it is as if the infinite meets our particular body-self aiming to bring to birth one of the possibilities into a being of its becoming. Our interpretation—our way of teaching, or writing, or cooking, or administering, or doing our job, or raising our young—meets and responds, attends to one of the possibilities the infinite offers us, even at the last moment in the way we approach the fact of death. We too assist in making the invisible visible.

In smallest terms of the consulting room, the unconscious needs conscious response for anything to take shape and come to be. In largest terms, the divine and human meet not in general but in specific forms of our particular lives that testify to the All. We thus offer to each other the light that came as lightning to us, the ground we made of it, the intent and suffering we gave to make its realness real in the here and now. Our particular time and place, our particular gift and flaw, draws forth into the world a particular version of the infinite, variations on a major theme of incarnation, like those celebrated by Beethoven, for others to hear and play. This yields nothing fixed but always contingent on the meetings, lost and found again, whether between conscious and unconscious, human and divine. Is the unconscious then the divine? Surely not, any more than is consciousness or anything else mortal. But surely, too, the unconscious is another passageway to and from the human and transcendent realms.

Before and After Body

We come round then to where we began, the preverbal language of the body, the protosymbolic, which is not solipsistic as clinicians know through the binding communications with their analysands through projective identification, unformulated experience, and nonlinear thinking (Anderson 2008, 56). Ogden writes of our earliest autistic contiguous position where we respond to shapes and edges (Ogden 1994, 140–141). I discovered with my patient Nancy that loss of words due to the placement of her terminal brain tumor did not mean loss of dialogue between us (Ulanov 1994). The sympathetic nervous system communicates beneath and differently from the cerebrospinal nervous system through collective emotions, body posture, organ speech, embodied presence in contrast to words. It makes me think of the mystical body in which we are "very members incorporate" having taken in the "precious body and blood" of God made flesh, visible, here, among the "blessed company of all faithful people," that "holy fellowship" where the unoriginated God dwells among us (*Book of Common Prayer* 1944, 339). The liveliness of this living God resists all reifying designations that would fix it into unalterable form. The invisible, nameless otherness of God before words, definitions, symbols, even images, evokes the *tehom bohu*, the void over which God's Spirit hovers and brings forth life, what Žižek refers to as the "murmur of the Real," which Torah scholar Rashi says evokes "wonder and astonishment . . . at the emptiness of it . . . a presence of nothingness" (cited in Zornberg 2009, xx).

Symbols of the feminine accompany, hover around, return and repeat such beginnings and ends, the body life and the beyond body life. This evokes another ancient symbol researched from Plato to Derrida: Chora, a category of being before words and logic, reason and image, a space and space-making that precedes and exceeds our concepts, from which emerges becoming into being. Lamborn suggests that the verb *chorein*, to make room for, is a point of contact between human experience and divine disclosure and is neither God or not God, but the depth of God, an open site where the divine may dwell and heal (Lamborn 2009, 229, 248; see also chap. 11, 40).

In the Church of Chora in Istanbul I was struck by two images of Chora as mother and Christ child. In the first mosaic, the child, bounded by an oval, dwells as if within the being of the mother, whose hands open and extend to the world, her blue-garbed being encompassing the child who dwells within her. In the second mosaic, she and the child are together enclosed in a surrounding boundary, the child now a separate being yet held within her arms and lap; now the child's hands open toward the world. The caption beneath the mosaics reads "Chora: 'Container of Uncontainable.'"

This image gathers all our paradoxes: of the All and our particular, of feminine symbols and the genderless beyond; of pliant receptivity and stonelike intent to bring the new to birth; of mortal body as site of incarnation; of singular subject and our shared existence of our subjectivities together; of psyche inseparable from body; of lightning flash that scares and illuminates us to become ourselves in transforming our society.

This essay was originally presented at Wake Forest University School of Divinity, Winston-Salem, North Carolina, as part of the Trible Lectures, March 2, 2010.

5

THE INFERIOR FUNCTION

The inferior function is not so much a knot to be untied as it is something that ties us in knots. It flummoxes us, slows us down, makes us feel as though we live with a roommate who brings a whole other way of thinking and proceeding that we just cannot understand. And we cannot change it! But it changes us. This ties us up in ways so new that it brings different energy, as if by knotting us up new life comes into us. Even so, it feels threatening.

Danger

It is dangerous to take up the inferior function. Inferior really does means inferior, which the *Oxford Dictionary* defines as "situated below; lower in rank, quality; placed at the bottom." Synonyms for *inferior* flesh out its meaning: "poor, low-grade, mediocre, low-quality, second-rate, not up to snuff" (*Random House Dictionary*). Worse still, we are trying to focus on the inferior not in general but as it applies to each one of us, to what Jung calls a function of our personality, a mode of activity and response in each of us that operates in a substandard way.

To touch what is inferior in ourselves makes us feel awful, and it incites this part of us. In facing what feels substandard, and to avoid resorting to generalities as though we were not involved, while all the time feeling vulnerable, I want to set a guideline. While reading this chapter, imagine I am talking to you personally, in your context, to your emotional situation.

It takes courage to do this. It is heroic to set out voluntarily to encounter this murky, touchy, undeveloped part of ourselves. An analysand reported a dream of opening an apartment door and being met by a barking dog. "What did the dog say?" I asked. "I don't know," he answered, "I don't speak bark." That is the inferior function! We come upon the unknown in ourselves; it barks at us.

To set this article in the context of Jung's theory, I want to create some boundaries to contain us, to hold us, as we venture toward what we do not know and what we do not like, what we feel when it touches us as if in our actual bodies, as something poisonous, entrapping, veering us off course into the illogical, immoral. Jung saw the psyche as self-regulating, pushing toward completeness and balance. He hypothesized a theory of personality composed of four functions: two rational, that is, ways of evaluating experience based on reflections that coalesce into making judgments (thinking and feeling), and two irrational, ways of perceiving that subordinate judgment to perception (sensation and intuition). Jung says he can give "no *a priori* reason for selecting these four as basic functions, and can only point out that this conception has shaped itself out of many years' experience" (Jung 1923, par. 731). By function Jung means a mode of psychic activity that persists as the same under varying conditions, a movement of psychic energy (libido) in a habitual way we orient ourselves in the world.

The same would hold for his hypothesis of two basic attitudes, extraversion and introversion, as a "state of readiness . . . a definite combination of psychic factors or contents which will determine action . . . in a definite direction, or react to external stimuli in a definite way" (ibid., par. 687), one of which would be our habitual way of relating to reality. In extraversion we move psychic energy to the object, adapting and making a place for ourselves in light of the object (ibid., par. 710). In introversion libido turns inward toward the subject; we weigh the outer situation against our subjective point of view.

In keeping with this theory, one of the four functions will be the most developed and will serve as the habitual way we orient ourselves to reality, both outer and inner. The second most developed function will aid us, like a good sous-chef, in cooking up our work and our relationships. The third function will be less developed, and the fourth will be undeveloped, appearing only now and then in an autonomous, unreliable way and, if we get into a neurosis, falling into the unconscious almost entirely. This fourth is the inferior function. The attitude of introversion or extraversion will characterize how our dominant function operates, and usually also the auxiliary second and third functions, but the inferior function will usually present in the attitude opposite to our habitual mode of behavior, making it all the more inferior because undeveloped and hence challenging.

To give the briefest description of the various approaches of functions and attitudes, each would begin dream interpretation from a different angle. The thinking type would look for the dream's basic structure; the feeling type would zero in on the dream's emotional hot spot; the sensation type would examine the facts of the dream, what is there, the images, the action, and so on; the intuitive type would sniff out possible directions at which the dream is hinting. Extraverts would look at the dream characters as referring to the real persons and one's interactions with that person; the introvert would emphasize one's subjective feelings or thoughts about that person.

Rather than discussing all the various combinations of personality types and the attitudes and functions within them, here we will focus on the realm of the inferior and the heroic task of facing it, going into that terrain, not unlike a Harry Potter movie where ghosts and brooms and spectral figures fly about.

Jung contended that all the functions and attitudes belong to each of us, and we won't get away with ducking out with only one or two. All of us must pay the whole bill. The pressure to individuate, to reach all the parts of our self and connect them into a living whole, will force our development of all these functions and attitudes within the limits of our personalities and social contexts. Equally important is that no one is a pure type but always a mixture. And the better we know people, including ourselves, the harder it is to type them, due in part to our own typology coloring our perception of the other's "otherness." The theory of functions and attitudes is just that, a theory, not a fixed essence but tendencies in us within specific contexts influenced by cultural customs, gender images, and historical pressures. Also, at different stages in life different functions move to the forefront to be developed.

I feel protective of our differences and our vulnerability to being labeled. I find that too much talk about types can serve as an intellectual defense against our task of approaching the inferior realm. So I do not want to get into who is what type, including myself. Leave that unspoken, even unknown. Focus on the realm of the inferior, which, alas, we can all locate far too easily, because there we are touchy, given to taking offense, subject to confusion and helplessness. We feel inferior, unable. We don't understand bark. We open the door and a rhino faces us and Jung says over our shoulder, "There, that is your inferior function." What are we to do with this? What vocabulary do we use, what caution do we take, what is the way to relate to this other?

The Function of the Inferior

Inferior has a specific meaning and functions in specific ways. Whatever our typology, we all meet in similar experience when facing what is inferior. Our experience may be differently accented according to whether it is inferior sensation or thinking, but the inferiority is the same. *Inferior* means all that we do not have conscious access to, all that is not under our conscious will but rather autonomous. We cannot put it to direct use but instead experience it through disturbing effects on our consciousness. An outsized emotion or mad idea erupts into our daily activity; an impulse takes over (Jung 1948a, par. 272). The quality of whatever it is that bursts into consciousness is archaic, unadapted, primitive. As Jung says, "It refuses to come along with the others and often goes wildly off on its own" (ibid., par. 245).

Such eruptions tyrannize others, and then they walk on eggshells around us, leaving us isolated. But these negative impulses overwhelm us. Because we are not in conscious relation to what stirs us up, we tend to project the cause onto the other, whom we then blame. But the other experiences us as crazy or just plain difficult and to be avoided. Feeling misunderstood and unaccepted only increases our sense of helplessness in the face of blundering behaviors, ideas, attitudes, and emotions that seem to happen to us.

It is no better if we blame ourselves, because we are in the realm of the archaic, and infantile fantasies overtake us. For example, a student trying to read a text she finds difficult panics when she cannot understand it. Negative fantasies overwhelm her with a persecutory illogical causality that turns to the past or to the future: her brain is burned out by her teenage drug use, or she is suffering incipient Alzheimer's disease which already afflicts her mother. These fantastic fears hijack her ability to stay in the present and marshal her resources to accomplish her assignment.

We need not look far for experience with our inferior function because it finds us. It is troublesome and feels imposed on us from the outside. The hallmark of our encounter is that we feel not only stuck, but stuck in a familiar, repetitive way. Here I am again at an impasse, not knowing what to do or how to proceed, not even how to think about how to go forward. I feel stymied again, threatened. We usually resort to trying to use the inferior function according to our habitual way of acting and understanding. So if I am swamped by helpless feelings in the face of bewildering facts, then let me make a map, a list of what needs to be done. But the very helpless feeling so overcomes me that the list does not get made or is interrupted by negative intuitions of the worst that could happen.

For example, a woman awakening to her very cold house one winter Sunday discovered the oil furnace had switched off. Knowing she was no good with such sensate tasks, she had paid extra for a policy that sent workmen out on the weekend. They discovered no oil in the furnace! "How could this be," she exclaimed, "a delivery was made just recently." Maybe her oil tank, still an underground one and now illegal, had leaked, they surmised. She reported to me that she went to pieces right there and then, yelling, "I can't take this, I cannot do this, I cannot manage this," and felt she was breaking down and could not catch herself. She imagined all the recently delivered oil leaking into the ground, contaminating the soil—a danger she had been warned against the previous summer when she was advised to have her tank dug up and replaced with the now prescribed above-ground oil tank, a chore she had forgotten to implement. That sensate task had simply fallen out of her consciousness. Now she felt flooded with shame, self-attacked and menaced. The danger of a leak and soil contamination, she had been told, was that the cleanup could cost thousands of dollars. At that moment the frigid house with no oil and the possibility of a cost of upward of forty thousand dollars just piled up on her, and she heard herself yelling "I cannot do this," meaning, she said, "I cannot cope, it is too much." She said she wanted to run to her bed and pull the covers over her head. In a panic she jumped into listing things to be done. Imagining the worst, she arranged for the man who refilled the tank to come daily to measure the oil to discern if the tank was leaking.

It looks like she was trying to use her inferior sensate function, but she was actually conscripting it to the habit of her dominant most-developed function of intuition. The sensate fact that she overlooked was to figure out how come the recently delivered oil was not there. Could there have been other explanations than the possibility of a leak? A connection to *all* the facts would have helped her feel calmer, and she could have considered alternative explanations of trouble with the oil delivery, a blockage of pipes, or a malfunctioning furnace. She learned a week later that there was no oil because the deliveryman shorted her order! He had run out and gave her less than her supply. The point here is that even when we try to use our inferior function, it is not sufficiently under our control nor at our disposal to be truly effective; we grab at it but do not give it the weight it is due, the reality of its otherness. We try to appropriate it to our habitual approach to things, to our dominant function, which then alienates us from that approach. In this example, had the analysand been able to consider a number of facts calmly and not pounce on the immediate solution of having the oilman come daily, she would have saved herself considerable cost and discovered that the oil company was at fault here for not delivering the proper amount of fuel. It came out all right, but she felt she had been caught in a whirlwind and thrown about, out of control, behaving hysterically, and exhausted when bumped back down to earth.

The Inferior Function and the Collective

This inferior functioning, where we feel swamped and do not know how to get at what we are after, brings us to a sobering fact: when we try to make our inferior function conscious, it drags the whole unconscious with it (Jung 1944, par. 193). Then we are in for it; we must deal with the unconscious, with the unlived life in us, not just the piece we need at the moment, but the whole tide rushing in and its undertow, which threatens to pull us back out to sea. Hence we fear pursuing the inferior function lest it drag us backward into unawareness. We want to avoid our inferior realm and get other people to deal with it for us, in our stead.

Even more is involved. For the whole unconscious means the collective unconscious, not just our personal repressed contents or our unused capacities but the *materia prima*, the original chaos, the slime, and the animal realm from which we have come. "Its roots reach back as far as the animal kingdom" which brings with it a "spirit of gravity" (Jung 1948a, par. 245). This "fourth function has its seat in the unconscious," which mythology symbolizes as "a great animal, for instance Leviathan, or as a whale, wolf, or dragon" (Jung 1955–56, par. 277). Hence opening the door and seeing the rhino there is not only to see the otherness of the inferior function in oneself, but the symbolic carrier of the inferior, the other in everyone and the animal as the symbolic carrier of the self (ibid., par. 283). This can be terrifying, and also a heart-stopping summons to our small ego to heed this "recalcitrant fourth" (Jung 1948a, par. 280).

The "dark and objectionable" nature of this primitive chaos, this primeval animal, makes us feel not only frightened but repelled, as if soiled, threatened with something poisonous, a monster, a madness, the jaws of hell, the ghostly (Jung 1988, 954). It can evoke in us vertigo, nausea, as if the earth is moving beneath us or the depths of the ocean are rolling under our feet (ibid., 1022, 1029, 1088). In addition, in the unconscious everything is mixed with everything else, nothing yet differentiated or worked upon, but just "a disorderly heap of possibilities," unwieldy (ibid., 954). We are like Hercules facing the Augean stables; the heroism that exists in each of us is called into being.

The collective unconscious also means the psychology of the mob, the lowest human; when we are caught up in the crowd, with "all the vices and virtues of the collective man. . . . there is something dangerous about it; it can overwhelm the conscious existence of the individual" (ibid., 1022). We feel unfree: "Inferior feelings that are now coming up . . . envelop him, encoil him completely and he will soon be possessed by them" (ibid., 1184). But we are in it; this is our life. With more consciousness, we see we "have carefully picked our way until we have found the hot water in which we are sitting" (ibid., 823). The student who could not discern the meaning of the text felt it was urgent that she go back to school to feed the underground reservoir of her work which had run dry. She put herself in the very situation where she had to face her worst anxiety of inferiority, for the sake of connection to something deeper.

The mob of the collective crowd is our mob; it is our tribe in society, it is all of us in the human family, and it is the animal world, all mixing and merging with the "cold-blooded saurians, the deepest down of all, the transcendental paradox and mystery of the sympathetic and parasympathic psychoid processes" (Jung 1955–56, par. 279). Even vestiges of prenatal memory press upon us, along with the voices of the ancestors, eerie, fascinating, elusive, tied to the timeless, pulling us away from the immediate moment in the world (from a letter dated June 7, 1932; Jung 1992, 94).

Our undeveloped inferior function, which lies in the collective nature of the unconscious, can present itself through any of the more familiar psychic complexes that Jung described as ego, shadow, anima, or animus. For example, one analysand, a man, faced images of a woman who was compellingly attractive, but he also had to deal with "her" craziness. In initial dreams his image of this powerfully luring woman included her psychotic episodes; then, in later dreams, "she" had shorter times of dissociation, moods that could get hysterical or anger that could overtake her. Slowly, as this man worked hard to relate to the feelings these images and experiences of woman stirred in him, her image harbored all these disseminated parts and brought them together into a cohesive personality. A woman analysand struggling against feeling washed away by self-doubt often dreamed of having a soapy head or that the shower curtain wrapped itself around her head, or once that a big hand was grabbing for her head in the shower. Lacking an effective persona—in fact, rejecting having to present herself in the outside world at all—this soapiness, this wet entrapment, pictured to her what happened not just to her thoughts, but to her capacity to think. A shadow figure can personify our inferior function and confront the ego, such as in the case of a young man almost obsessive about ordering his filing cabinet who dreamed of a raucous fellow who laughed as he kicked the cabinet, which burst into flames. A woman who came for analysis said she fell in love with her husband's capacity to talk in contrast to her own muteness, but now she thought she would choke him if he didn't shut up and let her find her own words. We can find ourselves fascinated by a person who embodies our missing extraversion or feeling.

Our psychological task, which calls forth in us great and persistent courage, is how to find ourselves in that crowd, that collective. As Jung says, "somewhere you have the secret of your particular pattern" (Jung 1988, 1401). Where we must look is toward the inferior function. In that specific struggle—to develop our way of thinking or articulate our deep feelings different from the conventional formula, to find our connection to sensate facts of life, to connect to our intuitions of possibilities hidden in the present moment that would open up the future—we find ourselves engaged in the task of reconciling conscious and unconscious, going beyond what Jung calls "that mere taking apart stage which is quite rational and explicable," that is, asking where did this problem come from, how am I to understand it (ibid., 956). We go further now into a synthetic process, which means, literally, getting all the parts of us in our specific location in the world together. Like a heap of jigsaw pieces, we try to fit them together, in fact, to grow the connecting tissues, to reveal the picture of the whole puzzle of us.

The Hard-to-Attain Treasure

The inferior function that we prefer to repress or "leave around the corner because it is so awkward and with the strongest tendency to become infantile, banal," nonetheless "conceals all sorts of symbolic meanings and significant relationships—they are the treasure-house of hidden wisdom" (Jung 1948a, par. 244). Jung likens them to the Cabiri, the dwarflike chthonic gnomes symbolizing the mysterious creative powers under the threshold of consciousness (Jung 1944, par. 204). In mythic tales these "godlets" also exist on Olympus, which Jung understands to represent the eternal striving of unconscious undeveloped impulses in the inferior function to rise from the depths to the heights, to unite the above and the below.

In this sense, the unconscious content, here in the inferior function, "seeks, and itself is, what I have elsewhere called 'the treasure hard to attain'" (ibid., par. 205).

More directly put, "the mystery always begins in the inferior function, that is the place where new life, regeneration is to be found" (Jung 1988, 954). We find this mythological motif in all three of the monotheisms and in Buddhism as well. The outlaw Moses becomes the leader of the Jews; the savior in Christianity is born of an unwed mother in the muck of a stable; Mohammed thinks the voices he hears mean he is going mad, until his wife and uncle persuade him to take them seriously; the Buddha deserts his family and position to encounter suffering, transience, and death, through which he breaks through to enlightenment. As Jung puts it, "the redeeming power comes from the place where nothing is expected . . . in a form that has nothing to recommend it" (Jung 1923, par. 440).

We find the treasure, or it finds us, in the inferior realm: "the functions that have lain fallow and unfertile, and were unused, repressed, undervalued, despised etc. suddenly burst forth and begin to live. It is precisely the least valued function that enables life" (ibid., par. 444). We protest, How can this be! We discover a mathematician living in the basement who speaks in numbers and formulas we cannot even grasp, and somehow we are to unite with this other, this complete stranger who approaches life from a point of view not only foreign to us, but unknown, seemingly utter nonsense. Or worse still, it is not a mathematician in the cellar, who has a point of view, an expertise, a vocabulary, an orientation, albeit alien to us, but instead we discover the lowest mob part of us where we are hardly individual at all, where everything to do with the sensate world—for example, schedules, work plans, papers, records, tax accounts, bills and notations of their payment—just get lost in a jumble. We not only do *not* organize them, we lose them. Our very employment is threatened by our inability to get a grip on ordering these basic facts of holding a job. Neglect of our body's life is another example, where fear or forgetfulness keeps us from having checkups or taking necessary preventive procedures or helpful medicines. We would not neglect our pet the way we neglect our body.

Yet at the mob level within us lies a creative will, a spark, a beginning of the new. The new never comes in the front door, civilized, adapted, advanced, introducing itself, but always barges in through the back door, or comes up the cellar stairs, or flies in through the window, disordered, bringing the treasure in a heap of stuff. But, Jung says, "the mob is the fertile earth or the incubator or the dung heap upon which creation grows. . . . the black earth: the black substance is needed in order to create something in reality" (Jung 1988, 1021). The earth, the dirt that heretofore made us feel soiled, is the undifferentiated stuff in the unconscious, in the inferior function. The earth, like black airy compost, fertilizes the power of growth.

It is there that the seed of the new finds nourishment, not in what is developed and had been differentiated into our dominant function. I think of the inferior function as often containing our wounds, and always certainly our deficits. Those are the unlockable doors where whatever wants to come in, whether a god or a rhino, can reach us at any time. We have built up no defenses there. Instead, we are more like a child, open, accessible, and vulnerable. It is the vulnerability, the unobstructed access, that makes us dread the inferior function.

These images of the earth and the child convey the ambivalent nature of this treasure, found in mire and in unguardedness. We could slip, slide into the mud; we could be badly hurt. New powerful life may spring up, may come streaming out of the unconscious, flooding into consciousness, washing away all the values we have built up. Or the new may call forth the dangerous and menacing aspect of the unconscious, the dragon that wants to kill it (Jung 1923, pars. 446, 448, 449).

These dangers protect against any fraudulence on our part, that somehow we are putting ourselves in the way of the inferior function. No. Life puts us there. The psyche puts us there in its ruthless urge to individuate. We do not have to do it, nor can we ape it or think we invent this encounter with the inferior function, that somehow it is on our schedule and under our control: "If one is there, one knows it; one does not need to ask. If not, one had better not dabble in things which are most dangerous and poisonous" (Jung 1988, 954). For example, we might think we can talk about having a transference to the analyst, as if somehow we were on top of it. But the emotional vigor of transference attachment shows that "the unconscious without pity holds them to the transference because something else is demanded or expected of them, some further development" (ibid., 956).

That further development is where the new comes in and where heroism is needed. The descent to the inferior function can go all the way to "the navel which denotes the place where the original life streamed into us through the umbilical cord, it is the place which is not well defended and which will eventually kill us, the place through which death will enter again (ibid., 1197). Facing our inferior function is always two-edged: we dread delving too deeply, lest the chaotic nature of what we find unravels all the parts of us, so that our functions, hereditary factors, social and political locations, inner images and ego and shadow parts will not hold together but disseminate, scattering like so much confetti into the world and back into the unconscious (ibid., 1196). Yet diving down is precisely what is asked of us, in a spirit of devotion, a humble attitude that gets us low enough to where the new trickles in.

Here we are the fool, the Dummling of fairy tales, not the queen or the wise man, but the inferior one who does not know what to do and so blows a feather and follows the direction in which it lands. Here we are dependent on helpers that others scorn, the animal or insect, the old witch, the dwarf. Here we are naïve, open to what is there and what is not there, simple, unsophisticated, not knowing any better way. Looked at from our most developed function, we appear foolish, ridiculous, pathetic. But we are willing (hence the courage) to expose ourselves to the new in whatever form it enters, which usually is in the opposite attitudes and functions from those we have already developed. We have the courage to trust what comes in, without worrying too much that we look silly and slow.

The inferior function, because it has been left behind, undeveloped, still has the qualities of original wholeness of the unconscious which includes everything—the mystical and the realistic, the profound and the banal, the religious and the profane. Thus the inferior function possesses a tremendous concentration of life energy and can become a source of renewal if we can let it come up in its own realm and in its own way. The person with a developed feeling function, for example, has, in the inferior function of thinking, deep thoughts, but they are not conventional or logical in the usual structured way; they are original and tinged with the sense of the whole of reality. The person with dominant thinking function has profound feelings that escape verbalization but resonate with heartfelt connection to others and, through them, to all others. The person with inferior sensation can find order at the deepest level, and it is from there they learn to schedule their appointments and order their records. But all this takes time. The inferior function is slow to our conscious pace, a wordless animal to our verbal skills. To develop our inferior function requires sacrifice.

Sacrifice and the Inferior Function

I want to include this notion of sacrifice in discussing the inferior function because on the personal level the inferior function feels like a sacrifice. It costs us; we suffer, flail about, find ourselves for a long time in a not-knowing place, in the dark, unable to see what's what or whether anything is growing. To consent to be slow, a not-knower, takes courage. We must sacrifice the swifter pace of our developed functions, live with the fear that we really are talking to a frog. We must give up feeling like we're on top of things, capable of mapping the best route, programming the stages of new development, knowing how long it will take and how we should proceed. For inevitably we want to approach the inferior function through our most superior one, and the sacrifice is to let the inferior work on its own initiative. We resist because it feels like an overthrowing of everything we worked so hard to develop and rely on. It feels as if we must waste time. We give up the old to let the new come in. "When the inferior function begins to work on its own initiative, it is experienced by the personality as a crucifixion, a symbolic death" (von Franz 2002, 91).

We may feel the dominant function we rely on is exhausted or unworkable, and that shocks us. One analysand, for example, said that after she had worked hard with her lawyer on her will, answering what seemed like endless questions, such as, What if this or that happened, then where does your estate go? she felt she would faint. With her intuitive capacities she could see the whole of matters and plot her course. What exhausted her with the lawyer was the endless series of concrete facts. She said, "Though not a drinker, I imagined slugging scotch to go unconscious!"

Sacrifice imposed on us by engaging our inferior function also has a collective element to it, because in our inferior domain we dwell in the collective unconscious and in the collective of society. The symbolic death we must undergo to let the inferior side of ourselves develop has collective significance. If we assimilate our inferior function, it feels like symbolic death, because it radically changes our personality and changes our behavior in society. That which was neglected in us and in our perception of others is now honored; that which was despised and avoided now has a seat at the table; that which we feared now brings us unsuspected gifts. Less hierarchy obtains; more equality reigns among the parts of our selves. The ego does not get away with dominating the agenda; it listens to the shadow, to the animus, and to other peoples' views. The Self by its nature includes all the parts of personality.

Our personal sacrifice to include the inferior bears directly on social and political efforts to include all the different religions, national allegiances, economic classes. Jung goes so far as to say if we do not undergo a symbolic death, genocide will result (Jung 1956-57, par. 1661; see also Ulanov 2007b, chap. 9). Our personal struggle for integration of all the parts of ourselves contributes to building social space in which rivaling factions may each gain a voice and begin to converse instead of kill. If we do not suffer the symbolic death of our presumed hierarchies, the rivaling parts seek to cancel each other in blind murderous ways.

The Treasure

What then is the treasure conveyed through the inferior function? Not only renewed gushes of energy, "but release from bondage and world-weariness" (Jung 1923, par. 435). The inferior function that we find stupid, immoral, or nonsense, Jung says, is "the only thing that contains the fun of living" (Jung 1988, 954). Our consciously disposable libido is gradually used up in our dominant way of functioning, and libido begins to regress into the unconscious, stirring up what lies undeveloped in us and around us, all that is inferior. A division builds up, our superior adapted way of functioning versus the inferior. From our struggling to bear consciously the increasing tension of their conflict, a symbol arises that halts the regression of libido into the unconscious, transforming it into a progression, forming an irrational compromise of the warring opposites that expresses both and neither in our own individual living unity of the yea and nay (Jung

1923, par. 169). This fills us with awe; the inferior function brings a sacred accent, a sense of being touched by the numinous. Whatever the symbol is, it conveys a freedom to be what we are and releases everything in us that had been held captive and unlived (ibid., par. 453). That which was dead comes alive.

But all this begins with our diving down into the first beginnings of the inferior function in us, with that open childlikeness devoid of prior assumptions, which allows us to see the new that brings with it "another guiding principle in place of self-will and rational intentions, as overwhelmingly powerful in effect as it is divine" (ibid., par. 442).

The symbolic death experience is trying to assimilate this new principle that works a fundamental change in our personality. Our superior function is no longer superior but has been plowed under to mix with the inferior. If the change is successful, we are no longer this type or that type, but a living mixture of a bit of each type. Successful assimilation of our inferior function brings the symbolic death of the theory of types!

Examples of this change of personality are a new sense of the symbolic level of living. We risk the death of concrete achievements and identification with our formerly superior function. On the conscious level, we experience things more as paradoxical unities than as rivaling opposites—the inner and the outer, the personal and the collective, the concrete and the mystical. When the inferior function is more integrated, its slower, more unconscious nature leads to a reality where this splitting into opposites does not occur. The question of which is real—for example, the inner relation to what this person represents or to the actual outer person, or inner realization of this truth or outer social action to plant this truth in the community, or connection to a sense of timelessness versus realizing accomplishment here and now in space and time—does not occur. They are the wrong questions! We reach another perception of reality as a paradoxical whole where both points of view in those questions simultaneously obtain.

You might object and say, "But this is just back to square one where, in the unconscious, everything is everything else." Yes and no. Because now we are there with consciousness, and that makes all the difference. We consciously can experience the value of each aspect which before split into either/or oppositions we felt we must choose between. We can entertain the unconscious, not be immersed in it but related to it. Consciousness can look at itself, at its own roots in the unconscious, not just through itself at other so-called objects. Conscious and unconscious are not so divided; each irrigates the other.

The catch, I believe, is to get to the point, the nexus, the meeting of our personal inferior function with the collective and the meeting of the human, both individual and collective, with what transcends us yet comes into us. This meeting point releases us to a fuller humanity, yet this new is not real unless we are living it. Then what was dead comes alive. This is the treasure: the livingness of it.

This essay was first presented for Jung on the Hudson, Rhinebeck, New York, July 27, 2007. It was published in Psychological Perspectives *51 (2009): 9–23.* Psychological Perspectives, *along with the C. G. Institute of Los Angeles, kindly gave permission to include it here.*

COUNTERTRANSFERENCE
AND THE EROTIC

E rotic passion bubbling up in analysis is one of the knottiest knots, often tangled up so tight it resists untying. Resistance comes into play to protect something of ultimate value; the fiercer the resistance, the more the life-and-death feeling around it. One's underbelly is exposed—one's hopes and dreams and even plots—and there is always the question, Is my loving valued? The analyst too is faced with tangles and entanglements and these can lead to messes that hurt the work, the analyst, and the patient. We are thus pressed to look into what we believe goes on in this work of analysis and the love it engenders between the analyst and analysand and for the psyche itself.

The Other Question

When focusing on the erotic in clinical work, we usually begin with the analysand, with the erotic transference. We ask what is constellated in the patient and projectively identified with the analyst, who becomes the love object, the one who recognizes the analysand's subjectivity which occasions a whole outpouring of response. In that spot, right there, of being recognized and witnessed, the analysand is usually young, not yet developed or differentiated, and the transference scoops up everything to make a bridge to the other, the analyst, a bridge that never was. Whether the preoedipal mother was never found, or the oedipal mother was never desired, or the father never reached, now right now, at whatever age the analysand may be, all this affect awakens and fire ignites in the analysis.

This is a dangerous time in the work, for at stake is the analysand's chance to grow, to widen and deepen his or her psyche and life in this world, and to secure a sense of being itself, a soul dimension not before dared. Mistakes can result in maiming. The analysand is in a tender condition despite all the force of emotion. Such dependence on the analyst, such endowing of the analyst with ultimate significance, can endanger the analyst as well—into inflation, as the one who knows, the one who brings the healing balm, or as the one who does not know, who may panic and rise above the affective heat, talking the fire to death, taking up all the oxygen in words, or being the one who falls into the fire and gets burned.

Such important junctures in an analysis have been written about by many clinicians, myself included (Ulanov 1996b, chap. 6–9). I want to explore the other side which is less talked about: eros and our countertransference. What do we bring into the analytic field in relation to eros before anything awakens in the patient?

A dramatic way to picture this question is to ask not of the child's oedipal complex but of the parent's erotic feelings for the child. Most of us fall in love with our newborns, and that loving all out with heart, soul, and mind contains the sensual, the sexual, the spiritual. Our children offer us potential for our own repair. All our unlived emotions flood in when holding this tiny baby, astonishing us that here is someone where before there was no-thing. We are given a chance to live at an emotional depth deeper than we have lived before.

I want to focus on how our relation to eros influences the clinical work we undertake. Where are we unlived erotically? Where do chinks exist in our erotic life, the young, undeveloped places in ourselves that might spontaneously pour out to another who recognizes and prizes us? For make no mistake, the psyche presses us to become all we can be, that ruthless instinct to individuation that cannot be lived except in relation to others (Jung 1946, pars. 471, 474). If we do not consent to undertake that journey voluntarily, it will be imposed upon us, urging us to live up to the moment of our death, in the spirit of Winnicott's prayer, "O God! May I be alive when I die" (Winnicott 1978, 19). Marion Milner said of Winnicott that he was on "excellent terms with his primary process; it was an inner marriage to which there was very little impediment" (Milner 1978, 42), thus evoking Jung's description of the complexity of the erotic field between analyst and analysand.

The complex erotic field contains two people's actual relationship to each other and both persons' relationships to their own depths, personified in images, clusters of emotion, and behavior of a contrasexual other within themselves who looks at life from a departure point different from that of their conscious gender identity. This other perspective introduces into consciousness gender fluidity, surprise that within oneself one moves over a whole range of masculine and feminine currents, with all their attendant couplings, at least imaginatively. The field also contains a reciprocal relating of the contrasexual other of the analysand with the contrasexual other of the analyst, unconscious to unconscious, as well as the reciprocal relating of the unconscious contrasexual other in each person to the conscious ego of each person (Jung 1946, par. 423). With such a field of potential erotic conversations, attractions, confrontations, and explosions, we wonder how will we get out alive! All these relatings comprise a veritable force field that convinces us how very serious this work of analysis is. Jung investigates how these mutual transferential dynamics symbolize human efforts to perceive and construct the wholeness of reality, in such images as the uniting of king and queen, sun and moon, lover and beloved, spirit and flesh, soul and god. In alchemical symbolism these conjoinings give birth to the precious *lapis* stone which represents not only the center of a person but also the center of reality (Jung 1955–56, par. 552).

Eros

Definitions will lend some clarity, not as a complete picture but as guidelines into this fascinating territory. Clinicians of different schools recognize eros as central to analysis. Freud links eros to libido as "that energy of those instincts which have to do with all that may be comprised under the word *love*." The nucleus of love—for Freud, found in sexual love—includes our drive to make unities within ourselves, with others, in the world, and in relation to the cosmos: "In its origin, function, and relation to sexual love, the 'Eros' of the philosopher Plato coincides exactly with the love-force, the libido of psycho-analysis" (Freud 1921, 90–92, cited in Lear 1990, 140–141). Loewald writes of loving the truth of psychic reality in loving the analysand "whose truth we want to discover" (Loewald 1970, 297; see also Ulanov 1996b, 398). The existentialist analyst Medard Boss believes the analyst must be imbued with agape to do therapeutic work (1963, 259–260). Ogden refers to private conversations we have with ourselves that are never exposed to others, but which turn up as an analyst's reverie stirred by the patient's unconscious that may eventually come out in an interpretation. I think these conversations are a form of love of our self, an ongoing conversation with our own subjectivity (Ogden 1999, 43, 114, 159). Kohut believes empathy, which sees the self and the world from the other's point of view, is itself the healing agent in treatment, thus recalling Freud's remark to Jung that "the cure is effected by love" (1981; McGuire 1974, 13). Both intersubjectivist and relational analysts emphasize the centrality of the reciprocal recognition of subjectivities of the analyst and analysand as the locus of therapeutic action, recalling Fairbairn's proposal that libido seeks loving relation to an other, not gratification. We are *au fond* relational, recalling Jung's dictum that treatment demands the whole person of the analyst as much as it does of the analysand (Jung 1946, par. 367). Jung grounds the relation of the two in their connection to the third of eros, and the converse as well: our relation to eros as a psychic force is embodied in relation to another. A wonderful example of this eros force, real in itself as psyche is real, is Kekulé's vision of the dancing couple—surely an erotic image—as the key to the benzene ring. This is the vision of what eros seeks: the *coniunctio*, the conjoining of the opposites, of the king and the queen, the mystic marriage, of the warring parts of us and of our world to create a living wholeness (ibid., par. 353).

Eros is the function of psychic relatedness that urges us to connect, get involved, poke into, be in the midst of, reach out to, get inside of, value, not to abstract or theorize but get in touch with, invest energy, endow libido. But relatedness does not mean relationship; that requires conscious participation, development of feeling toward the other and toward what is elicited in us in response to the other. The pull of the erotic is more wanton, bawdy, lusty, ardent, passionate. It is personified by Cupid shooting his arrows here and there, arousing our libido which we then lavishly invest in objects, others, causes, pursuits.

The pull of this daimon ranges from one extreme to another. Mozart's Don Giovanni pokes into one woman after another, opening her and abandoning her, for she wants passion and permanence, and he wants the chase, the conquest, the taking and the leaving. At the other extreme, eros is the dart of the golden arrow in the breast of St. Teresa of Ávila, whom Bernini immortalized in luminous marble. This arrow was "the liquid flame of love" between Teresa and her God in mystic union issuing in a life of works of love (Teresa of Ávila 1957, vol. 3, 282). That this penetration by the Holy includes the sexual is left in no doubt in Bernini's sculpture; out from under the luxurious folds of marble that depict Teresa's robe falls her bare left foot (the Discalced Carmelites, founded by Teresa, wore no shoes), a gesture of complete abandon, spentness, matched only by her mouth, open and slack, as if from consummated passion.

I stress again in defining eros that psychic relatedness, as libido with instinctive backing, is not equivalent to conscious relationship. It may initiate erotic embodiment in connection with another person, with one's God, with what conveys to us the loving of life, and the transpersonal source and value of it. Eros is like a huge spark that ignites our passion and then confronts us with the question of how we will live this fire in ordinary space and time. How will we nurture this flame into an abiding source of warmth? The early philosopher-theologian Origen described the Fall of humanity as the "chilling loss of the divine 'warmth' of love" (Drewery 1975, 33).

What then do we each know in our hearts of this spark, this urge, this flame? How did it come to us? Who or what was its object? For some of us it could be an actual object—a painting, a beautiful woman, a summoning vision. Or eros may manifest as a blind urge toward amassing something we have not yet differentiated ourselves from, so that we feel compelled to collect things—clothes and jewels or first editions or businesses to buy.

The most common understanding of eros is sexuality. Eros in the body is sexuality. Yet the sex drive transforms into eros, the life and love instinct striving for eternal forms of truth and goodness, a force for unity in our self, with another person, with life itself (see Lear 1990, 141–147). Yet such a spiritual development can also arouse again the sexual in the body, and then we feel the full force of eros moving us toward meaning as well as pleasure, toward a large receiving and giving, a sense of the splendid in the ordinary. Eros initiates us into the mysteries of desire to bond and believe in the other and ourselves as a unit, as a union that enhances both of us and even gives something into the world, benefiting others, as if our loving adds more to the sum of light available to everyone. It is in such junctures in analysis that professionals fall into ethical violations, for where spirit is, there will be sexuality, and where sexuality is, there will be spirit, creating flammable situations.

My clinical involvement with analysands for whom this has happened with their former analysts means a lot of hard work to find our way back to that juncture point when the work split, one fork going now toward what was called personal relationship and the other fork, which had carried the work, going into oblivion. If we can return to that pivotal point, often the prior good work with the former analyst can be secured, and the analysand can find his or her way through the thickets of desire to differentiate its sexual and symbolic levels. If we cannot reach that juncture point, the prior work is lost, and often parts of the patient too.

Two Kinds of Relationship

When the erotic is constellated, two possibilities of relationship offer themselves to us. The first is to an actual other to whom we feel drawn, by whom we feel arrested, toward whom attraction and fascination generate. The object is there and must be reckoned with as real; we did not invent it. The other is there, moving toward us, wooing or startling us, galvanizing our attention. As clinicians we need to review our lives and those remarkable others who interrupted our sense of self with a moreness we had not yet known. We need to ask, How did we respond? Did we flee? Pounce? Swoon? Pretend it did not happen? Did we try to talk it away with big theories? Did we demonize the other, especially if the relationship did not work out? Did we perjure our experience by reducing it all to our early object relations, or mere sex, or only projection, or to conclusions about what men and women should be? Or did we fall into inertia, away from the jazz beat of life fully alive? Or did we secure a solid relationship with an other, full of currents alive to this day? As clinicians we need to know where we stand with eros experience, where we are unlived, still to be lived, still willing to be surprised and live more. We bring our erotic selves into the work with our analysands: what we love, the unities we believe in, and those we still hope to grow.

Consciousness is our protection against falling into the soup with our patients. Consciousness can make a container where we do not have to act out or theorize away the bindings with our analysands. I remember being surprised at being pierced by a man saying with intensity that he wanted to take me off to a Caribbean island. I was surprised because I knew myself to be deeply in love with and contained in relationship with my husband and hence, I thought, immune to random attractions. My patient enlarged me and set me on a journey to discover how one could be deeply in love and thus pierced. I dreamed of very carefully driving around and around my big crescent-shaped driveway, up onto the road and back around the driveway's semicircle again and again with a big tiger in the car. Tiger energy! How to live with this?

The second kind of relationship offered to us in the sparking of eros is to psychic content evoked in us in response to the actual other or which arises within us and provokes interest in an actual other. This psychic content exists objectively in us: we do not invent it, we are not in charge of it, it arrives. As clinicians we need to be familiar with these happenings, for we bring this potential into our work as analysts, into the emotional field between us and our analysand. We need to ask, What is the psychic content stirred in me by erotic attraction? We need to be familiar with it so that it doesn't sabotage our work with our analysands. What has been my experience with this electricity, this setting something in motion? What is my desiring like, and what is it for? What dream images and imaginative symbols convey to me the meaning and the instinct in my erotic attractions and their spiritual pull? I felt currents of gender fluidity already present in myself as I listened to a woman speak of her first sexual meetings with a woman whom she loved at the same time she also felt love for a man. She rejected definitions and categories for herself: Was she this or was she that, or had she been this all along and only now discovered it? These were not my questions but rather of the currents that stirred her so profoundly, the sense of depths approached heretofore only by heights reached in her work as an artist. The erotic link between the two women transgressed their previous boundaries but seemed no less real. We looked into what their connection was scooping up that had not been included in her living, and we also asked, What was it unfolding in her, toward what unseen purpose?

Eros and Kinship

Eros brings with it a sense of purposiveness, a sense of going somewhere that feels important, that matters, that enlists body, soul, and spirit. It is this purposiveness that makes people break vows, betray others, create messes, sell all they have in order to pursue it. I think of young Matisse in the hospital after his psychological collapse, where his roommate suggested he take up painting to help his convalesence(!). Matisse's mother bought him a paint box, and he said of it: "From the moment I held the box of colours in my hand, I knew this was my life. Like an animal that plunges headlong towards what it loves, I dived in. . . . It was a tremendous attraction, a sort of Paradise Found in which I was completely free, alone, at peace" (Spurling 1998, 46).

What that purposiveness aims at in our own erotic life is not clear until we give it our full attention, working on both the outer relationship and the inner psychic content. We must flesh out the personal embodiment of such seeming intent, to bring over into living an aim that becomes our own, what we love and serve. An example for analysts, I would suggest, is our work on our own particular wounds in order to serve our profession, to be better qualified. I believe that is a right we must earn again and again if the work is to stay alive and meaningful.

The psyche presses for integration and for us to be and become all we can be, and that is what underlies our work with each patient, that they, too, be and become all they can be. Where eros leads shows infinite variety, as idiosyncratic as we each are from the other. But hidden in our personal stories is the larger aim of eros to serve life, to make unities, and that brings up to the surface another hidden purpose in all of us finding our own purpose.

In a deep analysis (and an erotic transference-countertransference field usually indicates depth), both the analysand and analyst are altered. The unconscious material between them is alive and presses for differentiation. The analysand coming to clarity about the hard facts of who they are, as Jung says, "make[s] up the cross we all have to carry or the fate we ourselves are," yet also means entering into the joy of being one's own particular person. The analyst too undergoes such a process, for "relationship to the self is at once relationship to our fellow man" (Jung 1946, pars. 400, 445).

The bond established by the analytical couple is important not just for those two individuals, but contributes something to all the rest of us, to society. It lays down another strand of uniting, sharing in common our differences, differing in our distinct ways of recognizing our shared existence.

We work as clinicians for this particular patient, and at the same time we are working for our own soul, promoting the coming to life as a person, not a discardable object, not dismissable collateral damage, not remaining sunk in inertia, not forgotten on the margins. As Jung says, the analyst is

> laying an infinitesimal grain in the scales of humanity's soul. Small and invisible as this contribution may be, it is yet an *opus magnus*, for it is accomplished in a sphere but lately visited by the numen, where the whole weight of mankind's problems has settled. The ultimate questions of psychotherapy are not a private matter—they represent a supreme responsibility. (1946, par. 449)

In the work of analysis, in the face of eros, we discover again and again that in making connection between conscious and unconscious, securing an open path for eros binding our two great mental systems, we also link to our neighbor and to his or her connection within themselves: we recognize our kinship. Yet eros presses further still, for the soul that finds its other side always in a "you" finds also that our combination of I and you are parts of "a transcendent unity whose nature can only be grasped symbolically" (ibid., par. 454). Eros leads to what we feel matters ultimately, what we are willing to die for, what with joy, with gratitude, we are willing to live for.

This material was originally presented in a symposium, "Responding to the Erotic Transference," at Mount Sinai Medical Center, New York City, March 8, 2008. Adapted from "Countertransference and the Erotic," Journal of Religion and Health, *vol. 48, no. 1 (March 2009), with permission from Springer Publications.*

BEHIND THE SCENES

7

BEFORE WE WERE
CREATING AND BEING CREATED IN OUR
ANALYTIC PROFESSION

I take up here where the knot gets tied linking us into what we become and feel we were all along. Discovering our vocation makes us feel deeply grateful that we found this work we love, in which we thrive. Indeed, we arrive where we belong. To be committed to being an analyst is to be forever working on our self, where it comes from and where it goes, and to look into which kind of service to the whole calls us, avoiding narcissism, and widening devotion.

My focus is on the numinous and the analyst, in the making of us, the breaking of us, in what got us going in this profession before we were. Jung describes the numinous as something beyond human will that alters consciousness; it is a quality belonging to a visible object—what we call mana, or genius, and is "extraordinarily potent"; it is the influence of an invisible presence which impacts us, arrests us, addresses us (Jung 1954b, pars. 383, 441; Jung 1940, par. 6). We may not understand such an encounter, but we never forget it. How does it alter our consciousness? We become alert to something there, an unknown X that sheds its own peculiar light, what Jung calls "luminosity" (Jung 1954b, par. 388), sparks in the soul, scintillae in the unconscious.

The Dark Side of the Numinous through Wounds

I begin with the dark side of this light, with the negative of its positive awe-inspiring nature, the wound it inflicts that brings us analysts into analysis in the first place, before we were professionals of long standing or newly accredited analysts or analysts still in training. For the mana power, the unknown X, may strike us in ways we find confounding, humiliating, and lead us to seek analysis. Many of us did not know we would come into this profession; we only knew we were caught and held fast, pierced; it was before we were, and we did not know something was creating us by undoing us.

We came into this profession through wounding by the numinous, through its darkest side—the fascination of a fetish or a sexual hook, the compelling need for middle of the night milk-food, the repeated linking up with the wrong partner, or the undertow of dead places inside us that we could not bring alive. We sought analysis as patients. Those of us who began analysis to train as analysts just took longer to arrive at the abysmal entry point of being a patient first, no longer rising above nor dodging out of the way of being addressed at the nadir of ourselves.

As Augustine says, you cannot give what you do not have, and so we could not be creating as analysts for others until we were first being created as patients. As Jung says, "the life of the spirit on the highest levels is a return to the beginnings" (Jung 1946, par. 439) and "inasmuch as you attain to the numinous experiences you are released from the curse of pathology. Even the very disease takes on a numinous character" (from a letter dated August 20, 1945; Jung 1992, 377). Before we were, the numinous came in the back door, through our wound, and only wrestling with it, and being wrestled by it, did we discover something beyond our ego living there, creating us.

The Numinous as Transcending the Ego

Reflecting upon this wound that resists our will and intellect turns our suffering into an encounter with something that transcends our ego. All of us here share the unfolding into becoming analysts. Who would have thought this possible? Who would have known there was balm in Gilead, a jewel in the wound, resurrection after crucifixion? The numinous is present in our becoming analysts.

Precisely here is the extra something Jung's approach offers analysands. The numinous is that which transcends our ego and compels our attention, often positive in a moment of stunning light or peace or bliss, but also even through the back door of our problems. This is the first meaning of numinous: it is beyond our ego and confronts us, positively or negatively; we cannot grasp it in ego terms; it evokes awe. With this sense of encounter a journey begins. The problems that beset us, serious as they may be, contain within them something else, a bidding, a summons, an engineering by something transcending our ego that points us toward a door through which we come to create what is already being created on both an individual and a collective level (Ulanov 2007b, chap. 8). For many of us, it is precisely encounter with the numinous that unfolded into our becoming analysts.

Individually, the wound that is an entry point is peculiar to our self. The work of analysis pays close attention to a person's particular details. The importance of the small things, the tiny features that make the process alive for the patient, leads analysand and analyst to come upon what needs to happen for something to achieve form (Balint 1993, 223, 227). When a woman, for example, says she lives in the posture of a "karate crouch," she conveys at once her defensive fear and her resilient aggression, a combination distinct to herself, not to women in general. Imaginative perception, that is, a sense of creating what we experience, yields increasing awareness that witnesses that we are being created.

Collectively, wounds we sustain as a people, a tribe, a nation, are also encounters with the numinous in its darkest forms. Stark examples in the opening decade of this new century are terrorist attacks in subways, office buildings, commuter trains, and restaurants, which shock us as being outside known patterns of war. Here the victim *is* the innocent bystander, no longer regrettable collateral damage but rather the intended target of the attack. The perpetrator here is not the soldier in arms in a hierarchy following an order from commander down to infantryman but rather one's neighbor, maybe even a gentle person, now incomprehensibly transmogrified into a mass murderer. Here the terrorist is not criminal or crazy in the usual sense, but one caught up in archetypal energies that may include a religious zeal exciting the ultimate sacrifice of his or her life, where religion is not about compassion and service to others but instead about murder of self and countless others, making them dead in the name of a living God.

Of all the groups responding to terrorism, analysts are called to look into such events to discern what addresses us through this collective wounding. What psychological injuries give rise to this horrific enactment of wounding on a mass scale? Is this a poor man's way of waging war, as effective as a rich man's planes and bombs? What identifications operate here that lead young people, sometimes with children and mates, to give over their egos into the power of the Self in its crushing forms? What do we encounter here that when reflected upon may indicate an unfolding path, one we find ourselves already on, but which when identified with unconsciously vaults people into enacting the Furies' vengeance? Asking these sorts of questions comprises one of our tasks and contributions to society.

Looking into numinous wounds—torments so profound to us as persons and in society that they hold us in their grip—means seeing something stepping forward. The wound becomes an encounter with something in the background. To try to discern it, to come into more direct relationship with this background, can only be for the good. Our greatest danger is to avoid the hard task of paying attention. Then we live in fear, in reactive retaliations, in exaggerated insistence; we are vulnerable to becoming assimilated to the Self. The change that comes when trying to perceive the background is that the impersonal milieu becomes a more personal encounter that may indicate a direction, a path to our journeying.

Trying to perceive the formless background gives us a new view of our foreground, as if standing at another point on the circle that contains everything. This containing circle, which Jung calls the *unus mundus*, "a potential archetypal world plan in the mind of God" before

God began creation where all the opposites are still unified, manifests sporadically in moments of synchronicity (von Franz 1992, 217). Then we glimpse the underlying unity of psyche and matter, of inner and outer, of the meaningful coherence of reality as an interconnected whole. In those moments we see what Jung calls the *creatio continua*, the acts of creating going on right now, displaying "a pattern that exists from all eternity," yet which is not determined by any antecedents (Jung 1952b, par. 967 and n17).

To experience these glimpses is to participate in creating as we are being created. Such firsthand knowledge, which touches the heart as well as the mind and brings clarity as well as beholding something ineffable, links our personal experiences of the numinous with the numinous in the background of our collective life, our shared existence with others. We gain a momentary perception of our part in the scheme of the whole, what religions call the will of God (see von Franz 1992, 257; Jung 1952b, pars. 924, 931, 948). Encountering what rests in our wounds, whether personal or national, initiates a second experience of the numinous.

The Numinous Entering the Ego

The numinous does not always stay in the background but steps over into concrete ego life within the bounds of space and time, historical and cultural location, with all the accompanying personal details. Mana comes into the ego and gradually decathects as we make something of the experience and assimilate some of the object's power to ourselves. We absorb our projections onto the numinous. Looked at from the side of the numinous, so to speak, this process of absorbing and giving form to the influx of potent formlessness of the ineffable contributes to the transformation of the God-image over the ages.

Here I want to focus on the ego side of the experience. As Jung says, in consciousness our complexes slough off their mythic envelope and enter into adaptive processes; they are personalized and rationalized, so dialectical discussion becomes possible (1954b, par. 384). The unknown X begins to be known: we create relation to it as we find it creating us; we name it as it reveals its hidden form, its "pure inconceivable *esse*." God's *hecceitas* manifests in our existence in "continuous activation of the Divine Names," the *ipseities* (von Franz

1992, 301). We are the ones who call on these names, who make narratives of our congress with them and create meaning out of our encounters with what creates us. For Jung, encounter with "the personified God-image in [our] psyche is *the* essential meaning of [our] existence" (ibid., 283).

Failure to connect with the background numinous leaves the ego high and dry in a desert of meaninglessness. This is illustrated by the plight of a man in his early twenties in the grip of depression from which suicide appears as the only way out to peace. He says of his life there is nothing happening: he is in a nothing job with no chance to get a good job; he feels nothing, there is nothing in his future. He has suffered a catastrophic disillusionment that life could hold possibility and around the age of twelve gave up the idea that he could make any difference. The hostility hidden in his passivity turns up in gruesome dreams of killing and nearly being killed, of having to pass a test and despairing that he can do so. In the transference he watches me like a hawk to perceive whether I have any hope for him, and he is ready to resist it quietly and completely if he spies hope in any of my responses. It is as if there is no numinous for him, except in the form of No-thing: nothingness blanketing his life, threatening to suffocate its beginning. He cannot yet make a narrative, a conversation, a form of the formless, a conversation between ego and Self.

At the other end of the spectrum is a woman in her nineties, remarkable in her achievement as a clinician and a social activist through her work in community, who drew on her African-American religious heritage to move her generation and her children's generation out of the slavery of her grandmother. She came for a specific symptom of hearing tunes, often the hymns or spirituals of her religion, which she experienced as communications. Could they be from the Spirit? At the same time, being medically trained, she sought consultation on possible neurological causes of these auditory events. She was in dialogue with this numinous happening. Sometimes she sang back, sometimes she argued with what the tunes say, and sometimes she responded with thoughts they inspire. In our sessions, I felt the background very much surrounding the foreground, as if she was approaching the border between life and death, and it was quite possible for her to entertain simultaneously that this symptom was nothing but an organic disorder and also a means God was using to speak to her. She was nimble enough to make something meaningful out of hearing tunes and enter the joy of it, while at the same time investigating it scientifically. She was in conversation, continuing her narrative of life right up to the moment of death.

When our affect, behavior, or emotion around the numinous comes into the ego, the ego changes and so does our perception of the numinous. We build up forms for the formless and enter into dialogue with it, finding the ineffable in ordinary daily events of our lives. This enriches living. We feel we come to witness some presence witnessing us. Creating is going on in relation to what creates us. A double discourse may develop, from both sides, so to speak, one in words and symbols, the other in scintillae, synchronicities, emerging moments of absolute knowledge. This conversation confers unity on scattered parts of the psyche and of the world, so that we meet, for example, in conferences to exchange perceptions of the intersection, the conjunction of the Vast and the All with the here and now.

The precious ingredient in such *coniunctio* moments is our ego. We come again into touch with what was and is before we were, but now with consciousness, ready to make something of what we experience. This is the key on which the whole lock turns, for without this willing consciousness (but instead a blind identification), we risk destruction. If our soul is in God, it is swept out to sea, the ego assimilated to the Self, losing its standpoint in the here and now in relation to others and caught in archetypal tides. If our identification is unconscious, then our distinctly human ego is at the mercy of archetypal energies.

Jung's warning is frighteningly apt right now: if we are unwilling to undergo symbolic death, universal genocide will ensue (Jung 1956–57, par. 1661). But to suffer symbolic death, there must be consciousness, an ego capable of shaping a narrative, carrying on a symbolic discourse that advances from encounter with the numinous. We make a hut, an ark, a tabernacle, an earthly house for the divine. The Self finds in the ego a receiver and transmitter. We have already seen massacres, holocausts, forced marches, systematic starvations, and oppressions of whole peoples based on race or religion or politics. For symbolic death to occur, we need egos full of readiness to respond to the numinous that already has engaged them.

As analysts, we have something to say here that can make a difference to the survival of the world. The first meaning of the numinous is that it is something powerful that transcends our ego consciousness and to which we must pay close attention. The second meaning of the numinous is its entering into our ego consciousness and changing it to enlarge it and/or defeat it (Jung 1955–56, par. 778). The third meaning of the numinous is *its* enlarged manifestation as a result of our egos engaging with it. The discourse doubles.

The more we are able imaginatively to perceive the numinous, the bigger it appears and the stronger our egos grow to see it. The unknown X elicits more ego, and more ego receives more unknowable. The numinous is not reduced to our forms for it but waxes into bigger forms that we are more and more able to recognize. It moves us by its inexhaustibility, its immensity, its generosity which seems to allow us to picture its reality in symbols and rituals precious to us both individually and as a people.

The Objective Numinous

In the secular version of this third meaning of the numinous, which we see in postmodernism, we focus on the ego's narratives and representations depicting our various registerings of the numinous, and we let its objective presence go (Anderson 1990, chap. 1). The question is not, Who is there? or even, Is there a there there? but rather, What do I (we) make of it? Focusing on the language we create to describe our experience of the numinous, we let the numinous itself go. We involve ourselves with the ways we are creating what we are describing. Representation captures our focus, instead of what is being represented. We emphasize our creating and leave off our being created, our dependence on an antecedent creator. This option does not lead to symbolic death but is the underside of postmodernism retreating into the ego world.

Symbolic death includes our relation to what is there as well as to our forms of representation for it, to include both our ego and the numinous as dialogue partners, and then to suffer their unraveling in the gap between our symbols and what they point to. We build up symbols, names, pictures for the numinous and converse with it in particular personal and social rituals. The ego builds up readiness, by which I mean consciously gathering the bits and pieces of what we know, assembling them to present ourselves attentive to the numinous.

The New Testament parable of the wedding feast comes to mind (Matthew 22:1–13). Jesus invites guests to the wedding feast who do not come. Their business or farm calls; they make light of the invitation and go their own ways. Then Jesus instructs his servants to go out to the highways and invite strangers along the road. They do come—the homeless, the unemployed, a free meal, an occasion! But one of them does not wear wedding attire, and he is seized and thrown out into the darkness. The point is thus forcefully made. Once we know that the numinous is, that the numinous bids us through our wounds, that the numinous impresses us as that which transcends our ego, that the numinous in momentous experience enters our ego consciousness, then we must dress up to meet it. It is not how grand our dress is—we may own little—but it is in dressing up, gathering our finest to meet the finest, the most, the momentous, that we show willingness to honor what presents itself in the numinous encounter. The ninety-year-old patient brought such flair to our sessions where she spoke of the numinous singing to her: she sported a delicate violet feather on her head to match her purple dress.

The dressing up is creating our forms to represent the numinous, to value it. We corral our lives in their disparate activities to assemble around this central conversation with what transcends us and yet speaks to us. Engaging in this conversation is what Jung calls the symbolic life. Religions go further into the precincts of the sacramental life (Ulanov and Ulanov 1975, chap. 4). Jung describes the religious attitude as

> careful consideration and observation of certain dynamic factors that are conceived as "powers": spirits, daemons, gods, laws, ideas, ideals, or whatever name man has given to such factors in his world as he has found powerful, or dangerous, or helpful enough to be taken into careful consideration, or grand, beautiful, and meaningful enough to be devoutly worshipped and loved. (Jung 1940, par. 8)

Symbolic death means we create as much as we can to house and express what is the most important, that around which our life and life itself revolves, and then we suffer its dismemberment, dissolution, destruction, because our forms, however grand, are finite constructions, mortal (see Ulanov 2007b, chap. 9). We create forms for what we name as ultimate, God, Self-experience, truth, beauty, and we know that none of our forms or names is it. What we create is dust.

The Numinous in Itself

Such a symbolic death, which if endured introduces a gap of nothingness, of mortality, between us and everything we have given our lives to build, launches us into a new consciousness. In our profession, an example would be learning all we can, training hard, working on theory, putting in the hours of analysis, supervision, case consultations, and self-analysis, and then putting it aside. As Jung says, "forget everything when you face your patient" (Jung 1959, par. 882). We sacrifice the ultimacy of what we are creating, and we go on creating it as if it is ultimate.

Paradox supervenes over intellect: we lose our rational constructions. We do opposite things simultaneously:

> Paradox . . . does more justice to the *unknowable* than clarity can do, for uniformity of meaning robs the mystery of its darkness and sets it up as something that is *known*. That is a usurpation . . . by pretending that . . . the intellect has got hold of the transcendent mystery by a cognitive act and has "grasped" it. The paradox . . . reflects a higher level of intellect . . . by not forcibly representing the unknowable as known. (Jung 1954c, par. 417).

We identify what really matters and commit ourselves to its vital importance, while at the same time we know it is not the first thing, not the utmost, the supreme endpoint. While committed wholeheartedly, we disidentify with our values. A space exists between us and them, dependent on the living numinous creating us as we are creating.

We explore the underlying real, the primary real, the *hecceitas*, through its various and numerous names, its *ipseities*, its forms of communication. We commit to purposes while at the same time we sense a background purposiveness that may unravel them. We withdraw our projections at the same time we entertain them as visions that make the whole visible, that bring within range the "Farnearness"—what Marguerite Porete of the thirteenth century calls God (Babinsky 1993, 155).

Our images of the heavenly city, of the peaceful lying down of lion with lamb, of the Kaaba at the center of the universe, bring the mystery into view at the same time we know the mystery is none of these things. We "become as little children" again for whom "the opposites lie close together," but now with consciousness, "not the unconscious child we would like to remain" (Jung 1952a, par. 742). This is the paradoxical consciousness of the child "born from the maturity of the adult" (ibid.). We are at once "never more than [our] own limited ego before the One who dwells within [us], whose form has no knowable boundaries, who encompasses [us] on all sides, fathomless as the abysms of the earth and vast as the sky" (ibid., par. 758). This One, grand and magnificent, also brings through the back door the wild thing, always alive and untameable, the All far beyond our comprehension yet whom we know best in the tiny particulars of our personal journey and the small cultural forms of our particular time. It dethrones our ego, wounding it, defeating it: "Whoever has suffered once from an intrusion of the unconscious has at least a scar if not an open wound. . . . the wholeness of his ego personality, has been badly damaged . . . a fatal blow to his own monarchy" (Jung 1988, 1233). Through that wound enters the "*influxis divinus*," and Jung says we "do better to disidentify . . . from the small voice within . . . through which the divine spirit manifests itself" and listen to it attentively to find a middle way between its opposites (Jung 1956–57, par. 1661).

This something more reveals itself as other than the forms we make for it, which it graciously consents to while also remaining a wild thing. As analysts we touch it in the joy we feel in the work we do. Beyond the necessity of our virtuous effort to be good analysts, is the joy of it that makes the virtuous life, for all its value, seem sterile in comparison.

Marguerite Porete writes of the country of peace. This lies beneath or beyond the unconscious of tumultuous affects and conflicting instincts that Jung and Freud describe. We reach this joy through a momentary spark that is also a brief aperture that shows the "glory of the soul," and the peace that remains "is so delicious that Truth calls it glorious food" (Babinsky 1993, 135–136). As a result one is "very free and unencumbered from all things" dwelling in freeness from feebleness and fear (ibid., 153). This is a passionate living with "the Ravishing Most High who overtakes me and joins me to the center of the marrow of divine Love in whom I am melted" (ibid., 155).

The alchemist Dorn describes the peace of eternity that breathes into the temporal world through the *spiraculum aeternitatis*, a sort of air hole where "the personal realm of the psyche," our particular wounds and potentiality, "touches the collective unconscious," Self meeting ego (von Franz 1980a, 109; Jung 1955–56, par. 670). From this "pivot point . . . from this nowhere comes everything which is newly created" (von Franz 1980a, 110).

Here we find our moments of joy, of our perceiving before we were, being created as we are creating.

This essay was presented at the Seventeenth International Congress of Analytical Psychology, IAAP, in Cape Town, South Africa, August 12–17, 2007.

8

LOSING, FINDING, BEING FOUND

K nots that we have trouble untying exist in our groups as well as ourselves, causing us social anguish that can deepen even into despair. What is the matter with us all that we cannot get along, even while we are devoted to helping people get along better and release blockages into easy flow back and forth? We felt this especially at the beginning of the new century with its explosion of violence in our country in the first year.

Here we are, Jungians of North America, midway through the first decade of a new century and millennium, living under the shadow of 9/11 in New York City and Virginia, 3/11 in Madrid, 7/7 in London, and 7/23 in Sharm el-Sheikh (not to mention repeated suicide bombings and reprisals in Israel and Palestine). The first two of these terrorist attacks, in the United States and Spain, we think of as having been committed by outsiders to those societies, while the attacks in the United Kingdom and Egypt were committed by insiders, citizens raised in those countries. Thus boundaries of insider and outsider begin to dissolve, as do explanatory categories of refugee versus citizen, poor versus middle-class, unemployed versus employed.

More frightening still are the dissolutions of boundaries between personal and collective, because the terrorists doing these attacks are not crazy or criminal in the usual definitions of these terms but seemingly caught up in transpersonal energies of the collective psyche and willing to make the ultimate sacrifice of their own lives for the God they serve. Such terrorist acts cannot be carried out without a group consciousness and a religious perspective. Only an unconscious identification with primordial images of the transcendent supported by a group consciousness has the power to convince potential terrorists that bombing people in subways or buses on their way to work or in restaurants for a shared meal is serving a living God.

In reaction to this blurring of boundaries, wherein neighbors of all sorts in ordinary life become targets of a holy war, sharp edges are drawn between groups; hard lines are instituted to combat this blurring. People think of stockpiling food and medicine and planning escape routes. But as with an immune disease, we do not know where exactly the enemy is, only that it can strike many places, without a certain cause to indicate where to defend ourselves. Randomness threatens, which only exacerbates our drawing still tighter borders as if to reconstruct precise containers in which to locate our security. Opposite to images of the global village, splits break out.

Rifts of all kinds are seen in North America: religious and political groups on the far left versus the far right; disputes about borders being too open and that must be closed to keep out those who would come in. And when we look beyond our national borders to the world we live in with others, more seemingly insoluble divisions threaten any sense of sharing a whole globe: Israel and Palestine, North and South Korea, Iraq and United States, let alone the rivaling monotheisms of Islam, Judaism, and Christianity and rivaling political styles of monarchies versus democracies. It is as though we have lost the blood of kinship, a basic hospitality to each other as humans, fellow beings, and the result is that real blood gushes out.

The solutions tried in Europe to establish space for different groups in one society—of separatism, multiculturalism, assimilation—have all failed (Friedman 2005). Even if, with Erich Neumann, we view marginalized social groups as bringing into the collective what has been left out and thus reenergizing society, at this moment we feel pushed to the edge of fearing that society as we have known it will be destroyed (Neumann 1969). We feel Eliot's "Wasteland," a "heap of broken images, where the sun beats" (1963, 53). Despair looms.

We Jungians have held out the theory and practice of the transcendent function as a source of help for such splitting. Engage the opposites, carry the tension between them consciously, wait and hope, and a creative solution will emerge, we have said in print, in presentations, in clinical work, and to our world. Yet we, too, are split in our own training groups, all of us, into rivaling factions that display what Henry Murray called "humorless hostility" (cited in Eisold 1994, 786).

We experience firsthand that Jungian analysis is not outside the collective but is part of its splitting. Splits embody concretely what goes on in the body politic, even the mystical body, whether we are referring to political parties, religious traditions, or divisions in training institutes. Cracks and fissures open up, gaps we cannot bridge, and helplessness threatens. The division widens, and the sides gather substance, weight. What we preach we cannot put into practice, for we do not hold the opposites and bear their tension consciously, thus inhabiting a space between. We sever instead.

The breakups in our Jungian groups all over the world, though seemingly minor compared to the violence of Serbians and Croatians, which results in rape camps and genocide, or of the Hutus and Tutsis, which results in machete massacres and thousands of refugees, or any of the other ruptures between peoples, are nonetheless on a small scale the same kinds of splits in our countries and abroad. The space between, which becomes instead a gap, fills up with hurt and rage. We dwell in breach of kinship, no longer able to view our theory as contributing to its solution. Meaninglessness threatens.

In that gap, that severance, where we feel helpless to fix the breakage, we can only wait with hope. The *I Ching* hexagram "Waiting" says, "Rain comes in its own time. We cannot make it come; we have to wait for it." But "disagreements crop up. General unrest can easily develop . . . and we lay the blame on one another." Surely all of us have been exactly in that space, falling into an us/them mentality, where the bad is for export only and we toss accusations back and forth between our rival factions. The sage advises: "Slander will be silenced if we do not gratify it with injured retorts" (Wilhelm 1950, 25–26).

Losing

What injures us so deeply that retorts rise to our lips? What are we losing so that in grasping after it we harden into opposition to those who just recently were our colleagues? We have in our Jungian institutes a laboratory to study splitting because we are suffering it; and with the usual Jungian method, we can look for what images bundle the tumultuous affects we bear on the personal, cultural, and archetypal levels.

Losing is the major image with all the connotations of defeat, undoing, destruction, privation, and waste that accompany loss. The personal losses get jumbled up with collective and archetypal images of dissolution. Clinical examples display on a small scale this same sense of a large tumbling into nothingness. A woman felt she descended into craziness when she lost the papers of an eminent person who would come into her firm. She felt knocked out, stunned, she said; how could she have been so careless! She said she felt "ejected from the universe; it was like a loss of sanity." Another woman said she was going along doing her work and had to refer to an important folder for her business and could not find it. Frantic, in a panic, she said she felt "out of the blue hurled into a pit, a hole of goneness." A third woman, said on losing a document crucial to her work, "You drop through life into an abyss; you disappear. I feel a sinking in my stomach and dread covering me like waters over my head; abysmal confusion, a crumbling of reality. I feel invalid, unable; it is truly awful."

We hear in these accounts the same sense of randomness, helplessness, and meaninglessness that befalls us in bigger traumas of splitting of our groups, our nations, our world. In these examples, the personal feelings of invalidity blend into a despair, of feeling exiled from the culture of the job because one has been so careless, and the feelings intensify to an archetypal image of falling out of sanity and being expelled from community into an abyss. One man said he felt "blanked," unable to think.

Collective losses pile on us from acts of terrorism, where a Suni doctor in Iraq is reported being afraid to walk on his street lest he be shot by a Shiite neighbor, as was his cousin. And when the cousin's family went to the hospital to retrieve his body, they were shot in the parking lot. Yet the Suni faction refuses to join in crafting Iraq's new constitution.

Collective losses also fall on us from natural disasters such as the floods of Asia's tsunamis and America's Hurricane Katrina. In such catastrophes we lose those we love, animals and trees we love; we lose our jobs, our neighborhoods, our houses, our securities. No food, no water, no clothes—all gone.

We witness these catastrophic losses, yet a hinge exists connecting them to our personal losses, in which we feel more implicated. We learn, after terrorist acts, after natural disasters, to picture with more imaginative aggression, more imaginative initiative, what might happen, what could happen, what will probably happen, and we learn that with better communication across groups or countries we might prevent or at least better prepare to help in such disasters. Our failure to imagine the whole and our little but vital role in it leaves us at the mercy of what happens, and hence we see our measure of complicity.

In images of losing the wholeness of our Jungian groups, we suffer disappointment in ourselves, even sorrow at a soul level, because as colleagues we do not get along with each other. We suffer de-idealization of our analytic enterprise; it is not as good or powerful as we thought. Individuation, assimilating the shadow, withdrawing projections from our neighbor—all these valuable concepts we thought we learned and taught and used in clinical work do not hold up in our own disputes but get buried under accusations, recriminations, hurt, and anger. We retrench to our side to make it firmer, clearer, to preserve truth as we see it, and split off from those who hold the equally strong fantasy that there is one right way and it is theirs.

We lose the container of our whole Jungian society and the ease of depending on each other. Because we live all our life long in continuous dependency on each other as partners in discovering where our ideas come from, our theory suffers too. Is our theory wrong, especially regarding the transcendent function? If not, how to live it forward in face of its breaking down? To lose faith in what we depend on—faith in theory, faith in justice, faith in each other, faith in our analyses—is to lose heart. We seem unable to house the diversity among us and must split instead.

A pivotal question arises: When is splitting repudiation and when is it differentiation? Kenneth Eisold, in examining intolerance of diverse views in psychoanalytic institutes, proposes that narrow-mindedness that can only repudiate is a social defense against anxiety arising from three sources: the conflict between belonging to a school of thought and being wide open to a patient's clinical material which may challenge that school of thought; the conflict of pairing analyst and analysand, supervisor and supervisee, within a psychoanalytic institute which subverts its sense of wholeness so that the institute then draws rigid boundaries of theory to secure its identity and exports the accumulating hostility toward rival schools of depth psychology; and the conflict between feeling the discipline is somehow outside society and superior to social reality while its institute is a part of that reality and aims to connect its members to the world (Eisold 1994, 788–790). Splitting, then, is a derivative of this unrecognized anxiety.

In Jungian terms, we may ask what are the personal, cultural, and archetypal layers of anxiety we endure that underlie our splitting, always with an eye to the relevance of our small sufferings to the large splits between peoples all over the world. At the personal layer of the unconscious, our anxiety swells in response to what we perceive to be power complexes in members of our group. In addition, we think we perceive members' unhealed narcissistic injuries—of feeling unwelcomed or excluded from administrative or teaching positions, of having their suggestions for training candidates ignored. We fear our ideas will be attacked in public or gossiped about in secret; we take offense. When we hop over such numerous tiny misunderstandings or hurts, gradually what was a grain of sand pushed under the rug becomes as big as a camel hump that in no way can get through the eye of the needle. Then, in every discussion of business or theory, this camel hump looms up to block communication. Personal shadow stuff fills the room and sucks up all the oxygen.

On a cultural level, the old Jungian order is deconstructed, no longer a unity carried by founders of institutes loyal to Jung as an internalized ego-ideal and able to quote "what Jung said to me." Early on different Jungian institutes were marked by varying emphases— archetypal or clinical (which is a false split, I believe), in conversation with other depth psychological schools or focusing exclusively on Jung's writings. But now schisms exist within individual societies and are often marked more by personal shadow material than by differing content. Through the shadow bits competing, Jungian groups are pushed into identifying with one faction or the other, forced into multiplicity. No longer held within one vessel or under one umbrella, the Jungian school threatens to disseminate, fragment.

Yet being pushed into multiple factions also brings in what was before left out by earlier, more unified focus. We are forced by the emergence of multiple conflicting views, for example, on how to train new analysts, to deal with our collective life together and the collective aspect of life. As Singer and Kimbles point out, complexes exist in a group psyche, too, and in the group level of our individual psyches (2004, 177). Defending against these "cultural complexes," we can flee into seeing them only as personal or as archetypal, thus avoiding the cultural, collective dimensions of our common profession as analysts.

On the archetypal level, images of chaos, gulfs, fissures, arouse our anxiety. Just as in clinical sessions, where a dream of the loss of the important document can take the person down to the loss of a loved one, and through that wound into the abyss of death, so here we can feel given over to turbulent images of nothing and everything, confusion and clarity, doubt and certainty, resolve and helplessness. Jung's counsel proves apt:

> More than once everything [we] have built will fall to pieces under the impact of reality, and [we] must not let this discourage [us] from examining, again and again, where it is that [our] attitude is still defective, and what are the blind spots in [our] psychic field of vision. . . . so psychic wholeness will never be attained empirically, as consciousness is too narrow and too one-sided to comprehend the full inventory of the psyche. Always we shall have to begin again from the beginning. . . . the work does not prosper without the greatest simplicity. But simple things are always the most difficult. (Jung 1955–56, par. 759)

What then are our blind spots and what is the psyche aiming at in all this splitting? (And remember we are using our splits as a way of exploring the psychic dimension of splitting in the world.) One blind spot is our belief that somehow we are doing this; it is up to us, our action, our failure, and we do not see that we are being done to.

Not by the opposing faction(s), for they too are being done to, but all of us together, in Jungian jargon, by the Self.

If we do not see this, then we feel doomed, under judgment, facing apocalypse, and all our tightening of boundaries, rigidifying of theory, will not avail. If we do see this Self action, then just as on a personal level when we see the Self emerging we are relieved of soul loneliness, so on a collective level we glimpse a bigger community in which we belong, so precious that we call it communion. Jung writes of such a vision,

> as Nietzsche says, "One becomes Two," and the greater figure, which one always was but which remained invisible, appears. . . . . [T]o the lesser personality. . . . the day of judgment of [our] littleness has dawned. But the man who is inwardly great will know that the long expected friend of his soul, the immortal one, has now really come . . . to seize hold of him by whom this immortal had always been confined and held prisoner, and to make his life flow into that greater life—a moment of deadliest peril! (Jung 1940, par. 217)

What confronts us in this moment of peril? What do we find?

Finding

New questions arise: Is the Self engineering something in the splitting? Is it destroying its symbolic forms to which we are accustomed to become newly embodied in the real world, which we do not invent any more than we invent the psyche? Is this a shift from the inner/outer boundaries to a new perception that must get into the lived body? What new patterns are we finding? As Jung says, the analytical style must not be clung to, and the sacrifice is terrible, as if we have lost contact with the unconscious, with the guiding Self. He says, "You must be able to lose contact, you never gain anything new without losing something. So risk losing the unconscious." Which is "ridiculous," he goes on to say, because "the unconscious clings to you so tightly that you cannot get rid of it" (Jung 1997, 1357).

What turns splitting toward repudiation is our desire to merge and become the other in a state of identity or, failing that, to annihilate the other, cast them out, call them damned, even kill them. Be like us, or be opposed to us. Repudiation wants merger or evacuation, identification or obliteration. We want to preserve the precious theory we know; we want to conserve the precious values we endorse; we want to safeguard the precious God we serve. We need the astonishing courage of Emily Dickinson, who faced into the experience of what critic Kenneth Stocks said she found to be "the reduction of the human" to life in "a seemingly indifferent universe" (Stocks 1988, 6–7). She explored this new predicament where, "under the pressure of the new science—economic—technological order that had not only subordinated real human value to its own necessities but, in her own words, had left 'The Heavens stripped— / Eternity's vast pocket picked'" (ibid.).

What turns splitting toward differentiation is the strength to look into what is happening as Emily Dickinson did, to let the parts separate and stay separate, with a capacity to be alone with our vision. That is an alternative to thrusting one part forward to make it everybody else's whole. Turning toward differentiation means opening to unknowing, even to losing without the guarantee of finding anything as good as what we have known, relying only on hope in things unseen. Hope means we dare to yearn, desire, expect, dream of, hunger for, in the absence of appearance but still in trustful anticipation that what we hope for will come. Hope means courage to risk toward what is not yet. Hope means modesty in recognizing our limitations and those of our "side," the limits of our vision, and the limitations of our failures. Differentiation alters the vision of unity from sameness to seeing that what we have in common is our differences. Hope means seeing our libido withdrawing from the old form of the opposites in our group and stirring up new possibilities. Jung puts it, "One can say that the psyche no longer feels wholly contained in the dominant, whereupon the dominant loses its fascination and no longer grips the psyche so completely as before. . . . [It] fails to touch the heart. A 'sentiment d'incompletude' produces a compensatory reaction which attracts other regions of the psyche and their contents, so as to fill up the gap" (Jung 1955–56, par. 505).

The new possibility we find stirred up by splitting is the reality, once again, of the shadow. Shadow energies invade, even take over, and crowd out our actual dispute about the third thing—the theory of the transcendent function, of the Self, of the best way to learn. And separation from shadow stuff must precede our assimilation of it. We cannot get into conversation about differing views of the Self or how Jungian training best proceeds, which are the bases for the splits, unless we pick up all the relational issues that we hopped over. The problem was not that we differed but that we hurt each other when we differed; not that we are conscious of thinking of the other as evil, but that we act it out concretely by calling each other names and excluding each other.

Such concretization of shadow impulses obscures a deeper threat of reformulating what we believe in, in the face of maybe losing it because we are questioning it. Yet getting caught up in interpersonal shadow issues can be a defense against facing chaotic images and tumultuous affects at an archetypal level, that the Self we counted on is destroying itself in its symbolic form to get earthed in a new living body of society and theory (Jung 1997, 1314). That is where hope enters, expectant longing that we are cooperating with a bigger thrust from the Self to unfold in new forms we do not yet know. If so, it means not-knowing, un-knowing, must now abide with what we do know. Jung's insights push us into a bigger order, beyond our ego idea of how things should work. Being a Jungian means risk, for only his theory incorporates destruction of its terms and of the analyst as the aim of analysis. And the experience of this, as Jung says, "is the important thing, not its intellectual representation or clarification, which proves meaningful . . . only when the road to original experience is blocked" (Jung 1955–56, par. 777).

But issues of shadow must be faced; as Edinger puts it, we must "give it profound acceptance—with all its sinfulness, with all the guilt it generates—if the individuation process is to proceed" (Edinger 2004, 82). It helps to remember here, whether talking about our splits or those in the world, that sin which separates us from the ground and center of being is not just intentional act; it is the state before this that such action indicates.

Methods we use in clinical work apply here. Manifestations of Self always take place in a context, a location both personal and cultural, that modify their archetypal depth. So each of us in our separate groups begins with what is there in front of us. Here the rival faction, the enemy neighbor, may be seen in a new light: still an enemy but making visible what we see as bad. Our neighbor coagulates it for us, carries it for us. What they are in themselves we do not know, but as our subjective-object, we can clarify what most deeply threatens us, even name it to ourselves as evil, wrong, bad. We locate the shadow and look into it, and become full with its menace. Repudiation moves toward differentiation when we face what is facing us and do not hide out in personal or cultural complexes. Insofar as we see even the archetypal Self as a bridge to reality beyond the psyche, we face, through this shadow stuff, the cosmic void.

Thus it is fearful to fall into the hands of the living experience of what comes through shadow stuff. As Jung says,

> The contents that rise up and confront a limited consciousness are far from harmless, as is shown by the classic example of the temptation of Christ, or . . . the Mara episode in the Buddha legend. . . . they signify the specific danger to which the person concerned is liable to succumb. What the inner voice whispers to us is generally . . . negative, if not actually evil. . . . The inner voice . . . makes us conscious of the evil from which the whole community is suffering, whether it be the nation or the whole human race . . . [and] brings the evil before us in order to make us succumb. (1934, par. 319)

The catch is to succumb, but only in part. If we completely succumb and the ego, whether personal or collective, is overcome, then "a catastrophe ensues. But if we can succumb only in part, and if by self-assertion the ego can save itself from being completely swallowed, then it can assimilate the voice, and we realize that the evil was . . . a bringer of healing and illumination" (ibid.).

We find that to succumb in part changes our approach to shadow stuff. Not only is our enemy also our aid in seeing what we are trying to become differentiated from, but we see the bad in the light of the good. Jung says, "in dealing with darkness, you have got to cling to the Good, otherwise the devil devours you" (from a letter dated November 24, 1953; Jung 1976, 135). Here opposites rearrange from opposition, each seeking to quell the other, to cooperative contrast: that we must cling to the good when facing the bad, to better discern the good when aware of all our negative affects that the bad arouses (from a letter dated June 28, 1956; Jung 1976, 314).

We re-collect, once again the cutting edges that sever connections inside and out to anything competing, because we sense we are held in a larger perspective of the Self moving in us. Here, paradoxically, is where ego assertion is a sine qua non. While succumbing to despair over intractable shadow problems, at the same time we gather into awareness all we are given to be (Ulanov 1996b, 12–15). We hold fast to what we value and belong to while simultaneously confronting the infection seeping in of vengeance, justification, indignation, righteousness, retaliation. We hold to the good in order to face the bad.

By having the split-off other group carry the bad and thus circumscribe it, define it, we become more differentiated, more able to see with what we contend. By our experiencing what we succumb to as bad, we feel the despair of ever bridging the gap between us and within us. By asserting what we value, we define it more clearly and lean on its accumulated strength to face the rift, the breakage of communication.

This is strenuous work. Our ego participates by imposing forms, narratives, on unconscious material coming up in us and others, thus putting the *massa confusa* into a shape or figure in which it can then be assimilated. With luck, we avoid the twin dangers of insisting only on our formulations, which petrify instinct, or of just going out to sea, swept away by the impulses, affects, images of the unconscious shadow (Jung 1955–56, par. 603).

We are stretched between the animal and the spiritual. The gap between them, and between us and our neighbor, transforms into space between us and within us. But only if our ego participates fully, creating this third space and finding itself created in it. We glimpse that this third space is what the Self has been engineering (Ulanov 2007a). We begin to feel a stirring of kinship, to see that we share the same boat as fellow strugglers, sister sojourners, refugees rowing between good and bad, hoping to fulfill the promise of our discipline of analysis.

Such an ego-stretching moves us into the paradox of securely identifying what matters to us, to what we pledge allegiance, to our position, and simultaneously to disidentify from that position. We locate what we love and hate; we identify where our libido is, what we find it poured into, and because of that solidity, we see beyond it. With the poet Milosz in his song to Orpheus, we go down into the hell of our shadow conflicts and into the death they deal—in us, in our groups, in our nation and world—to seek the one we love. With the strength of what we loved and lost—such as the wholeness of our Jungian societies or of a world without terrorism—we bring it almost back to this life. But this life, with all its color and scent, proves richer than the beyond. The poet says of Orpheus:

> It happened as he expected. He turned his head
> And behind him on the path was no one.

> Sun. And sky. And in the sky white clouds.
> Only now everything cried to him Eurydice!
> How will I live without you, my consoling one!
> But there was a fragrant scent of herbs, the low humming of bees.
> And he fell asleep with his cheek on the sun-warmed earth.
> (Milosz 2004, 102)

We embrace how much this life fills us, claims us, while paradoxically feeling claimed by what transcends it, is beyond it. We find ourselves being found just as we deeply locate ourselves not only in what we lost but in what finds us in the here and now.

Being Found

What finds us and what happens to us as a result? We find ourselves being found and that radically changes our consciousness. Grounded by re-collecting both our shadow bits and what we value, we discover our limits, that we are not the sole authors of our splitting: it also happen to us. We thought we were splitting the groups, or at least the other faction was doing so. We perceive now that something else is the subject of this drama; we are a bit player, necessary, essential to witness it, but not central. No longer above the splits nor inundated by them, we see that something comes upon us, happens spontaneously. Our job is to be the jar for its containing so we can attend to it, behold its happening.

When near the numinous, we are near danger of identifying with it or splitting away from it. We must not overpersonalize it into our problem of schisms (to avoid looking at it). The Self, as Jung says, engineers its own destruction as a symbolic form in order to come into living. If it becomes too reified and hence subject to fanaticism, or too spiritualized and hence off the ground, the Self destroys itself, says Jung, as a symbolic form, to incarnate again in a living body of individuals who respond, relate, witness, live it (Jung 1997, 473, 1314). We attest to this process, verify it, endorse it. It captures our attention.

The painter Rauschenberg describes something like this in relation to creating a painting, saying there is never a definitive way of doing things. "He wanted to be unfamiliar with what he was doing, to keep things open until the last moment and not to work 'schemingly.' He liked to think he was collaborating with his materials, rather than trying to make them work for him, and . . . as much as possible to keep his feelings and taste out of it" (Tomkins 2005, 72). Rauschenberg says, "I don't want a painting to be just an expression of my personality. I feel it ought to be much better than that" (ibid.).

Jung describes this event in alchemy as assimilating the Christ image to one's own self, as "an involuntary experience of the reality represented by the sacred legend" (1955–56, par. 492). It is the reality that undergoes the change; we are affected by it, but it is doing it and having it done. The *materia* is the star of the drama; we are the witnessing narrators. It suffers; it dies; it rises.

We do not identify with the transformation going on. We suffer the paradox of its objective happening within the intimacies of our subjectivity, both individually and shared, which means collectively, such as, for example, in religious rituals. We feed this objective process going on outside the ego by perceiving it, giving it libido, becoming conscious of it. We live simultaneously both in our small ego identity and feel paradoxically thrust out of it. Jung says this is "the real experience of a man who has got involved in the compensatory contents of the unconscious by investigating the unknown, seriously, to the point of self-sacrifice"(ibid.).

We are involved in unconscious compensatory events through the painful splitting going on in our groups and in our world. We look into what is unknown in the analysand who repeatedly loses things. We ask what kind of attitude it would take to keep from losing things, how would this person have to live differently not to lose things. We inquire where the losses take the person—into some emotional space or some line of thought unreachable any other way. We inquire into the meaning of our own splitting. How are we to live together as societies devoted to Jungian analysis? What kind of attitude will make it possible to hold conversations between our differing groups? We feel the necessity as analysts to try to understand terrorism in order to contribute to the world's efforts to prevent it. Our profession investigates the unknown and participates in the self-sacrifice.

Our analytical attitudes do not protect us from splitting. Jung describes it: "the transition from a psychological atmosphere into the collective atmosphere of the world is a most painful procedure . . . and therefore it is quite justified to symbolize it by a lot of sacrificial blood" (Jung 1997, 1357).

The blood flows into our living rooms through television coverage of splitting around the world and within our own nation. Boundaries dissolve at the same time they are asserted with a vengeance. Borders are defied at the same time they are tightened to define separate cultures. As a world, we are transitioning into one world, *unus mundus,* where familiar inner/outer distinctions and us/them oppositions are both exaggerated and nullified. Subject-object thought forms dissolve at the same time we see afresh our dependence on each other not as objects but as subjects who make our unfolding possible. Jung brings us back to the "psyche which covers both conscious and unconscious, the whole being. . . . expressed by the Self, by the greater thing in which we are contained. That can never be lost, but you can lose consciousness of it . . . you can lose consciousness of being led by God" (Jung 1997, 1361–1362).

Being found in this larger container, what can we offer to this transition? What are we conscious of losing and finding? We are conscious of the loss of wholeness as we experienced it before splitting happened. We are conscious of the weight and grounding of the shadow stuff in us, in others, around us. We are conscious of a greater chaos that throws all the parts together, including ones we do not know. We are conscious that we are not doing the splitting to the degree we thought. A something more, what Jung's notion of Self aims to express and point to, is engineering this transition, and we find we are mediators of its actions. Our consciousness of it, our witnessing of its processes, makes it accessible to conversation, communication, contemplation. We disidentify with our subjective viewpoint at the same time it conveys what transcends us. Consciousness becomes an organ, like an eye or an ear, to perceive what supports, subverts, and transcends it.

Hope emerges. If our struggles contribute to the whole, this counteracts a despairing sense of helplessness. If our view of the whole is relativized, deconstructed, to make space for the emergent new, this counteracts our sense of randomness. If all the splitting makes space for what is making itself known, which we are to mediate and witness, this counteracts our sense of meaninglessness. We need very strong ego-legs to do this, but also flexible knees that will bow. We are at a time of "profoundly felt need for a spiritual authority transcending egohood. An authority of this kind is never the product of rational reflection or an invention of the moment . . . it springs from traditions whose roots go far deeper both historically and psychologically" (Jung 1955–56, par. 520).

Our individual experience is bound up with the meaning of the process as it applies to the collective psyche. The Self reaches toward us in these great upheavals of splitting. The identity of the whole, the *unio mystica* with the potential whole world, that we fantasize we knew in a *participation mystique*, before consciousness divided it up into subjects and objects, now asks us to recognize consciously its unitary being, its ground beneath and among and in the midst of all splitting. The new thing is that we see the whole and bring consciousness to the whole while our consciousness is one part of the whole. We are in the whole but not submerged entirely, as we are as infants at the beginning of life. Now we have an ego point of view that sees, beholds, reflects, attends, while knowing the ego is small, slight, easily knocked over. Yet it is a seeing eye that sees its own limited scope and its necessity.

A space in between opens. The edges that cut off connection create a space in between our faction and the opposing one, our country and the enemy, our religion and the ones we fear, our training group and its rival, our joyous planting in this life full of children, nature, animals, greenness, and the nothing of the vast beyond. We live in that space in between as we help create it. This is a different way of living from the embattled identification with our side of the splitting.

Projection changes. It is still a defense against the bad; we still struggle to withdraw our projections and assimilate them, but now we are grateful to our enemy for showing us the psychic object we deposited in them. The opposite side of our splitting shows each of us what shadow stuff is presenting itself to which we must succumb in part. We recognize the projections we must work to integrate. This is familiar.

More startling is the new idea that we must project onto the numinous, the Self, especially the good, in order to relate to it at all. In order to get ahold of the reality to which our sacred legends point, our projections about it make it visible so that our consciousness can then respond. We cannot take in the good if we do not help picture it, create it, make it graspable (Ulanov 1986b, 174–179; Ulanov 2001b, 104). In this way our consciousness functions as an organ of perception at the same time we disidentify from it.

Registering this paradox delivers us into a deeper one: Is this mysterious power to create reality that contains and confronts us located within us, outside us, or springing up in both locations simultaneously? The Self and the ego share the same mysterious substance, but are these psychic centers of the same core inhering in and bestowing from the center of reality?

An approach to the answer comes from Barry Ulanov:

> It is not our part in the looking process that matters at this point, but what is looked at. . . . really to see the world. . . . [A]s we come . . . to receive others and otherness with ease, we may begin to bring ourselves into the picture. . . . one who has earned the role of mediating consciousness. . . . [seeing] the intentional interpenetration of subjectivities, by the multiple mirroring of people, and places, and things exchanging images in open and oblique ways, including the animate and the inanimate. This is the way our looking will be rewarded. This is the way we will know that we really have looked and seen, for what we have seen will clearly reflect our seeing. (In Ulanov and Ulanov 1995, 178–179)

This essay was given as a plenary address at the Conference of North American Jungians, At the Edge between Hope and Despair: Confronting Cultural, Political, and Clinical Dilemmas through Analytical Psychology, Chicago, September 22, 2005. It was also presented at Jung on the Hudson, Rhinebeck, New York, July 2006. It was published in Quadrant, *vol. 37, no. 2 (Summer 2007) and is published here with permission.*

9

THE MANY IN THE ONE,
THE ONE IN THE MANY

R elation of the Many and the One is a knot tied throughout
the ages. Is it One, or is it Many? They are different and with
different consequences. Together they form a knot that stays
tied and reveals its nature as paradox, a both/and. They cannot and
must not be split from each other.

The age-old mystery of the Many in the One and the One in
the Many bursts into the twenty-first century with new vigor. In
what has been called the postreligious era, we see religion at the
heart of international and national conflict. Fundamentalistic
assertions of the one right way, whether in the true God or the true
politics, are felt by adherents to be the solution, not the problem.
Through such core beliefs, whether from the right or the left,
connection is secured to archetypal verities that the opposite position
seemingly shreds and scatters.

To separate spirituality and religion in order to erase the conflict
between them is an evasion, I believe. In the field of Jungian analysis,

where we recognize the psyche's spiritual dimension, we still fail to reach across the splits between our institutes, to transform our differences into vigorous, meaningful conversation that would deepen our perception of psychic reality. Here the Many split the One into opposing camps.

Relational psychoanalysts find fault in notions of the One—of a true self or a "mentalized, de-eroticized, masterful" self (Flax 1987, cited in Rivera 2002, 346). They favor instead a notion of self-states that link or dissociate, thus finding freedom in the self's multiplicity (Bromberg 1993, 396–397). Jung begins the Red Book, saying that he had attained all he wished for—riches, fame, marriage, wealth— we might say a full unit. Yet his soul went missing. Going in search of it took him down into multiple encounters with frightening figures, terrible insights, horrific acts. He discovered there was no one meaning, no one interpretation. Indeed, his soul disclosed chaos as the other half of the world that must be included (Jung 2009, 235): "Behind the ordinary the eternal abyss yawns" (ibid., 305). Jung swayed in response, and then, even worse, saw that the bottom swayed: "Life has no rules. That is its mystery" (ibid., 298–299).

Experience of a vital missing part turns up in our clinical sessions, too, where this lost sheep, isolated from the community of sheep, derails the whole personality. The unity cannot function without this missing part, any more than the one lost sheep can function without coming home to the others. Multiplicity—as unguessed assertions rearing up from our past or as spontaneously compelling primordial images—splits up our sense of being of one piece. Instead we feel like confetti, tossed into the air, a feeling triggered by losing our job or our retirement funds in the economic collapse and losing with them a vision of a future; a feeling triggered by the emotional desertion of a partner, the death of a child, loss of faith in life's good purpose, an illness of the body or of the mind, or worries about our earth, the air, the sea glutted with spilling oil.

Yet we know from our personal and professional experience that multiplicity and unity go together, alternate, create a dance between them, a rhythm of being and becoming, unless we get caught in their extremes. The Christian doctrine of the Trinity provides a fabulous picture of unity in diversity, distinctness in sharedness, which sets

Christianity apart from the other two great monotheisms while at the same time joining them as one of three. Jung writes, on the one hand, "the unconscious . . . unlike consciousness, shows only the barest traces of any definite contents, surprising the investigator at every turn with a confusing medley of relationships, parallels, contaminations, and identifications" (1954c, par. 440). As Origen said so long ago: "each of us is not one but . . . as many personalities as he has moods" (cited in Jung 1955–56, par. 6 n26). On the other hand, the "unconscious has [a] tendency to personify itself in a uniform way, just as if it possessed only one shape or one voice. . . . [and] conveys an experience of unity" (Jung 1954c, par. 440). In short, "the unconscious gives the impression of multiplicity and unity at once" (ibid.). Their conjunction is neither merger that absorbs all in oneness nor severance that dismembers their partnership into multiple factions.

The Many

Within us we encounter the Many in autonomous complexes that change our thought, behavior, and/or emotion when we come under their influence. In addition, "primordial images can rise up anywhere at anytime quite spontaneously, without the least evidence of any external tradition" (Jung 1955–56, par. 103). Outside ourselves, we find persons, objects, and events that present multiple perspectives, potencies, and problems. Clinicians recognize right from infancy the alternation of splitting and healing, integration and deintegration, and stages in multiplicity itself. The Many moves through different forms, so it is important to keep in mind the background of unity, of the One, in reviewing them. In mythic imagery, the oneness of *prima materia* seemingly contains the multiple, the various, all in one place so to speak. In the Genesis creation story, God gives up "primal unity of 'God alone in the world'" for the sake of manyness, of difference (Zornberg 1996, 5). Although that brings conflict and opposition, it also brings "proliferation of His image" and hence recognition of God's sovereignty (ibid.). The Tower of Babel story makes the same point: unity desires not sameness but complexity; the many recognize the One.

I have a clinical example of a middle-aged woman who found this mythic oneness in her parents' endorsement of one containing view that seemingly she never left, never moved out of; the analysis began with its breakdown. Her mythic background might be likened to a Sleeping Beauty who awoke not to the prince's kiss but to sobbing at what she had lost. As she put it, she did not know where to place herself in reality. We had to find the many—preferences, aims, satisfactions, objections, refusals—which she never before dared to allow to surface. Her nervous collapse necessitated this opening to multiplicity in the midst of an abiding connection, a oneness between us different from that which she had with her parents. She felt that our oneness encouraged her manyness. Though she was in her fifties, it was as if I were in the presence of a small girl whose undifferentiated life had broken open. She dreamed of being served dinner with her parents and the waiter bringing her a tiny child's spoon. She said she thought of herself as being five years old. She married a man also under the spell of primal parents, though his were negative, accusatory, and condemning. This couple woke up to the fact that they had practically no adult relationship and now faced multiple fallouts: his over money—is there enough energy here? Hers over sexuality—is there any eros between us? Over a period of months her weeping gradually ceased as she felt held in the ongoing unity of the work we were doing. Her uncontrollable tears were communications to be looked into, registered as feelings, thoughts.

The Many and Threat

Images central to the Many circle round its dynamics. At one extreme is the Many as myriad, portrayed in a patient's dream of seeking refuge in her bed only to find the mattress erupting into countless insects flying upward. How can we relate to such tiny bits of life? How impersonal and scary! Would the analysis be a net, or a simple beholding of what was? The Many as dust is similar in its boundless state and makes us think of famine-torn countries where dirt flies up the nose, into the eyes. Yet dirt holds a hint of unity in having come from the one earth and its need for healing wetness. Even myriad insects bespeak the sympathetic rather than of the cerebrospinal nervous system, conveying a psychic organizing along collective emotional lines, not individual and intellectual (Jung 1952b, par. 957; see also Ulanov 1994, 68). Unity lurks in the background, hinting of paths for the analysis to find.

The Many as myriad and dispersed conjures up the recent increase of autoimmune diseases that infiltrate the body, are hard to locate and diagnose, harder still to treat. Instead of the old model of getting rid of the invader, banning it from the whole self, treatment now means living with the intruders—allergies, blood diseases, skin attackers, fibromyalgia sabotage energy and muscle.

In the external world we see preoccupation with countries' borders—to lock out those stealing their way in or to open to the uninvited guest. Similarly, terrorism replaces the iron curtain, the stark division of us versus them, with manifold indefiniteness. Now it is perhaps our neighbor who parks the car loaded with explosives in Times Square or our fellow passenger on the plane whose clothes or shoes begin leaking smoke of an intended bomb. And from deep under the sea a gigantic explosion of the *Deepwater Horizon* in the Gulf of Mexico in April 2010—takes not only human life, but poisons with the spewing oil the one environment that holds all of us.

Dust and boundlessness stand in contrast to fragments as an image of the Many. Fragments are differentiated; they present themselves as shards resulting from the shattering of trauma. Our synthesis of self can be smashed into bits, splintered into fractions that seemingly can never be added up to a whole number again. Our body knowledge cuts loose from affect, mental confusion clouds our ability to perceive, torrents of energy let loose without channels for expression, boundaries blur between self and other, history is blotted out by forgetfulness. Here is Winnicott's notion of disintegration into smithereens, going out of existence for a second or two, a sure death while still alive. Yet such cracking up can reveal itself as a defense against the ruin of disillusion it imposes, so that we get stuck in distintegration to protect against the risky hope for unintegration which is unity at rest with multiplicity (Winnicott 1963, 58, 61). There we feel the One at ease with the Many. We can let all the pieces drift and dream apart and together in the hammock on a summer's afternoon or at a swimmer's relaxed pace through the water.

The Many as parts gather more coherence than fragments. Parts show the Many in distinct forms—the dissociated grudge, the undared hate, the evaded hope, the consent to passion and to one's necessary path. Gathering the parts is familiar to analytic treatment, to allow each one its distinctness, even its "god," its ruling archetypal image. We allow the complexes to speak, to show their root and trajectory. Jung believed in the wisdom of nature and in paying attention to it, not assuming our human order is best. He felt forced to recognize a different kind of science that included what he called magic and soul: "Magical understanding is what one calls noncomprehension. . . . We need magic to be able to receive or invoke the communication of the incomprehensible" (Jung 2009, 314). Here our personal path includes the impersonal project of the psyche itself, to move all parts of us around a center, excluding none.

The Many threatens us with ambiguity, loss of secure meaning, and loss of faith in one interpretation. We want one word to protect from the boundless. Jung writes in the Red Book, "You cry out for the word which has one meaning and no other, so that you escape boundless ambiguity . . . from countless possibilities of interpretation. The word is protective magic against 'the daimons of the unending,' which tear at your soul and want to scatter you to the winds" (2009, 270). Can we glimpse that in our splitting from other members of our group, from our human family, we all are defending against this threat of being scattered to the winds, of reverting to mere dust with no toehold on the enduring real?

The Many and Liberation

The Many brings liberation as well as threat. What presents as dust and fragments may also exchange with scintillae, sparks that illuminate points of beginning in the swamp of darkest dark (Jung 1954b, pars. 388, 392). Like a fish surfacing briefly, our eye sees in an instant from an opposite angle a possibility that bequeaths a sense of hope. I am thinking of clinical examples like addiction to marijuana, which, counter to an orderly schedule of behavior to cure it, may disclose an intent to lay back, to claim time for oneself, not to please others, not to bend one's being to accommodate standards outside oneself. Compulsion to pornography may hide a quality of desire that is missing from one's lovemaking with a longtime partner—an all-out yes to desire, a drive to climax that is not doubted or self-guessed.

Pornography may also show a masking of rage that needs to be faced instead of smuggled into what looks like eros but sabotages it instead. Shoplifting may recover a small child's right to have the world bend to her desires in illusion of creative unity.

The missing part may show where some essential bit of self is sheltered in repression, dissociation, bursting out periodically to assert its claim. At the very least, to see what the lost part conveys may induce in us a burst of laughter that comes from recognizing the proportion of things, that what we think is the right way is but one strand, not the whole. The absurdity of our position explodes into mirth. All these other strands weave a bigger world.

Our connection to the Many liberates us from being captive to the one right way of doing and being, captive to a punitive superego, a tyrannous ego ideal, captive to the harsh powerful trauma that befell us, captive to allegiance to the family myth, to the one theory of the psyche, to the nation's persona, to a God who encapsulates us in a cult. Perceiving Many as opposed to One, allows us to emerge from unconscious identification with the other, be it our complex, our mother, our political party, or our God, to live in spaces of manifold ways of being.

Connecting to the Many may bring redeeming power to us. Not only freed from these inner and outer compulsions, we connect with something wild and free beyond our ego constructions. We find permission and impetus to be, to grow, to improvise ways of thinking and acting that may seem a mere byway at first, but which create a path that is our own. Jung finds in the Red Book that "we create the meaning of events," that "the meaning of events comes from the possibility of life in this world that you create" (2009, 239). And this leads to a different seeing of God: "The meaning of events is the supreme meaning, that is not in events, and not in the soul, but is the God standing between events and the soul, the mediator of life, the way, the bridge and the going across" (ibid.).

The One

If redemption through the Many means space for choice, reverie, acts of imagination, the One promises wholeness, completeness, and calm through gathering the many into one (Jung 1950, par. 624).

These are positive images of sustained continuity and of belonging. In analysis the regularity of appointment time and space, built-up memory between analyst and analysand, created connections between each other as well as between past and present and, even more, present and future impart a sense of unity behind the apparent multiplicity. When the work goes well enough, both feel something growing, springing from a root that has taken root, unfolding a self that abides, growing its present and future. The woman who awoke from near fifty years of childlike sleep—despite children, job, and vocation as an artist—concentrated on her enlarging self now as her own, not parceled out to others under the rubric of making things pleasant for them and never consulting her wishes and thoughts. She found her growing self in the freedom to engage her own points of view. Here the image of the One was the past negative encapsulation of an inherited worldview from parents and then husband. When this overtook her, she fell into a profound sleep from which she could hardly awake, saying once, for example, "I slept my summer away."

Another analysand searched endlessly for the missing sense of self in past decisions always reviewed as possible mistakes: a different road should have been taken. And future time was running out; he was getting older. Will he have missed his whole life? Here the sense of having a unit self that was his precious own was fugitive at best, hiding in phobias and supposed missed opportunities, despite a thriving career and family. Anxiety obliterated his feeling of himself as One, which turned up in the transference as nonstop talking, "to keep you," he said, "from getting to anything important."

The One and Threat

Such negative images of the One include stasis: being stuck, stagnant, enmeshed, codependent, bound. Eruptions occur in the transference or countertransference to break up this captive being, to make a mess, to get parts to emerge and start growing. Necessary as that may be, it may feel to both like dismemberment and loss. As the Sleeping Beauty woman said, she did not know how to be anymore. I remember another case where I felt alarmed at the loss of my attitude of attentive warm interest in an analysand; I felt cold as a hard stone (Ulanov 2001c, 433).

What is amazing about a sense of having a unit self, the One coming into being, is the seeming silence of its arrival. Working in analysis on an analysand's traumatic wound releases the psyche's contraction around that injury both to defend against and to deal with its pain. The symptoms that manifest that contraction soften, even disappear. The patient's sense of an underlying trustworthy oneness increases. Another way we experience this growing unity of self is as release from binary thinking—where the solution is this or that, not both; where this is good and that is bad. Jung says in the Red Book, "you free yourself from all distinctions and thus are freed from the curse of knowledge of good and evil" (2009, 301).

Even massive collective traumas that wipe out not only our sense of self but any language or image in which to register the notion of self can, in certain remarkable humans, yield a sense of something that endures, something that can be found again. Such persons bequeath to the rest of us a glimpse of Oneness that must be seen, even when the artist himself is not sustained and succumbs to suicide. I think here of the painter Rothko, who insisted on asking, What do you see? He saw his reds as prevailing against the darks, and even saw in the late black Chapel paintings a coming forth of seeing and the seen (Rothko 2009, 93). I think also of the poet Paul Celan. Born in Romania, he grew up with the German language, which he lost as a victim of the Holocaust. Silence fell upon him to describe the extinction of parents, country, belonging, as well as the discourse to give voice to it. His poetry creates a new language to speak the unspeakable. When he won the Bremen Literature Prize twelve years before his death from walking into the sea, he said: "There remained in the midst of the losses this one thing: language. . . . But it had to . . . pass through the thousand darknesses of death bringing speech" (cited in Felstiner 1995, 114; see also Hamburger 1988, 18–24).

A process of ongoingness as the One replaces our dividing up everything into parts—us versus them, good versus evil, sane versus mad, inner versus outer. Dimly we discern a growing that enfolds all the parts "so that despite multifarious modes of manifestation, they are at bottom a unity" (Jung 1955–56, par. 660). Indeed, "Mephistopheles is the diabolical aspect of every psychic function that has broken loose from the hierarchy of total psyche and now enjoys independence and absolute power" (Jung 1944, par. 88).

Our Role in the One

The Devil refuses to belong to the whole whereas in the image-making language of the psyche we see the Many gathered into the one symbol. For example, Phanes, the child-god in the Red Book, displays many beautiful names for the ever replenishable One, of inexhaustible freshness and preconceptual beholding that this divine child symbolizes. His names include Shining One, Father of Eros, golden bird, resplendent day, immortal present, gushing waters (he is depicted in a painting; see Jung 2009, 113, 301, and n211).

This human capacity for symbol making—to make something of what is there and what is not there—gathers unconscious whiffs, currents, undifferentiated affects into specific images, thus clothing them with matter, the joy of incarnation. The value of particular personal existence comes to the fore. Even experiences of synchronicity, which momentarily disclose that we are somehow part of a greater whole, a surpassing Oneness, nonetheless require our personal, particular emotional response, our surprise of meaningfulness in the coinciding of noncausally related events, to be real. We are the Many for its Oneness. Without our wonder and impress of meaning, we would not register synchronistic experience or the Oneness of matter and psyche it implies.

We experience this symbol-making capacity and meaning-making response as being linked to something beyond our perception but nonetheless present and lasting. Jung says "the supreme meaning never dies, it turns into meaning and then into absurdity, and out of the fire and blood of their collision the supreme meaning rises up rejuvenated anew" (2009, 230). It feels like a larger purposiveness that we translate into our personal purposes and beliefs. We intuit a transpersonal center or presence as source. Jung makes clear that purpose is not the linear achievement of a goal, but circumambulating around the center, all points of entry looking to that point. Its Oneness compensates for the diversity of our many positions around it, all of which become relativized, no longer the only way or even the best way to view the heart of the matter. The helpful implication is that our unity, our ability to share in Oneness, does not depend on identical convictions, but rather on all of us looking to the same point of origin as the nucleus in our midst.

The center is empty, not in the sense of vacancy but in the sense of transcending our ability to grasp it in its entirety. Jung says it is "something unknowable which is endowed with the highest intensity. . . . This brings us directly to the frontier of transcendence, beyond which human statements can only be mythological" (in a letter dated June 13, 1955; Jung 1976, 258). In the Red Book he says, "the myth commences, the one that need only be lived . . . the one that sings itself" (2009, 328).

The remarkable thing is that we can have "conscious, reflective knowledge of these hidden processes," and it is in the imagery of the One that we attain to it (Jung 1954c, par. 447). For in the round dance that replaces the Last Supper in the apocryphal New Testament, Jung sees that those who remain at the edge of circling round the center and do not identify with it remain isolated (ibid., pars. 415–429). The relation of the One and the Many is pictured as "the single point in the centre and the series of points constituting its circumference. . . . to impress upon the mind the . . . relation of each point along the periphery to that centre" (ibid., pars. 418–419).

Jung sees this as an image of the Self "embracing the conscious and the unconscious"; the unconscious "has no assignable limits" and "continually creates . . . the unity of the many, the *one* man in all men" (ibid., par. 419). Three things happen: through identifying with this One at the center, we are anchored in transpsychic reality that recognizes our uniqueness because it "forms the basis for the archetype of the *anthropos*, the Son of Man, the *homo maximus*, the *vir unus*, purusha, etc." (ibid.). Finding Self is finding the heart of reality that transcends our psyche. The second thing that happens stems from recognizing that all of us have access to the center. Relating to it means feeling related to our neighbors through sharing "the all-embracing One . . . the one psychic substratum common to all" (ibid.). This One brings us as the Many into relation with itself and with itself in each other. The third thing that happens is seeing that this heart of reality beyond and within each of us needs us in order to come "into actuality through the concentration of the many upon the centre. . . . it is dependent on being perceived" (ibid., par. 427). The Many and the One mirror each other and come into existence together. In analysis, we know this when we find our own growth is spurred by our analysand's growth and vice versa and that together we sense that we participate in something that is showing itself.

The Many and the One

When we have the Many we also have the One. The One is not exhausted by its dispersal but shows its plenty in holding all its variousness in being. The Many does not disappear in this holding but appears within the One as hints, associations, on which we can elaborate. We amplify its fullness into differentiating parts. Their dance, their back-and-forth rhythm, their coming together and spanning outward into separate instances, displays the generosity of their complexity.

In analysis, for example, a patient's association sparks in the analyst the memory of a dream the patient had a year ago. Consciously the analyst could not have remembered that long-ago dream, but oneness undergirding the treatment links in this fragment of the Many. The result is intensification of connection between analysand and analyst and of the whole arc of their work. The myth of this particular analysis sings itself.

Mercurius is a good symbol of this paradox, displayed as the medium in which the conjunction of Many and One take place (Jung 1955–56, par. 658). As "mediator between body and spirit," "the sweet smell of the Holy Ghost," "the 'marriage-maker' between man and woman," he also is "that which is to be united" (ibid., par. 659). In short, "Mercurius is . . . the *unus mundus*" (ibid., par. 659). We experience this mercurial motif in analytic sessions when something happens to make the analysand feel held, not just to the main thread of the analysis but as if our work connects to something over our heads and beneath our feet, like the angels in *Hansel and Gretel* at the heads and feet of the sleeping children, a sheltering whole of earth and heaven.

In such moments we discover that we also make the *unus mundus* by becoming aware of how the upper and lower meet, interchange, separate, unite. Our symbol-making function creates unities that assemble multiplicities like a bridge spanning the personal to the beyond, as if we "submit to suprapersonal decrees of fate . . . serving a king" (ibid., par. 540). Our personal constructions incarnate the parts necessary to make up the whole. In the Red Book, Jung says that in the individuation process we differentiate the Pleroma and blind creative libido into experience of ourselves in the "eternal moment" in which being flows through us, and which needs "the devoted efforts of the conscious ego to come into actuality" (2009, 354 n123; see also Ulanov 2010, 11). With this foundation in the beyond, we feel grounded in our uniqueness and right to exist. This is the second creation of the world, the *unus mundus* (see Edinger 1985, 230).

This Oneness is different from the uroboric beginning because of our explorations, efforts, mistakes, and potencies. The new ingredient in the *unus mundus* is our consciousness of our selves and of the transcendent whole, made up of linking its many parts. We discover that the unconscious seems to take the same attitude and action toward us that we take toward it: "The Stone declares: Protect me and I will protect thee" (cited in Edinger 1985, 228). For example, the person addicted to marijuana who shuns it as contemptible can nonetheless be held fast, entrapped. When she takes an attitude of curiosity, to look into what and when and how marijuana beckons and to what it leads, she begins to feel a margin of freedom. The problem shifts to what lies behind the marijuana and to what it communicates.

Even more potent is the discovery that the conjunctions of One and Many into an enlivening dance is contagious. We sense the same activating motif in others and in groups. Our particular constructed forms for the all of oneness that hums with various differing parts displays the wholeness of the whole and our place in it, like a facet of the multifaceted diamond, as one patient said so long ago. We meet in our multiplicity in the One, in our belonging there together with others, and share similar tasks, similar exiles, but not identical ones. To do the work of analysis, analyst and analysand must become lovers of soul in each of us, the One in the Many.

Multiplication of the One in the Many

The Many in the One transmits knowledge. It shows itself. It multiplies itself. It creates itself in sparks which catch over there, borne on the wind above the trees, hidden along the ground, running under the leaves, swift like a bolt of lightning. A scintilla, an odd small gleam in an obscure dream mass, a bright spot of distant reverie draws near.

In dense text, turgid in its prose, blinks a tiny flash of illumination that calls up another text long forgotten; they link and in an inkling ignite, shimmering. In tense meetings crowded with conflicting opinions, a receptivity dimly glows across the room, hidden in another's comment; it shimmers, and an arc of connection leaps across the distance, a possibility of conversation blinks beneath the conflict, dispensing warmth to solve the impasse.

Each time we must nurture the spark, the gleam, the dim unconscious hint, and "the unconscious reacts by enforcing an attitude of devotion to life" (Jung 1957, par. 36). The One spontaneously incarnates in the Many, assuring us to trust it, to let it do the making whole. We do not have to do it all; it will do it. Our work is an essential part, not the whole, only a part. In the analytical session this brings comfort and release from conscientiousness that can slip into coercion. The analyst can trust the psyche in the analysand to communicate the distress that is being defended against, to bring in the lost sheep and repair the community of sheep. The analysand can trust the psyche working in the analyst not to get hung up on mistakes or to force interpretations. We can together depend on what we are creating between us, and what is creating us, like water finding its way through the thicket.

We witness this multiplication of the center that embraces the circumference in the manifold names for God: "the arcane substance has a 'thousand names,' but essentially it consists of the One and Only (i.e., God)" (Jung 1958a, par. 633; see also Hind 2004). In Islam we need the Many to find the particular name to connect with Allah today. We find such generative presence in stories of miracles. Only God creates out of nothing, the nothingness void; we create out of scraps. Elijah asks the poor widow for a bit of bread and water (1 Kings 17:11–16). She will give him her last scrap of meal and drop of oil, without knowing he is a holy man. But then her nearly empty cruse of oil and barrel of meal do not empty but replenish. The miracle of loaves and fishes displays that our meager scraps are more than enough, multiplying to feed five thousand with much left over, reminding us always to begin with what we have, not what we think we should have in order to begin (Matt. 14:17–21).

In each of these stories an easily overlooked beginning gives the key to the lavish outpouring. The holy one thanks God, the One over all, and then the bits magnify into plenty. In alchemy the tincture, the *lapis*, the *radix ipsius*, the first root from which everything grows, the *uroboros* that gives birth to all, this "everlasting food" is never exhausted but spreads to others (Jung 1946, pars. 526–527).

In analysis we experience this multiplication, this spontaneous renewal of the tincture, when we see that our humiliating problem links to a human problem and maybe even to what Jung calls God's problem. Connecting these multiple dots releases us into a flow of energy that we do not originate but channel into working on our problem, now without humiliation and isolation at being so caught. We feel we contribute something to the human family and even to God through our suffering and working on this problem. This buoys our efforts, sustains us, indeed, feeds us. Our path not only includes our problems; our problems show us the path, what we are here to work on for the good of the whole community and, dare we say, the cosmos.

If our personal plight links even to God, then our work expresses devotion. We not only consolidate, we serve. We feel our efforts lodge somewhere. The freedom of our limits gives way to recognition of interdependence; we belong to a larger whole. Finally, then, reaching "the eternal moment," we register the transpersonal psyche touching our personal problems and potencies, as something objective within our subjectivity. We are the Many of its Oneness. It is consolidating and manifesting the unity through all things. In linking multiple parts to a unified Oneness, and feeling Oneness ebb and flow into the diverse, we see we are one of the parts of this whole God in and through and among us. In that sense, we do not become whole, One or Many, but partake of its Oneness in our Many.

This essay was presented at the Seventeenth Congress of the International Association for Analytical Psychology, August 22–27, 2010, Montreal, Canada.

IV

PSYCHE, SPIRITUALITY, RELIGION

10

Is There a There There?
Or Is This the Wrong Question?

T he first question of this title is knotty indeed and is never completely untied, its strands once and for all laid out clearly. Gertrude Stein's criticism of Oakland, California, that "there is no there there" proves useful to us when changed into a question. All our discussions turn round this center of inquiry, whether we are seated in meditation, on our knees in prayer, in a clinical session seeking desperately for a felt sense of something holding us in being, or gathered together at some (safe?) distance from the necessity of asking, Is there a real spiritual object, a there that connects with us here, or not?

Here and There

Decades of clinical work with analysands who seek not just a solution to a specific problem but resolution about their connection to aliveness convince me that the hereness of daily life sustains itself only in a felt link to a thereness that is real. A middle-aged woman says she can't get herself into living touch with reality, with its center. Decades of teaching students preparing for ministries in the world, who anchor their spiritual formation in a keen sense of thereness of God, persuade me that such links to thereness do not happen without the hereness of psychic life in all of its vicissitudes. A life in touch with spirit thins out psychological defenses and digs up secrets of the heart, even the secrets of God (I Corinthians 2:10). Authentic spiritual practice does not remove us from the world but brings the world into us. As Ricoeur says, the sacred is the area of combat (1970, 531).

My departure point, then, grows from the space in between the here and the there, neither evading the question of whether there is a real spiritual object (indeed a subject) there whom I behold, contemplate, to whom I speak, cry, confide, nor excluding the radical change in subjective experience of spirit here, described as oceanic, bliss, mystical, mother-infant oneness, illusion. As Gadamer reminds us, any horizon we claim "includes everything that can be seen from a particular vantage point"; to lack a horizon is "not to see far enough and then to overvalue what is nearest to us" (Gadamer 1975, 269). To have a horizon "means not to be limited, but to be able to see beyond it" (ibid.). To have a point of departure includes the point as the image of primordial beginning, the origin where we come into being. Euclid started his geometry with the point as oneness, that which has no parts, indivisible, genesis (Edinger 1995, 57–58). The late artist Andrew Forge radically changed his painting from realistic forms to what he called daubs that were points of colors building up moving masses, the blues that Jung calls the flow of experience and Andrew calls *February* (Jung 1988, 1233; Forge 2007).

In Analysis

People seek analysis to gain access to aliveness in themselves, to find and strengthen that conversation going on all the time between the me to whom life happens and the I who makes something of it (see Borges 1957, 246–247, cited by Ogden 2001, 141–143; see also Ulanov 2001a, 139–158, for an example). We use word, image, sound, texture, and even taste to describe these interchanges between conscious and unconscious that help us find and create our own voice, our sense of our own self with which we converse with others. To find our original voice, the voice that goes on originating us, we know moments of just rightness, like a gong with full sonority that conveys presence of something more that cannot be captured in symbols. Such moments can only point toward what is there, outside our means of understanding. Some human voices are so unique that the voice is never lost, and we, hearing it, can always gain access to that moreness. Think of Mozart's aria "Dove sono i bei momenti," about lost love, or Duke Ellington's "Come Sunday," about lost life, or the joyous combustible body and spirit in his "Something Sexual."

But a person must be taken as a whole, not just one fragment, so the patient also brings to analysis all the protections against aliveness. Strategies to obfuscate, block, or bury psychic pain also figure in the conversation within the person and between us in an analytic session, evoking my own defenses and pain as well as associations that may show a way through them. I listen in on the conversation going on already in the analysand, and my own conversation within joins in the conversation between us. Spaces between us and within us multiply and symbols are constructed and found to embody what is being said and what is being omitted, all of which point to what is unspeakable yet present in these layers of discourse. A man feeling quite dead despite success at no longer drinking his way into oblivion says he lives in a grey space where nothing happens; he hasn't got the real goods, he cannot imagine a beginning and feels tied to the wheel of meaningless, though lucrative, work. I feel the drag of greyness down into wordless nullity, my mind also going blank, as if the two of us are falling into sleep and might dream a way to life.

An opposite example is a woman who, after months and months of working through trauma, dreams her living room enlarged "into a bigger square, more space, in radiant light, vibrant, arresting, and pleasing. It glows," she says, and I am struck that this is not a special space segregated by its sacredness, but her actual living room, now made bigger, suggesting a here-and-now expansion into fuller self. She called it "the Spacious Square."

In contrast to symbols that make a bridge to the there that cannot be captured here is the religious sacrament which is the experience of the there here, not the memory of it, nor the description of it, nor knowledge about it. It itself is experienced, created now, of presence bestowing itself, not to be understood but to be received (Ulanov and Ulanov 1975, chap. 6). We know precious instances in our lives where the primordial presents itself and we are present to it, where all falls into place, even evil, where entire reality feels contained in this one whole moment, our own whole experience. The person following a spiritual path is one who gathers these moments, like musical notes on a staff, into the sustained awareness of what that there is that infuses the here and now and makes it sing.

Spiritual practice builds up muscles so that we can withstand moments of joy, as well of those of dread and annihilating anxiety. How to bear the full register of beauty, of truth? Would our backs break? Our ears burst? One way is described in Ezekiel: the "bright presence of the God of Israel makes entry," and Ezekiel falls "face to the earth" (43:1b). "The Lord's presence [is] a sight that brought me to my knees, face to the earth" (44:4c, Knox translation). Then follow long descriptions of exact measurements for temple building and specifics for altar sacrifices. That seemingly obsessive laying out of procedures bears the weight of making real in the here and now the moment of the All facing Ezekiel.

Spirituality and Religion

It is important, I suggest, to note the distinction between spirituality and religion. The former is in fashion, the latter not, when religion is perceived as coercive rules and regulations that focus on the cage while the tiger jumps out. Worse still, religion comes with a bad name borne from acts of terror as devotion to one's God. Yet religion is center stage in world politics, carrying the heft of embodied experience that can make spirituality seem airy in comparison.

But spirituality offers ample freedom to find and create our path, to see and not ignore the gap between the symbol and the reality symbolized, a gap that can transform into a space for conversation. We glimpse then that the conversation going on in each of us between conscious and unconscious and between us, now doubling those registers, is multiplied again. Our conversations between self and other, both personally and transculturally, mirror the back-and-forth between all human symbols and the ineffable divine. The divine mirrors us, and we may discover that our job here on earth is to mirror it. Multiple conversations thrumming forth and back gather all of us as parts into a whole that makes up reality.

One important way religion and spirituality have been contrasted began with Kierkegaard. For him religiousness A circles round *our experience* of God, which might be best compared with what Jung calls the symbolic life, where we see through symbols to the reality to which they point; we live *sub specie aeternitatis* where layers of meaning intersect (Kierkegaard 1941, 493–498, 507–508, 516; see also Jung 1939c, pars. 625–631). Religiousness B looks to our experience of *God*. It is this One, this Thou, this Holy Other on whom we dwell. How we experience the divine Subject, what functions that experience effects in our lives, what benefits it accrues, are all secondary, tertiary, of less importance. Rizzuto sums it up: "Religion is God-centered. Spirituality is subject and experience centered" (2007, 42).

A contemporary version of this contrast is, paradoxically, taken from Freud, who discards the spiritual object as projection of wishes for consolation and judgment onto a heavenly father to avoid our facing the harshness of reality and the insistence of the unconscious, for which we have the ability to respond, to take responsibility. Freud seeks truth, not our experience of truth (Blass 2006, 23–24). He finds the spiritual object does not exist independently in its own objective right and proffers instead what Oskar Pfister calls an illusion of a future in psychoanalysis. Nonetheless, for Freud it is the objective real God that matters, not just our experience of God as self-expression. A believer's spiritual quest for the "true God from the true God" (from the Nicene Creed, *Book of Common Prayer* 1944, 326) seeks the objective God also and sees that whatever human language we use, it never can describe the God who breaks all our categories and discourse.

Subsequent analysts shift away from truth of a there there to emphasize instead our spiritual experience of a there, even raiding religious vocabulary while denying its referent. They explore spaces in which an individual feels brought into aliveness, feeling real, and glad to be so. The mystics believe that the inspiriting aliveness at the center of us that makes us feel authentic is the same as the center of reality, what Teresa of Ávila calls His Majesty, and what John of Ruysbroeck says sends forth the Sparkling Stone.

We could argue that the transcendent there had gotten too far away to be felt alive here. The swing of analysts back to self-experience, for example, in Winnicott's transitional space of illusion where we meet and mix internal and external, subjective and objective, provides a compensatory balance (Winnicott 1971a, chaps. 1 and 4). Such a reinvigoration of spirituality can be fruitfully explored by examining the space in between our God-images and the God they represent (Ulanov 2001b, chaps. 1 and 7). Loewald, though objecting to Winnicott's subjective-object zone for the infant who has not yet developed any sense of subject or object, explores religious experience as the instantaneous congress of primary and secondary mental processes that yields, for example, a moment of *nunc stans* when all that is, is now. Eternity is not endless moments of time, as conceived by secondary conscious mentation, nor is it outside of time, as pictured in primary unconscious mentation. It is everything now (Loewald 1978, 62–69). The here swells to the promise of abundant life, of the cup running over. Kakar respects the wonder of mystical life and treats it as part of our humanity (1991, ix). Bion's O comes closest to joining clinical and spiritual experience, but he disowns the religious implication (Grotstein 2007, 137). There is a there there, O, which we become but do not know. Living it here is in the flesh, incarnated, which we often thwart for fear of psychic pain that must be borne, all the losses mourned, all the absences faced into before they can be filled up with living presence. In Christian terms, this is like the piercing by the sword foretold by Simeon on seeing the Christ child, who reaches through the individual to the whole community and even the cosmos.

Each of us has our O or transitional symbol or eternal moment through which to navigate the connecting point between the All and the Vast and the small personal here-and-now life we lead. For Ogden, I suggest it is language, the marvel of words, found especially in poems. Borrowing from Wallace Stevens the words "the nothing that is," Ogden says it "is everything we have not concocted with our words and imaginations" (2001, 71). We give up our inventions, even those that bridge the here to the there and let it be "an experience that asks not to be figured out, not to be reduced, not to be understood" (ibid.). Jung talks about the devil of understanding that grasps at mystery and denudes its symbol so that we lose our spiritual muscles, no longer taking strength from spiritual paradox (1939c, par. 665).

But not to get caught in the gods of religions as too far away from the here-and-now lives of persons and societies can expose analysts who revivify spiritual experience in psychic flesh to an unintended reductionism. The there now falls back to mean mother-infant oneness, to early object-relational patterns repeated as adults, to transitional space, to self-experience, to archetypal depths of the psyche, to the enlivening power of illusion. The there becomes the unconscious, or some version of coming to terms with it. The dominating emphasis falls on representation, that is, language (Kristeva, Ogden), mathematical function (Bion), life theme (intersubjectivists), relational pattern (relationalists). The there turns out to be really on the human side of here, at best unconscious and in that sense transcending ego limits, but not securing a foothold beyond the psyche.

I do not think this will do. One does not pray to oneself, even if that self locates in the distant past or the unconscious. In clinical terms the question is, What is the mutative agent that yields psychic blockage to transformation, that liberates us from our captivity to complexes, addictions, depressions? This is not an abstract matter but involves life and death, at least psychically, and often bleeds over into communities. Mental suffering erupts into Columbine and Virginia Tech massacres, to setting bombs in political meetings, to bringing down planes full of passengers over innocent countries.

Healing

In my clinical experience the healing agent is not interpretation, nor even the bond of loving that can grow between analysand and analyst but through those linkings to something more that moves and involves both participants in enlivening process. It is that link to something more, a there there, that does the trick (Ulanov 2007b, chap. 7; see also 2007a, 591, 601–603). How that connection is described or shows itself varies from person to person. I would go so far as to say that the specific complex a person suffers is one of the means through which the saving link forges itself. The unconscious itself proves a medium through which the there reaches us, and in that sense psychoanalysis adds another line of hermeneutic to spirituality. One does not just get over what one man called his perversions, for example, but finds the meaning of them for him hiding within them (Ulanov 1993b; see also Ulanov 1996b, chap. 3).

I agree with Antonino Ferro that the number of derivatives of O are infinite; I find helpful his amusing cooking imagery (2008; see also Ferro 2005, 1–2). The beta elements, the raw sensate stuff of existence, are like the tomatoes, and the kitchen instrument that he calls a *passopomodoro*, and I call "the thing that mashes apples into applesauce," is like our mental alpha function, which squeezes the juice from the tomatoes, transforms them into edible substances for sauces, drinks, and seasonings, analogous to pictograms that we then connect into narratives that create the stories of our lives. Yet this engaging picture of psychic and spiritual transformation still leaves us with the question, Who authors the alpha function? Who is the big container that contains all our alpha functions that work the health, richness, protein to feed us with the infinite derivatives, or should I say the derivatives of the infinite?

A note on method comes in here. I follow where the aliveness is most evident. So if a patient asks, What does this dream mean? I often respond, Where does it touch you? We circle round it in a process of association, drawing bits and pieces of affect, memory, thought, or word picture that come to mind consciously. We also follow what spontaneously derives from unconscious experience and might, for example, manifest as a symptom of falling asleep right in the session, or a burst of anger so great the person strides around the office, or an image impressing the person so deeply it is as if what Jung calls archetypal resonance emerges in an immediate sense of being at a crossroads, fording the river. In this method of associative circling (circumambulation), we are not uncovering a preexistent content or meaning, but participating in the creation of something coming alive. Such a process throws ties between the unbearable and the bearable, the unspeakable and the spoken, between heartbreaking sorrow and the seriously funny, transforming the gap between those opposites into spaces of conversation.

Alert to what is there and not there, two vectors emerge. One, regressive, reduces to instinct, object relations, or archetypal dominant, calling into the present past hurts, energies, conflicts, ancestors, and images. The other vector, progressive, ushers in future unfoldings by present nudges that shift attention to a color that now clothes the threatening abyss with a furze of faintest greenness or to a passion to embrace an abandoned part of oneself over the humiliation felt by its forlorn weakness.

This sort of associative method by analogy always leaves space to say this is like that and does not revert to the symbolic equation of this is that. But at some moment, the analytic pair come to the point of knowing no more, even knowing nothing about what this means, and then they throw the conflict, the image, the symptom, the dream, the impasse back into the bath, to use one of Jung's alchemical terms. We throw the conscious thing back into the unconscious which is like a river of being. There it finds its own life, and in Jung's method, the self-regulating nature of the psyche rescues the struggling ego by setting it within a larger whole, as if, so to speak, in conversation with the self. Consciousness is both "absolutely indispensable . . . because it is the organ of awareness of the self. . . . [and] is a smaller circle contained in a bigger one" (Jung 1988, 408, 417). We are waiting on what alchemy calls the arcane substance (the mutative agent) to do its work, which can only happen in conjunction with our utmost effort.

The Weight of Hate

Spirituality and psychology often merge in practice until up against the weight of hate. Then we must find what we believe in, that for which we are willing to sacrifice. Under hate I lump all the pain that makes us foreclose the space between us here and the source there, whether we find it through our psyche or ancient traditions. Spirituality will not hold up if it cannot survive an emergency trip to the hospital. Psychological work will not last if it does not yield a sustained conversation with what we recognize as the origin point.

Hate includes the violence done to another (whether by ourselves or to ourselves), treating that self as if of no account and to whom no accounting is owed, and then denying one has done such. Robbing the other of agency, rendering the other invisible and inaudible despite total liberties taken with their body and soul, infects the self with rage and destructiveness borne of the perpetrator's own denied captivity to power or to the fear underlying grandiosity. Hate includes the violent horror at death and loss of all kinds and our panic that we will be lost in mourning rather than come through to mourning our loss. Unable to bear the hole in our ground made by loss, we cover it up with steely vows, manic activity, or procedures of self-holding that both rescue and entrap us. Hate issues from turning away from accepting the strain that loving puts on the other person, that they may refuse a chance at fullest life. Hate that springs from such pain can break the thread of connection with our own experience so that we evacuate it, projectively identify it into others and into whole groups, pervert it into distracting behaviors, numb it with substances and attitudes of denial, thereby killing a part of our own aliveness.

Hate stems from being overwhelmed in the face of so much suffering in the world, so much worse than our own that we grow ashamed of our pain in comparison. Then we seek to be in charge of destructiveness, losing the thread to external reality by trying to account for too much, recalling Winnicott's remark that the other side of identifying with a global village is annihilation. We may, mistakenly, try to inhibit our instinctual responses, believing it is our destructiveness that makes the other fail to respond, instead of seeing that the root of absence lies in the other or in interfering circumstance. We live then with the volume permanently turned down.

Hate that covers suffering may sever ties with external reality so that fantasy reigns unchecked and then demands for itself severe restraints from the world, like a totalitarian government that dictates every move and thought to control the threat of unbridled fantasy. Even creativity can overrun personal life, gobbling all the time and energy, if used to escape suffering. One may produce fine paintings or books but not live from a sense of self.

One of the most dangerous results of suffering expressed in hate is the foreclosing of the gap between symbol and reality symbolized. Terrorism gives the most frightening example, simply because of its scope, but the same foreclosure occurs in mental illness. In New York City, for example, a man came to demand his money back from his therapist because he felt no better and to threaten the therapist if refused. But finding the therapist busy with a patient, he went to the adjoining office and stabbed to death the therapist there, who was taking a bit of time to herself. The abstract reigns; the personal is lost. Any object will do to vent rage. The symbol, here of helper, is equated with this generic other called therapist. One will do as well as another.

Similarly, in religious terms, feeling entitled by that foreshortening certainty that knows the truth means there is no point talking. It is not as if you are the enemy; you are, therefore you are to be killed. My deep hurt at not having something vital to my well-being recognized, my emptiness, my political need, my god, impel me to act. There is no space, no procrastinating function of thought, no analogous as if. What then to do? We should study those in refugee camps who do not become terrorists, where deprivation and suffering do not issue in hateful actions.

Spiritual and religious traditions offer us help of great insight. In Judaism, when Moses asks at Sinai, "Who should I say sent me?" the answer comes, "I am who is; I am who is with you." This is not a name to latch onto, not a dormant content now revealed, not a thing to be possessed, but a presence in relationship. In Christianity, Jesus says repeatedly, Do not call me good, but him who sent me, thus refusing to be reified, made graspable. In this way Christ brings the end of all religions, evidenced in the New Testament Book of Revelations where there is no temple; the Holy is present throughout the city. The resurrected Jesus tells Magdalene, Don't cling to me [that is, do not fall into identification with me as God] as I have not yet gone to my father who is my God and your God (John 20:16). He goes back to the source; he does not identify with the source, but directs her to the source.

When we succumb, for all kinds of poignant reasons, to our hate, we fall into identification with the there that is there, and close the space of conversation with it in the here. The psychological becomes the political. Clinging to the source, identifying the source with our version of it, we insist others identify with our version too. We forget the subtle genius of Marguerite Porete, a thirteenth-century mystic who calls the center of reality Source without Source (Babinsky 1993, 46–47).

The remedy is sketched, I think with great humor, in the book of Daniel (Daniel 2; see also Jung 1935, pars. 245–247). Nebuchadnezzar has a scary dream and commands his wise men first to tell him the interpretation and only then will he say the dream. That is all of us when we fall into identification with our theories, our traditions. We know and can declare what it means before we hear what it is. This is psychoanalytic sadism and theological bullying, both a kind of terrorism to the soul. This is symbolic equation, appropriate at a stage of early development, but lethal if persisted in. No gap exists that could become a space of converse where we could say this is like that or as if that. Instead it is that, this equals that, thus excluding others' views and the space between the symbol and what is symbolized, otherness itself.

Daniel meets Nebuchadnezzar's test. He does not go directly to the dream problem but goes, as if around it, to the author of all dreams and interpretations, to the mystery underlying the fact that we dream and that dreams bring meaning. Like Krishna's counsel in the *Bhavagad Gita*, Daniel does not cling to the fruit of his actions but goes to the source of ability to act. He prays to his God for guidance and deliverance; from that vantage point he then speaks to the dream and its interpretation.

Similarly with our hate, we cannot seek its cure directly because it will fix us to the spot, ever inflamed, ever turned to stone. We need to see through association and analogy, as did Perseus looking not directly at Medusa with her snaky locks but at her image in the shield given by Athena. Through the image he could cut the hating head at its root. Murakami tells the story of a woman who was taken by her driver (not unlike Krishna the charioteer for Arjuna) to hear the solemn truth that she carried a stone of hate in her heart (2002, 85). An analysand associated to this story to describe her own (stone of) hatred. When we recognized the voice of her hate, a sense of her agency created movement in her self-judgment and self-defeat and led to a surprising clarity. Her hatred formed the principal life-giving tie to a mother who hated her. Feelings of sorrow and mourning for what she and her mother missed together washed over the stone again and again, shrinking its size to tiny pebble.

This patient's experience gives a clue to understand the exalted counsel of Krishna to Arjuna that helps all of us find a place for destructiveness and thus aids us from being crushed by the overwhelming suffering in the world (an overwhelming that issues in hate and blame and in enforcing our schemes of justice which in turn wreak more injustice). Arjuna does not want to fight; the horrors of war bring only suffering. But, Krishna says, that is not ours to decide, for both sides will be destroyed anyway in time, by time, by me. Krishna counsels that our job is quite different and shows the place of the human-centered approach in the nonhuman-centered whole. Our job is to see our task here and do it with discipline and devotion and without attachment to the fruits of our action. That is how we serve the there here. In the words of T. S. Eliot, this is "the expanding of love beyond desire" (1943, 36). Neither withdrawing into renounced action nor insisting on our version of result of action, we devote our energy to the specific task in the here and now and thus contribute to the order of the whole. We leave the results of our action up to the there there, beyond our control. With our best discipline, and with all of our heart, soul, mind, and strength to the there, to Krishna in this story, we unite our action with cosmic purpose (Miller 1986, 36, 38, 40, 44, 47–48, 53–54, 60–61).

Each religious tradition offers its own response to the place of destructiveness. Each psychoanalytic theory offers its view on how to deal with destructiveness. Which tradition we live out of and which theory we commit to in our work turns around which there we believe is there and how it makes itself known here.

Is This the Wrong Question?

Is is there a there there the wrong question? Yes. But it delivers us to the right space where all our conversations here intersect with what is there. Hate gives a clue to how it happens that our question is wrong and right, not so much answered as that we grow beyond it. Hate, as awful as it is to endure in its exhausting ravages, also begins asserting: I do too count; I am; I am still, despite your denials, or my own; I do matter and must be recognized. At first all we see is the self in protest, insisting on its life and value. We are led to see, however, the pivotal impact of recognition from which all communication flows. Our self needs recognition, not ownership, in order to be. That holds as well, I believe, for the there we seek. Otherwise, as Ricoeur says, we reify the subject of religion into an object and that is dead-making, a possession to be fought over (1970, 5).

Can we let the space exist between ourselves and the ineffable? We try to name it in gesture, word, or image, in ritual that stutters toward, stops in silence before, gathers up the sequential history of the there with its simultaneous presence, so that the container contains and bursts, the tiger and the cage escape any net we create. Imaginative efforts to address the there in the here bring it and us into being at the same time they are defeated. The here makes possible the there and yet without a there, no here exists.

A clinical example comes from the woman fighting for months against the long-term effects of trauma. Two dreams in succession she feels give her a foothold, a new beginning space. In the first, she is at a conference and sees a beautiful blond woman desperately trying to find her husband. Distressed for his well-being, she asks six men to help her find him. The dreamer says she is watching this as if it is a film and says out loud, "Oh God! They are going to rape her!" She then goes on: "Then it is as if I am she, and it is I they will rape. I stand and face these men. I say, 'Kill me if you must, but I am not going to let you rape me. You are not going to rape me.'"

Many strands of the dream suggest themselves, but what struck the dreamer forcefully was her potent resolve to stand against this violence. She recognizes her own feminine self and will not tolerate being treated as if not here, not mattering. She stands for her life, even if it costs death. This new response recognizes as it undoes the trauma of years ago.

In the second dream a woman says to her that she can speak up and, if she needs to, she can go from her terrace all the way down and around through the Strait of Magellan. She remembers from school that Ferdinand Magellan led the first expedition to circumnavigate the globe, proving that the earth is round, not flat, and revealing the Americas as an entirely new world. Through these associations and analogies, she opens to a wholeness that defies her flatlined suffering as if it would kill her. The dream woman recognizes the dreamer's capacity to break through to a revolutionary new perspective: through her navigation of personal trauma she enters the surround of the whole world. She penetrates through her suffering, like a passageway to an entire change of orientation. She sees the world is round, a roundness of the whole, that comes around to the beginning again but opens to something so different that it is like the discovery of new continents. And she can get there from here on her own terrace. Her personal human location here meets the nonhuman-centered whole which means not only the large human community but also its placement in the larger whole of reality.

Recognition is the key—of the self here, a there there—and to get it means seeing what is left unrecognized, denied. Recognition that underlies communication that springs from it comprises the nexus point of conversation of self to self, self with others, all of us with the world that transcends us, and our world set within the cosmos.

The need for recognition applies to everyone and to society. Wendy Doninger looks to places the repressed abides in society through the novels of late nineteenth-century fiction. For Conan Doyle, "it was shipped to the colonies"; for Robert Louis Stevenson, "it was masked in psychoactive drugs"; for Oscar Wilde, "it is captured in a portrait"; for Bram Stoker, "it falls into the deep sleep of the undead" (Doninger 2007, 252). But we cannot know all of ourselves, as individual or society, and thus bear the return of what was banished unless, as Jung says, citing the alchemist Dorn, through meditation one knows "*what* rather than *who* he is, on whom he depends, and whose he is, and to what end he was made and created, and by whom and through whom" (Jung 1955–56, par. 884). Then we can recognize all we are, share the weight of it.

So I press the question, Does a there really exist that knows about the here that we each and together are? The question yields no certain answer. It seems too silly, literal, childish. It appears to be too narrow, too explicit, stuck on the goal we define, blind to everything left out. Yet in spiritual and psychological practice, we act as if in relation to a being, power, meaning, reality that is real and there. In our moments of blinding joy or deliverance from death, we want to find whom to thank; in our moments of re-collecting the full arc of our lives, we want to see we were where we belonged and to whom we go on belonging. Yet the question is never really answered once and for all. In reaching the end of an analysis, for example, if the conversation persists—the conversation which the person started in our work with their self, with others, and in response to what to them bespeaks the point of it all, the divine, the unoriginated, the there—then I know the work succeeds in ending.

We grow beyond the question, Is there a there there? It is the wrong question but delivers us to the right meeting: to moments we are known and know we are known and know that something essential is being created right now in alive experience. Yet our conversation with the there here and the here in relation to the there is not filled up with knowledge nor uncovering something now revealed. It creates space for the new to come in, for our fresh perceiving, imagining, arriving at insights we did not invent; synchronistic meanings usher us to dwell conscious of the whole (see Ulanov and Ulanov 1982, 104, 107–108, 115–116).

This wrong question functions like Jacob's ladder, which comes to an end in his beholding the Lord God (Genesis 28:12–13); it leads to an end of itself in beholding what we perceive as the source. Pressing this question is a tiny version of Job pressing his question about the justice of the Lord breaking the Law He established, until it was answered, finally, not with an explanation but with disclosing the whole that encompasses and transcends the Law. Job's theophany transforms his suffering into his intercession for his friends and for us who, like his friends, dare not persist in our wrong questions. The real there needs embodiment here, to be experienced as real; we need a here for a there to be there.

The here is us, full of our peculiar problems, cultural locations, spiritual practices, psychological complexes. Our problems do not vanish, any more than Jesus resurrected appears in a different body from the wounded one at his death. It was precisely through the wounds that he could be recognized as beyond them. Similarly, our wounds may become points of access to the there. I think of the traumatized woman, so typical of trauma victims in her radical vulnerability and creeping self-doubt about what really happened to her. When able to recognize herself and move into spaces of conversation where she feels recognized and validated by another, her extreme vulnerability does not fell her but appears as radical openness, strength to see what is and not. Her confused self-doubting does not vanish but appears as the ability to tolerate ambiguity, to see what is there and not there from several perspectives at once, thus demonstrating capacity for empathy and otherness.

Analysts who go toward the spiritual describe the change effected in our consciousness. Freud talks of perceiving the id beyond the ego, Winnicott of the mystic communicating only with his subjective objects, Loewald of a consciousness that unites our verbal and protoverbal secondary and primary process thinking, Bion of our becoming O, Ogden of a qualitatively new experience expressed through metaphor, Kakar of "unknowable ground of creative experiencing" (Freud 1923, 300; Winnicott 1963, 185–186; Loewald 1978, 73–74; Bion 1970, 70; Ogden 2001, 41; Kakar 1991, 28). Yet all step back from recognizing as real the spiritual object (Subject) that evokes our spiritual response.

I agree our consciousness changes in response to spiritual experience. I would describe it as reaching again that childlike (not childish) consciousness, the second naïveté Ricoeur enjoins, echoing the New Testament injunction to become again like little children if we would see God (1970, 543; see also Ulanov 2007b, 20–24, 238–242). This consciousness is childlike in being without prior assumptions, daring an openness without resistance and with a trust that we will not be destroyed by blasts of reality (Jung 1923, par. 442). We renounce our preformed, prefabricated protections and take what is offered, and even sometimes steal it or wrestle for it, persisting in our desire. This return to childlike open response where we gaze upon what is induces play, spontaneity, and original response. It also requires sacrifice, even what Jung calls symbolic death, and Marion Milner describes through the imagery of the crucifixion (Jung 1956–57, par. 1661; Milner 1937, 139, also cited in Parsons 2006, 129). We renounce knowing, prejudgments that reify into prejudices, all that we assemble into pictures of the ultimate from choosing the know-it-all tree of good and evil. We accept not knowing, while we go on building new pictures, new theories of the ultimate, devoting to them the utmost concern while we also know they are not the ultimate.

This childlike consciousness is not a return to childhood but borne of the consciousness of the adult, one capable of that space of conversation, capable of reflection, constructing, imagining, and making analogies about the nature of reality. What is different about this consciousness is its childlike openness to reality without prior assumptions joining our adult consciousness of thought borne of experience. We have spiritual muscles to withstand the paradox of immediate, direct vitality of experience, inexpressible in its realness, and simultaneously to create representations and constructions in time and space that express this primary realness. We know that the other, even what we find as there to us here, is at once both our hallucination and a separate reality external to ourselves. We accept our dependence on the whole yet also carry our depending and exchange it with others we are lucky enough to have love us and with cultural creations that hold all of us, such as paintings, music, political visions of justice, institutions we honor, particular landscapes that convey our place of belonging.

A middle-aged woman said she thought of herself as five years old and dreamed of herself dining out with her parents and the waiter bringing her a tiny child's spoon to use (see p. 148). The image regressively made available a means to feed this small child aspect of her grown-up personality. Yet also, through that very part of her now dreaming into consciousness, the tiny girl suggests a progressive symbol of a new self coming into being for her to take care of and nurture, in contrast to her being the child. This tiny new consciousness, symbolized by the child she was and is coming to be, both regressive and progressive, bespeaks great funds of energy for life to unfold into the future even though she is an adult woman. This child symbol conveys a capacity to see life freshly, without prejudices built up over fifty years, and yet joined to reflection on what unfolds as a woman with fifty years of experience. A child consciousness sees with an openhearted immediacy without all the arguments about the fittingness of mediating terms, practices, or representations. The thereness of reality is accessible, and one is vulnerable to its presence. She dreams she is asleep and wakes up in the dream; she wakes up to this new possibility coming into consciousness that had not been there before. The childlike open consciousness can be a place least expected from which redeeming appears. With energy for life as an ever-creative base from which new development is born, a child symbolizes playful, eager vitality held within the whole of family, culture, historical era, even the cosmos. The child is full of life, not in control but in relationships that bring the whole into being, making a personal link to what transcends us.

Yet, we go further. The advance of the spiritual into visibility brings not just a change of consciousness. It brings a there into view. In order for our conversations with it to intensify, we must risk describing it and its relation to us, the there we find addressing us here. Jung stands out as daring to undertake this task; and he has been dismissed as a mystic, sidelined as major source of psychoanalytical wisdom. The there that is there is an experience of something found, or of a presence that finds us, inexpressible in our terms of here. Yet the privilege of finiteness requires making our experience of transcendence into forms we apprehend. To perceive, we must apperceive. To speak to ourselves and each other about what is there, we must make something of it, as we know it is making something of us.

To ask, Is there a there there? is to press right up to the edge only to discover this is the wrong question, but responded to by a mutual beholding. Our conversations with self and other and the whole—what Ernst Cassirer calls building up symbolic forms that make up the spiritual organs of our universe of meaning—intersect with the there speaking through dream, theory, mathematics, painting, or the science of the brain (Cassirer 1946, 7–11). Such intersection conveys a presence to which a click in us says, yes, here is aliveness, here is real, here is it, here is God. This is like those moments in yoga of weightless balance when standing on our head. All falls into place, even though our usual perspective is turned upside down.

Then we know our conversations partake of an ongoing, universal, common one. We know the good belongs to no one, lives as presence not possession. The there becomes humanized in our experiencing. Living it here, the here expands beyond the human to the whole round world. We inhabit the spaces made by our multiple conversations, of mirroring the there and it mirroring us. Rilke speaks of the radical significance of this mutual beholding:

> Catch only what you've thrown yourself, all is
> Mere skill and little gain;
> But when you're suddenly the catcher of a ball
> thrown by an external partner
> with accurate and measured swing
> towards you, to your centre, in an arch
> from the great bridgebuilding of God:
> why catching then becomes power—
> not yours, a world's.
> (cited in Gadamer 1975, vi)

This essay was originally presented to nine speakers speaking just to each other in the Symposium on Spirituality and Depth Psychology, August 4–8, 2008, Wasan Island, Canada.

11

What Do We Do If We Cannot Forgive? If Forgiveness Does Not Happen?

This is one of the most difficult knots to untie. It causes us great strain. This title introduces us into a terrible field where great suffering occurs. Forgiveness involves an offense, an offender, and a victim. And, we hope, we believe, a grace may also happen that, like the merciful dew falling from heaven, dissolves the urge to revenge and the bitterness that accompanies it. But does it? Sometimes, maybe even often, no. Forgiveness does not happen, or we do not want to do it, or we want to and cannot. This inability or refusal or insistence on some other way persists despite religions urging us to forgive for the good of our souls and psychological and spiritual leaders insisting we forgive for the good of our health and our shared existence together. I want to look into this absence of forthcoming forgiveness (or is it a presence of something else?), despite the strain this exploration puts on all of us. For such a subject calls up old wounds that still can bleed openly many years later.

A Subject of Strain

Why then take up this subject? Because it is part of the task of all psychologies and spiritualities of the depths to contribute to the growing of our emotional and psychic capacities. The great technological advances of the twentieth century and the beginning of the twenty-first far outstrip advances in our relations to each other and to all parts of ourselves. We need to catch up, for the sake of our literal survival, for the sake of our children who need to find workable alternatives to shooting down those who called them the scum of the school, as happened at Columbine; for the sake of workers and college students who feel so discounted and humiliated they shoot their employers or professors; for the sake of whole groups of people who feel so oppressed by their rulers that when they get the upper hand they massacre those who used to massacre them. Caught as individuals or societies in uncontainable, repetitive excesses of vengeance, we destroy peace and its possibility of thriving together in simple happiness of being.

We need to look into this hurt we inflict on self and other and the rage it evokes. Those of us working in spiritual and psychological disciplines need to bring to public and political awareness the fact of psychic reality and its emotional impact on our feeling alive, real. For it is from that experience that we recognize each other as persons who have the same kind of mental life, whose creative core is worth protecting and promoting. From such recognition grow our sustained efforts to foster the rights of everyone.

All religions urge forgiveness when offense injures and even kills (Briggs 2008). Christianity addresses forgiveness with particular verve, stressing that we must love our enemies (Matt. 6:12), forgive them seventy times seven (Matt. 18:21–22), look to our own sin before we feel entitled to throw stones at the woman caught in adultery (John 8:3–10), forgive others as God has forgiven us, as Jesus prays from the cross to forgive those who kill him for they know not what they do (Luke 23:34). The Amish stress even further that we must forgive if we hope to be forgiven by God, and they lived up to their belief in their astounding response of forgiveness of the man who held their schoolgirls hostage and killed ten of them at Nickel Mines, Pennsylvania, in October 2006 (Kraybill, Nolt, and Weaver-Zercher 2007, 15, 46, 48–49).

Mental-health experts also exhort us to forgive, demonstrating the benefits for blood pressure, stress reduction, and release of toxic emotions from the body. Who among us would deny themselves such benefits? Although it does strike me that forgiveness here is more psychic hygiene than its own surprising marvel. Everyone tells us to forgive wrongs done to us. Let go; do not keep that toxic anger in you. Align with eternal energy; do not get stuck behind the rock in your path. Reconcile for the sake of the world as well as peace within yourself. Do not be snagged by the small grudge, nor hoisted by big injury, feet dangling, ungrounded, flailing, flapping in the wind. Get over it. Move on. Life is too short. Don't poison yourself with fantasies of vengeance.

But what if we cannot? Are we to add shame and scolding to the original injury, pathologizing ourselves or the other who does not forgive? To say let it go or to impute stiff-necked refusal only humiliates those of us who are not doing what they desire to do but find themselves unable to do.

Social Location

Forgiveness lands us smack in the middle of our social world with others, and even in a larger field of interconnectedness of all being and nonbeing. It is an intersubjective phenomenon. For example, some discussions about the possibility of forgiveness turn on the condition that the offender feel and show remorse, that we cannot fix the rope bridge between us if it has been hacked off from the other side. Forgiveness makes us feel helpless and dependent on the other to come forward with apology, repentance. But others insist that forgiveness is unconditional. We are not to be controlled by the offender's behavior but must reassert our subjective agency in our freedom to forgive the trespass against us, regardless of what the other does or does not do. Forgiveness wells up from the depths of our own subjectivity, which links us with a transcendent source beyond us.

Forgiving or not forgiving finds its deeper social location recognized by psychoanalysis and, in different terms, by spirituality. These disciplines recognize the fact of the unconscious and the fact of spiritual reality in which we all live and thus increase our personal and interpersonal capacities and skills. What each of us does both reflects and changes the whole of us all together, either through unconscious communication or through seeing or blocking the spirit in which we dwell. For example, when forgiveness works, it offers, as Hannah Arendt says, "possible redemption from the predicament of irreversibility" (1958, 237), interrupting the chain-reaction of injury answered by retaliation. What is unfolding when we forgive that dispels vengeful repetitions? What is the new constellation in the emotional field we inhabit that attracts a different energy into incarnation?

I think of Paul Kagame in Rwanda instituting a form of South Africa's Truth and Justice Commission. In Rwanda these public meetings are called Gacaca; there the perpetrators confess their deeds, and the surviving victims and their families grant or withhold forgiveness. Kagame legislates the political requirement of these meetings and also that perpetrator and victim are to live side by side, forsaking retributive justice and breaking the chain reaction of murder that controlled Tutsis and Hutus alike. One of the murderers says of President Kagame: "But the Rwanda of today, I don't know if it is a miracle or what—but there is a man. A single man . . . without Kagame the genocide would come back. . . . There's a man. Just one. There aren't two. . . . For the first time in fifteen years there is near universal agreement that there is possibility of peace" (Gourevitch 2009, 49; see also Digeser 2001). But the underside is that Kagame stands accused of exporting the violence to the Democratic Republic of the Congo where atrocities have multiplied, including the horrors of drafting children to fight and the grisly mutilations of women in rape.

Individual Location

My approach focuses on the individual person and on connecting to the social, the archetypal, the universal through the particular. Further, I want to focus on the person who has been injured by another and cannot forgive, to look into what is going on here. Is the absence of the forgiving act actually the presence of something that must be noticed, brought into conscious awareness and discussion? For my cultural location is the psychoanalytic, where we get at what is happening unconsciously in the face of deep hurts and of the rage they inspire.

Hurting that needs forgiving calls up wounds that we fear damage us forever. They cast us into a no-man's land, without compass, at a boundary behind which lurks struggle, failure, irretrievable loss, and death (Ricoeur 2004, 460). These wounds inflict mind-numbing trauma such that we can hardly remember what we long to forget. Such trauma isolates us, makes us ashamed before the excess of our suffering, unable to move on. Psychodynamically something has us in its grip and it is too painful to think about or to work on consciously (Ogden 2009, 48, 92–93). In this field we are held fast but also abysmally confused, as if a psychotic part of us cancels our capacity to think and feel our way through what we are enduring (Bion 1993, 43). Advice to "move on" condemns us to feeling crazy.

These wounds are intensely personal yet they take us to the edge of what is human, to the realm of the monstrous (Kearney 2003, 3). The injured one, in the rage engendered by the other's act to erase him, can identify with the terrorist who flies a plane into an office building filled with civilians. This fantasy is appalling. To discover the monster of destructiveness within oneself terrifies. A chasm opens; the floor of the psyche gives way to boundless depths where conventional borders between good and evil, human and inhuman, disappear. Where are we then? We are face to face with the urgency of drive, instinct. We must behold it, not sentimentalize it. One woman dreamed: "I said to a young woman, do not play ball with the bear. It is the bear's ball." The dream statement counters a cozy human feeling about fuzzy bears, teddy bears, playthings, gentle games with a ball rolled back and forth, to make the younger dreaming part of her face the idea that this is a wild animal, instinct bound, not within the human field, that can suddenly attack and maul, even kill.

The dream confronts us with questions: What are we to do with savage bear energy? What connection does it have to our spiritual universe, to the joy of living? What link does monstrous energy forge with our highest symbols of meaning? The wholeness of the whole includes this link.

Such a perception inquires into the relation of spirituality and psychic reality. Although I have some criticisms of the currently widespread repudiation of religion in favor of spirituality, often stimulated by bad religion that impinges on and hectors our experience of psychic reality, nonetheless here I draw a distinction between the two (see p. 166). Religious traditions can be understood as embodied spirituality, that is, they recognize our finitude in their achievement of definite forms of ritual, doctrine, texts, and history of practices of worship, meditation, mindfulness, and prayer. All these form one pole. The utter freedom of spirit that blows where it will and comes from we know not where (John 3:8) forms the opposite pole. In crises of injuries that need the healing of forgiveness, we land somewhere between the two poles. Floundering there, unable to forgive, we enter a kind of spirituality found in psychoanalytic culture, which is to face into the unknown, to risk encounter with it (Stein 2002, 13).

Here we meet the unconscious, not the valuable constructed spaces of traditions and practices of religion, but the "unknown as it immediately affects us" (Jung 1958b, 67). Here we make our way bit by bit, responding to body nudges, intuitive hints, following what happens, trying to discern any guidance from dreams, risking a different kind of consciousness and danger. Jung writes, "the ego is brought face to face with an unknown superior power which is likely to cut the ground from under its feet and blow consciousness to bits" (from a letter dated June 13, 1955; Jung 1976, 260). Like explorers, the analytical couple—and the inward couple of our ego encountering an unconscious figure—proceed supported only by trust that the core mysteries of aliveness seek us as much as we seek them.

The topic of forgiveness makes this exploration deadly serious. The kinds of laceration that require forgiveness take us through layer upon layer of harm we do to one another and straight into the vacuum of evil. To examine and not impose where spirit blows, surprises, upends, is to discover ourselves pulled beyond accustomed ego shores. Like navigators looking for the passage to India only to discover unimagined new continents later named the Americas, we too do not know where we will land or what we will lose in the trying. We travel beyond accustomed ways of doing things, of understanding them; we exceed our God-images and our concepts of how the mind functions. Bion describes it as proceeding in darkness by way of darkness to arrive at darkness, thus recalling those mystics who arrived at blackness, not light, as the apex of meeting the Holy or those Buddhists who arrived at great silence, the sounding silence of the non-ego.

Suffering: What Is Hurt

What then is the hurt that requires forgiveness as its panacea? This kind of hurt penetrates the privacy barrier rendering us helpless to shelter our self; it steals into a necessary sanctuary of integrity that protects our sense of being a subject who is an agent in our own life. This kind of hurt wounds our connection to ourselves as a person in our own right, disordering what Winnicott calls our going on being, disrupting what Jung calls our subjective relation to the objectivity of the psyche living in us. Our particular means of being alive in and by our self is invaded and disturbed; we feel we are without resources and have no rest anywhere. Whatever the incidents that dealt the blows, erasure of our reality has resulted. The other has behaved toward us as if we are of no account, so no accounting is necessary. Not just our value, our mattering, but our very facticity has been obliterated, wiped off the map, and the weight of such a wiping out is denied as being of no importance or even as not having happened. The other's behavior toward us has blanked us, vacated the space we used to inhabit. Nothing is there now, not even no one.

Such hurt is described in psychoanalytic literature as trauma, and indeed it is, with all its debilitating effects. Can we survive this? is the urgent question, and we do not know the answer. For not only has the hurt happened, but it has been denied that it happened. Whether we speak of rape or holocaust, massacre or abandoning intimate relationship as if it had never been, justifying wiping out the other takes center stage. The one injured loses his or her life or the life lived in intimate relation. But worse, the injured loses his or her self; the lost good object is the self as valid, resilient, able to see what is and is not and to make something of the experience. Instead, we are shut down, unable to experience our own aliveness. We cease to do the psychological work, both conscious and unconscious, in our dreaming and thinking, that would find and create the meaning of what happened to us and to our world. We are invalid, hollow, wasted, fruitless, cast into futile vacant silence. If we have the nerve to protest, we are challenged as to why we are making a mountain out of a molehill, why we can't let go and move on. Silenced by nonrecognition that any hurt happened or that it counted for anything, we are left for dead or buried alive.

The burial affects our society, our shared existence with others. Our particular voice is subtracted from the whole chorus. Further, the human capacity to symbolize even the worst events and the hope for finding meaning in them that redeems the suffering inflicted falls into a wasteland. Accumulated trauma brings down a culture. Each grain of sand mounts up until there is a camel under the rug. Groups split apart, warring against each other, no one meeting the deranged camel, only riding it to attack the other and otherness itself.

The social trauma amounts to the symbolic level being almost wiped out (Kristeva 1989, 223). Suffering falls mute, a dumb affliction like the pathos of the hurt animal. The animal part of us splits away from the spiritual, the monstrous energy from its transformation into symbol. We cannot find ways to represent in word, image, attitude, or ritual the buried alive hurt that has become unspeakable, even unnamable. Instead of absence instigating expression, or at least catharsis, it remains blanked, at best inchoate, but erupts periodically in compulsive behavior. Like all trauma that reaches to precincts of evil, it becomes a "traumatic impossible memory. . . . that petrifies remembrance" (Kearney 2003, 142).

For the injured person the trauma buried alive in the unconscious goes on nonetheless; the reality of the offense eclipses the reality of the present and strips us of our ability to think and dream about it, that is, to work on what happened (Symington 2001, 107; Ogden 2009, 32). We suffer the disturbance unconsciously, and it interferes with our capacity to do anything with it. We live on the borders of communication, voiceless. In analysis, a person may just stare blankly, or weep uncontrollably, or fall into barren silence. Socially we lose converse with the horror that befell our culture, be it the racial or sexual divide in America, the anti-Semitism in Europe, or the terrorism in the Middle East or Africa; the examples proliferate and can reduce us to hopelessness.

How Does the Hurt Show?

What is buried alive in the individual's unconscious and in the collective unconscious in our culture may not be known, but it can be shown. It shows itself. Repressed contents are not dead but dynamic, exhibiting a process of energy going to the object and changing us as subject. The injury inflicted speaks through the body, through behavior, through acting out. Our bodies, like beasts of burden, must carry the heft of our erasure, making us wake up in the early dark hours of the morning, the wolf hour that savages us with a feeling of being devoured by anxieties, made less, diminished, in a sleepless vacuity. Or, during the day while functioning in our jobs, obsessive thoughts may push us around and around as if in a washing machine without bringing any lightening of the load, no whitening of the stain of annihilation. In such states, we do not feel erased; we do not have an experience of nothingness. That hiatus of observation and voicing of distress has collapsed. We are erased; we are nothing; we are eradicated. The only sign of life is the obsessive around and around process working autonomously in us, unceasing, making rest impossible.

In such states we feel caught in a vortex of energy beyond our control. Seized, the injury reiterates itself in frantic emotions and obsessive thoughts of how to get free, how to keep sane, how to hold onto one's self which seems increasingly vitiated by mounting stress. This vortex isolates us from those around us, or they, sensing our distress, counsel us to let this go, move on from this suffering that only makes us feel more trapped. We would let go, but it is not us holding on; a greater power grips us, shakes us like a rag in the wind, hits us like a ping-pong ball from one extreme to the other. We have become an object in the world, objectified, an item, no longer a subject. We have lost the good object of our own subjectivity; and we have lost all others as subjects, for they live outside the ring of our obsessive enactments.

We resort to tactics or solutions that worked for past troubles only to find them useless now. We turn to long-standing beliefs that have secured the ground under our feet over the years, only to find the bottom has dropped away; there is no ground. We feel crazed, deeply frightened; we fear for our survival and do not know how to help ourselves. All this may land us in the analyst's office. But we may fear the analyst will not understand the gravity of our spiritual as well as psychological condition and seek to fit us to a theory or a medication program, not hearing the voice we cannot find.

The social version is no better. What to do with this unconscious energy pushing around within and between us, like gas leaking that could ignite into conflagration any moment. What we cannot contain, what we cannot recognize and hold, will be projected out of us onto an other, onto a group of others, onto Otherness itself. We ring all the changes from branding our enemy, to labeling a whole different group as the source of the enemy, to attacking the spiritual fact of otherness symbolized by God. There is no God, or God is so distant we know God only in exile.

Bypassing words and symbolic representations, our story tells itself by repetition—reenacting in action what words cannot describe (Miller 1981, chap. 3). On an individual level we reiterate hurt done to us by hurting those we love, even our children, making them feel obliterated from our attention and concern, as if they too do not matter. We fall into the gap between what we would believe and belief that exceeds reach. Our perpetual air of suffering and complaint drives people from us, and we feel further removed from human congress. A colleague criticized his sister for still going on about her divorce ten years before, time itself having been destroyed by her stuckness in the hurt of that rupture. A colleague who quit her job, blaming the company for bad treatment, which was true, went off on holiday as if dealing intellectually with the rupture would be sufficient. She was thrown off her horse and confined to physical therapy in order to learn to walk again without pain. Quitting her job looked like a free act, but the accident revealed the other side, of being thrown, hurt, and disabled by rejection. The hurt is an alive thing and must be dealt with in an alive way. Repression just leads to action against others and ourselves.

On a social level we may repeat in action toward others the affliction they dealt us. A cycle of retaliation and revenge begins and appears irreversible, stretching over decades, even centuries. Prejudice, discrimination, persecution, and genocide become possibilities, taking shape in the histories of communities and nations. Eventually only payback matters, for we are all now no-thing, no-where, of no account.

We can make no sense of this non-sense wherein mutually we conspire in our destruction, first me to you, then you to me, then me to you, and on and on. Catharsis of rageful pain only inflames, causes more pain that must be let loose on the other and even on the fabric of being itself, declaring nihilism the ultimate in truth and value.

The Danger of Forgiving

Danger looms all around. The hurts that require forgiveness deepen toward the abyss of evil itself where we are mired in offenses we can neither punish nor forgive, acts and withholding of acts that destroy bonds of connection, and even of lamentation (see Arendt 1958, 241). I think of the silent women marching in Argentina with pictures and signs of the Disappeared, those loved ones removed from this earth without a trace, vanished from sight and sound. This intensity of destructiveness goes on forever, seemingly demolishing time and space. How could we forgive such massive robbery, such irretrievable loss passing into oblivion and denial?

Forgiving can risk hopping over the hurt inflicted which transmogrifies into affliction's daily assault on the soul. We paper over rotting holes in the walls of our being, both individually and collectively. The weight of hate (see p. 171) in response to such violation must be reckoned with: What to do with it? How to carry it? How to gain release from it? Forgiveness is costly, not a cheap grace that Bonhoeffer so long ago warned us against. The hurt can break your back, throw you off your horse, obsess your mind, steal your sleep, reduce food to medicine necessary to survival. It costs time, energy, devoted attention, and money for analysis and for methods of peacemaking to tend to the rot introduced into our psyche and soul. The hate testifies that something grave has happened.

In order to survive we build up those self-states uninfected by the hurt and dissociate the traumatized self-state. We can use a false forgiveness to wall off the traumatized state (Bromberg 2006, 200). If we hop over the hate that marks something terrible that happened, we treat the part of ourselves to which it happened as the Disappeared, a part that vanishes from view and cannot be found. To use the stronger parts of our self radically to dissociate this hurt part only breeds what Grand calls a "malignant dissociative contagion to evil's reproduction"

(2000, 156). Evil appears and disappears, committed and denied, ravaging self and others and treated then as if nothing is happening, so it can go on happening, appearing and disappearing. The fact that mortgage brokers succumbed to monstrous greed, selling contracts they knew would bankrupt borrowers and cost them their homes, was passed off in the economic collapse as "everyone was doing it." The whistleblowers got fired or transferred to other sectors of the business. Genocide explodes into palpable horror and is denied as the mass graves are eradicated. Incest victims are presented in light of day with the perpetrator endorsed as a normal relative, the reality of his role as a perpetrator obliterated (ibid., 14–17). Like a spreading infection, evil contaminates in exact obverse to the multiplier of livingness symbolized in the *lapis* stone of the alchemists or in the host that embodies the connection between Christ and the Source he incarnates. The depravities of evil are disavowed as not really real or disowned as not really ours but let loose abroad, uncontained to occur all over again.

The person who cannot forgive or for whom forgiveness does not happen, weighed down by hate of what was done to them, witnesses to what is truly, really happening. Even wanting to forgive and trying the prescribed steps in forgiving, the fury bursts out of them to announce the fact of injury—what happened and what consequences it wrought (Worthington 2003). Such rage makes the Disappeared appear again, no longer vanished as though they had never been, no longer diverted into the false intrapsychic path that Laing named "mystification" (Laing 1967, chap. 3). The victim is told that she made it up, or just imagined it, or is not remembering accurately, that it didn't really happen that way or it was just her upset, full of her projections, not what occurred (ibid.). But the rage says no. Hate engages what was done, and memory recovers history.

The weight of hate levies its price. It can take us down to the precincts of evil. We can feel our self as victim becoming the perpetrator, to do to the perpetrator what the perpetrator inflicted on us. The boundary separating the two dissolves in reactive fury, reversing who was the terrorist and who was the innocent civilian office worker in the building as the plane flew into it. The victim full of rage is inflamed with fantasies of retaliation against the one who stole their soul, or struck blows to their existence, or rubbed them out as a valid existing person. The horrors of destructiveness now flow through us to compound the destructiveness we suffered. We feel deep shock that we can identify with a terrorist or fantasize annihilating the offender who made us feel we were nothing. We now become the one we repudiate, but with a different motive— not only to retaliate but to penetrate their denial, to wake them up to their horrible action, to acknowledge the injury they inflicted. Our hate aims to make them conscious.

The injunction to forgive, ingrained in the culture, as with the Amish, or ordered by the government, as in Rwanda, puts the brakes on this psychological dissolution of boundaries between good and evil, keeping one safely on the side of forgiving. The extraordinary actions of the Amish forgiving the murderer of their children grows from a culture that from birth locates its citizens as creatures of God who will forgive us if we forgive those who hurt us. The aftermath of forgiving this murderer shows in the parents' struggles to secure forgiveness (Kraybill, Nolt, and Weaver-Zercher 2007, 135). For the non-Amish who do not know this ingraining of a cultural container imbued with the necessity to forgive in order to receive God's forgiveness, the weight of hate busts the container we would have but lack. For me, in a psychoanalytic and spiritual culture that includes the unconscious, it is a different matter. We must look into the hate and see what its weight presses us toward, including its dangers.

The Danger of Not Forgiving

The danger of not forgiving looms in our being caught in masochistic collapse or sadistic explosions of rage at others. Trapped in a reactive position, we feel controlled by the offender rendering us valueless; we can fall dumb, become, in Kristeva's words, abject, a no-thing, a nothingness, so that even language gives up and we cannot represent what is happening to us (see Kearney 2003, 91). Our inner conversation is nulled. We fade away into meaninglessness. Psychologically, we describe this state as being locked into a complex where we suffer a deficiency of consciousness, of freedom, of neighborly support. We struggle against the shock, even incredulity, that someone could invalidate us and refuse knowledge of it. We struggle against this evil; we suffer its wounding, we undergo it, and we can go under.

The rage we feel in response both promises release and threatens to lock us into new imprisonment. Caught in vengeful emotions, toxic hate shoots like electric volts under the skin, radiating out from us so that people become wary of when our next eruption will be set off, and we become afraid of when our next scheme of revenge might capture our fantasy. People do mad things to the lover who hurt them—putting salt in the gas tank of their lover's car, or worse, attacking them physically, maiming them, or spying on them. People hurt by a colleague defeat their colleague's promotion, scotch their important interview, or spread malicious gossip. On a social level, we create laws that restrict and segregate, customs that diminish others, strategies that humiliate, and conspiracies that kill. The danger of not forgiving is to be locked into passive reacting, giving the offender power to define us as discardable. We do not connect to the astounding freedom not just to repudiate the theft of our soul, but to revision our self as an active agent, a subject linked to unexpected, unpredictable resources of aliveness.

If forgiveness happens, the victim is released from being in the past and released into choices about the future (Arendt 1958, 241). Uncoerced by exhortations to forgive, forgiveness sometimes bestows itself as a grace, falling like the merciful dew from heaven, surprising us. For what we need when imprisoned by trauma is not forgiveness but liberation. When caught in addictive cycles of hurt and vengeance, we need not forgiveness but to be set free, unshackled. We do not forget the injury, but it does not determine us. We are subjects to whom something pivotal has occurred. We carry the hurt in us but are not awash in its turbulent currents. We do not condone what happened but mourn it.

As active subjects we find again our inner conversation. All the parts of us assemble and speak to one another, and hence we can converse with others, no longer locked out of human congress. We dream again when asleep and imagine again when awake, and though our reverie may conjure horrific images of suffering, we awake refreshed, feeling good. For the trauma is now in us. If we can dream it, we can work with it consciously and accept the night dream's unconscious work with it. We have the trauma; it no longer has us. The danger of not forgiving threatens endless obliteration of this active subjectivity.

The weight of hate plays a crucial role. The hate testifies to what happened and does not allow the hurt or the self to whom it happened to disappear. Our hate refuses the offender's definition of our self as not worth communicating with, mere refuse to be disposed of. Hate is the first sign of re-seeing, re-specting our self as an agent with subjectivity, free to find and create in aliveness who and what we may be. Thus our hate stands with our soul threatened by the other's theft. Hate voices protest and active efforts to speak to the other to make them see what they have done, even if they knew not what they did. Our hate thus carries a gift for the offender; it seeks to penetrate the other's denials, to awaken the other from his or her own captivity to disavowal. Wrapped in the hate hides the gift of admission: to acknowledge their behavior and denial of it to themselves, to the ones wronged, and to be thus admitted again to human family.

The weight of hate—if we consciously can bear its pressure to retaliate in tension with our desire for liberation from the captivity of trauma—supplies the energy to do this work of recovery of self and other. Hate signals the arrival of a new attractor in a field of repetition that shifts the archetypal patterns to new trajectories (Conforti 2007). What is recovered is the lost good object of the self as active subject, no longer a discountable, discarded item. What is recovered is also the object as a subject, not just as perpetrator.

Winnicott writes of objective hate that separates the action from the person doing it (1947, 199). Ricoeur writes of fault participating in nonbeing, of loss of our wholeness (Ricoeur 2004, 459, 463). To engage the hurt that was done contains its dissemination, encloses its harm into a locus differentiated from the subject who now sees it and from the doer who does it. Hate gives the energy to do this, indeed riles us continually until we articulate in communicable terms to our self and to others the offense to which our hate testifies. This representation releases the victim from the transgressor and reestablishes the victim with the power to name.

We recover the lost wholeness of ourselves as a subject, not the original innocent goodness our self knew before this suffering, but the self who had innocence in us and now has suffering in us. We are no longer lost in the suffering; we contain it even as it still has power to hurt us. This renewed contact with the self we were is the subject to whom we show compassion, mercy, even forgiveness for all the suffering endured. We come home to our self and welcome the self who comes home. In some remarkable instances, forgiveness wipes away all the suffering as tears from our eyes.

The weight of hate presses on the object too, recalling the perpetrator to the status of subject who can relate to herself or himself and even, maybe, to others (Gobodo-Madikizela 2003). Accusation makes a boundary around the evil behavior, makes it relatable, introduces a space between the act and the doer of the act, a space into which the perpetrator might enter to engage the act he did (see Grand 2000, 153, 154, 158). Inner conversation might be rescued from mind-numbing denial. A differentiation is introduced between the perpetrator as subject who, in recovering ability to name his act, sees himself as a whole subject separate from the perpetrating part of him that he must mourn. That part does not vanish but now resides in him, to be carried by him, engaged by him, no longer compulsively driving him to hurt others, even if unconsciously. The danger of not forgiving misses this chance to realign with the person we were, now changed by suffering, but not lost to it.

Two Kinds of Witnessing

Some proponents of forgiveness assert that the offender must show sincere remorse and repentance before forgiveness can be granted. That was a premise of the Truth and Justice Commission in South Africa and is carried into the Gacaca of Rwanda, for example. The offense must be stated in all its gruesome detail and consequences and witnessed by its effects on speaker and hearers alike as a bad act, even an evil act, even though not (usually) intended as such. The act may be described as following orders with dire penalty if refused or as collateral damage, or the doer may claim to have been controlled by an imperative complex or acting unconsciously, that he did not know he was doing that and still cannot believe it. The perpetrator's confession and contrition help the victim be able to forgive and may stimulate the perpetrator to move from being entrapped to possibilities of self-renewal. A new beginning, not based on spite, rage, or vengeance but on mutual sorrow, though fragile, may be reached. Both are liberated from a prison of payback, an emancipation that may engender faith that out of the Gilead of "ghastly awfulness," of the "hopeless case," comes the beginning of balm (Tutu 1999, 269). Proponents of this view argue that forgiving, to be real, must be intersubjective, a back and forth between persons, not the horrible monologue of encapsulated suffering.

Others assert forgiving must be unconditional, regardless of the offender. It is "without exception and without restriction" (Derrida cited in Ricoeur 2004, 468, 478; see also Oliver 2004, 183–184). This way the giving obligates no debt to be paid in return and testifies to the marvel of forgiveness, its impossibility, and yet here it is, surpassing reason and expectation. Forgiveness opens a future no longer determined by the past.

My sense is that forgiveness, always miraculous in its advent, can work either way, with perpetrator confessing remorseful apology or without such, the forgiveness leaping forth supported by its own nature. Not something we achieve but a gift given to us just as much as a gift we give along to the offender. But I do think witnessing is prerequisite and of two kinds.

The first comes from a different arrangement of intersubjectivity than that depending on the perpetrator confessing regret. Trauma does isolate; trauma generates, if we can stand it, hate that introduces testimony to what is disavowed. To withstand the force of hateful emotions and not succumb to their toxicity, I believe we each need a witness to hear us. We need a witness to our witnessing in order for our hate to testify to the offense denied and to transform into energy needed to become immune to the other's offense defining us. This is personal and intersubjective. The witness sees the whole person we are, not defined by the offense done to us. This allows us to recognize and reinstall our subjectivity—and in some cases, though not all, to see the subject of the offender behind his offense.

This witness to our witnessing is one who can listen and hear us. This can be the analyst; it can be a religious figure alive in person or alive in symbol, the God to whom we pray. It may be a poet, a singer, a composer, or a nameless nobody, a neighbor in suffering. But it must be a someone, palpable, nearby, there for the long haul, who witnesses to our witnessing to the offense that cries out for forgiveness that we do not give. We depend on a witness to the hate with all its weight, with all its energy that enables us to drag into consciousness the mute suffering we cannot digest or overcome. We need an other standing behind us, endorsing our standing for our self, not abdicating our self to the perpetrator's treatment of us as discardable. Hate says, "No. I stand here; I am a self, a subject, not determined by your behavior."

That hate heard by another allows us to transmute it into firmness, for example, in drawing a line against the other repeatedly acting out against our self so that we lose our capacity to think, to respond genuinely, but instead become entrained in the other's violence, whether in the analytical relationship, the parent-child relationship, or an intimate connection of any kind. The other witnessing to our hate's witness to what happened helps us uncover the energy that hides in our hate and use it in a positive form instead of just gnashing our teeth or thrashing about repeatedly in distress. We cannot witness to our self by ourselves. We need an other to back up our backbone, as we differentiate hate from the energy expended to deny denial, to repudiate annihilation, to reconnect with our pretraumatized self. Our hate transforms into strength to discern and be done with repetitious reenactments.

But just here we embark on the second kind of witnessing, also intersubjective but different. The first intersubjectivity renews the bond of person to person, so precious it can only be named as love. In the second form of witnessing, we witness to and feel ourselves witnessed by a collective, objective dimension. The psyche confronts us in the magnitude of our distress like an objective other, amplifying our distress to an archetypal level, so we feel not just the present hurt, but earlier trauma. We are ripped open, as if the bottom has dropped out from under us, not just wounded but sensing we can lose our mind, not just angry at the other's behavior toward us but aroused to monstrous hatred whose energy exceeds our standards of good and evil, right and wrong. On the personal level our hate stands up for the subjectivity of our self. On the archetypal level we, the subject, gaze upon the object of the psyche's own projects and energies arranged in patterns that exceed our constructed symbols.

In this second kind of witnessing we see the objective world of psyche through the particular subjectivity of our self. Not the subjective through the objective, but the objective through the subjective. That is the culture and spirituality of psychoanalysis. In religion, the frame is known and given in doctrine or ritual. For example, forgiveness is to be found within the frame of the Trinity in Christianity (Jones 1995). The spirituality in psychoanalytic culture does not have a certain frame but looks into the unknown by giving devoted attention to experiences of our subjectivity.

A dream illustrates these two kinds of witnessing: the dreamer sees that her mother, who is driving the car, is unconscious and that her sister in the backseat is sleeping. The dreamer pushes her mother over to get in the driver's seat and yells to her sister to wake up. At the same time another dream image is present—a large wheel, all its spokes connecting to a center revolving around and around a still point and also pulsing in and out. When the dream ego, recognizing her lack of effective mothering and sister closeness, takes charge of her dream car, this archetypal image of the wheel confronts her. The wheel appears side by side or in the midst of her capacity to dream the hurtful loss of mothering and sisterly intimacy without being disabled from taking charge of her own life. The images address her particular subjectivity on a personal level. The dreaming psyche also provides an impersonal archetypal image, that of the wheel which, in the history of symbols, represents cyclical movement, becoming and passing away—the sun with radiating spokes of warmth and light, the wheel of life in need of redemption, the wheel of doctrine, the wheel of the cosmos in its constant cycles, and the wheel symbolizing God as unity in multiplicity. How to bring these two levels together in a person's life? How to perceive the interweaving of these two levels already together in one's own life? This comprises the interplay of the two kinds of witnessing that are sharply etched in the tasks around forgiving.

What is scary about being caught in a powerful complex around forgiving or not forgiving—of feeling hate dissolve our conceptions of right and wrong so that we can imagine identifying with violence and becoming a perpetrator ourselves—is the sheer energy, the terrific weight of hate that could wash us right out to sea, forever gone from shores of human community. The isolation suffering imposes is undone by these two kinds of witnessing, between self and self and between self and psyche. Taking a stand against the offender treating us as refuse, indeed not admitting the offense ever happened, introduces this second kind of intersubjectivity with the psyche and with figures of spiritual reality. The energy of hate that changes into drawing new lines to protect subjectivity also means perceiving that subjectivity in everyone.

We are each and all subjects in our own right, entitled to respect and shelter in each other's regard. If our hate for being disregarded can be witnessed by another, it can move from reactive retaliation against the offender to witness to the fact of the outsized energy of our hate itself combating the egregious destructiveness in the other toward us. Our subjective emotion opens onto encounter with depths of psyche, an objective something that shows itself and exceeds our personal narrative. What is this energy? What does it want from us? What is its place in our life and in life itself?

Our personal experience with our own reactive hate opens to archetypal affect, what I have called monstrous hate, shocking in its intensity. Our personal question about destructiveness in us, in our subjectivity, opens to the question of the objective place of destructiveness in human life, in creation. The larger question about the place of destructiveness in life addresses us through our particular experience of the weight of hate in relation to forgiveness.

To gain a space, a hiatus, between the instinct to retaliate and choice of response is to enter a pause in which we reflect on the task we are given and the place we hold in the immense wheel of all things. Together, task and place unite the personal and the cosmic. We thus witness to the truth of our small subjective self and, looking through its particularity, witness the large objectivity of reality in which we are all held, interdependent and interconnected, each with all things mirrored in the divine. We glimpse archetypal patterns that shape reality and see afresh our contribution to this wholeness of the whole.

Such witnessing can change our suffering to some degree. We may see that it does not all come from the offender but also from burgeoning archetypal energies that insist on coming into being in daily life and pressing us to shape them in our particular lives and communities. Consciousness, puny as it is, intercedes in the insistent form of the field constellated by the injury and adds something new that may shift the archetypal energy into the flesh of the personal in a livable way. This kind of meditation supports our capacity to gaze, however briefly, on the monstrous energy that forces its way into being humanized if we can stand the process.

The Inner Check

But the outcome all turns on the inner check of the mammoth energy that initiates its transforming process. I am indebted to John Peck for this phrase, though we agree its origin remains mysterious (Peck 2008). Something curbs the outpouring of the weight of hate and allows us to bear it within instead. This check starts the process of the containment of violence and a willingness to suffer the tension of its opposition to our wish to receive the blessing of forgiveness. This inward suffering replaces violence for export only, onto the other tribe, the alien neighbor. Richard Kearney, in his discussion of monsters, also sees the check to violence coming from recognizing the monster within ourselves; the other threatening us confronts us also from within. If transformation occurs, we learn that evil does not equal otherness and that the monstrous energy transmutes to support our symbols of highest spiritual meaning (Kearney 2003, 5, 65).

But what causes the inner check on which depends our release from repetitive rounds of destructiveness? Its mystery can be described. I believe the revolt against helplessness in the face of offense inflicted by an other begins in hate that protests as much as it threatens retaliation. In the very monstrous energy itself, something arises that could go either way—out into the world as violence or inward as self-attack. But when witnessed, revealing the beginnings of agency recovered, new action is still possible despite the evil suffered (ibid., 104). Only if we feel the full fury, the full force of monstrous emotion, does something arise in it to check it. Half measures will not do; it seems we are asked to be hundred percent in it in order to fuel its countermove. Hence premature or false forgiving threatens dangers.

Yet the reining in, to turn the energy a different way, does not rest entirely in our hands either. Our psyche presents images that confront us, as if to show in the psyche itself a brake, a limit. The psyche's image encloses the energy and evokes our ability to respond to it, which leads to our responsibility to and for a monstrous energy and also to unfolding possibilities for our living with it. One analysand received in a dream only the word *mercy* and understood it as a legal term to do with justice, an action that only comes from within, not imposed but an act done to another because "inside I make a decision, not changing my feelings, but [choosing] a possibility of going forward." It opened her, she said, to "a deep instinct in me for life which had not been obliterated [at the hands of another]. I will live; I will survive and that is stronger in me than what was imposed on me." That reflexive reflection, that encounter, starts the energy of injury evolving into new forms.

A dream may appear relatively harmless until a horrific image comes in at the end and shows the psyche's picture of the dreamer's relation to past trauma, triggered by present trauma, thereby calling forth monstrous emotion from which liberation from that trauma might unfold. One woman dreamed that she refused to move her room from a place of women to one mixed with men. The dreamer follows a young woman who supports this stand, which is then depicted as belonging to a young woman who will not move from her upper-story apartment which is only one room but decorated in lovely colors. Two other women join them, and the four gather to go out to dinner. Not until approaching the steep steps going down does the dreamer see that the young owner of the apartment has no feet! She manages without feet, with stumps, and makes no fuss about it; she is used to it, even going up and down the steep flight of stairs. In addition, there is a layer of olive oil on the stairs to ease her descent. The dreamer is shocked, horrified.

This dream called the dreamer to attention: look at this, this is a young part of you, and a feminine part of you that must be housed as feminine, not mixed with the masculine; it is afflicted. The shock was double: the severing of her own standpoint—getting around with stumps—and that she had adapted—no protest, no mourning, no pain of loss, but instead an attitude of let's not make a fuss, even in the face of danger of slipping and falling on stairs made slick with olive oil (an oil associated with the feminine).

Not having her own feet to stand on rendered the dreamer extremely vulnerable to others' standpoints being thrust upon her and especially to the residual definition of herself as discardable inflicted by trauma at another's hands. A gush of pain, loss, horror, and rage swept over the dreamer in response. She no longer adapted, not protesting, but felt the full weight of colossal emotion of so many parts—rage, pity, tenderness, violent wish to harm—that it was as if she became a monster, half human, half beast, with talons and a tender heart, yet sharp fangs and brutal intent. But the dreamer dreamed the dream and was not swept away by tumultuous affect (Grotstein 2000). The inner check locates, in the psyche's picture of itself, both expression and limit through dream image. The psyche communicates and contains the horror through image.

If we have eyes to see and ears to hear, we witness to the psyche showing itself while making a boundary, an end point, a breaking point to its showing. Hence the inner check resides in the psyche itself, as well as in us. And it resides between us, that is, between the dreamer and the dream image bundling the horror into a narrative, a picture that expresses the narrative's full freight. To confront the monstrous side of hate and the amputating effect of the crushing impact of destructiveness on the ego's standpoint is no small matter, and one fears to lose one's mind, one's soul, one's very life, or at the very least one's footing in life. One could go under. We are afraid to hate, but if we do not dare lest we suffer more, we can be wed to loss, only to resort to hate to try to revive (Kristeva 1989, 7). More is needed to make the check effective so that in bundling the outsized energy, it reveals its role in supporting our highest symbols of spiritual meaning.

Still another source of inner check presents itself, a source that exceeds both personal and archetypal layers of the psyche. This source is pictured in those highest symbols of spiritual meaning. The Lord in Genesis checks the flooding of his destructiveness and marks it with a rainbow: "I do set my bow in the cloud, and it shall be a token of a covenant between me and the earth . . . which is between me and you and every living creature of all flesh" (Genesis 9:13, 15). Religions of all denominations testify to the tense relation of destructive and creative energies at the core of reality. We experience that tension in our own moral dilemmas where we want opposite things to be released and to be reconciled. Holy scriptures present these tensions and thus give us space in our subjective struggles to see the objectivity of such struggle in the whole of reality.

Healing: The First Witnessing Again

The two kinds of witnessing indicate that healing takes place on a personal level and on an archetypal level and enjoins cooperation of religion and spirituality. In the first witnessing we can look at our hate because another witnesses our experience of it, and that seeing initiates change. We begin to stand for our self in the face of the offender's objectifying us as a thing. When the hate we fear and justify and thrash around in, especially if we are exhorted to forgive, is beheld instead, it transforms us from victim to one who accepts this monstrous energy as belonging within, not for export. No longer the victim, we now must engage this monstrous energy and determine what it is, what it shows, where it belongs. This task now devolves on our regained subjectivity, and this breaks the isolation imposed by the initial trauma. The hateful energy conflicting with the forgiveness we desire pulls the ego from its familiar shores, widening its reference point to the human family but also decentering it.

We see our hateful energy as certainly ours but also as part of the human problem with the cycle of hurt-hate-revenge. This heals our humiliation and shame at being so caught in this complex; we open to a struggle shared with others who suffer their versions of the same repetitions (Jung 1935, pars. 229–232). Each of us clashing with these emotions contributes to our joint grappling with them, each of us contributes our small but dearly won insights into our common efforts at resolution. Even our suffering contributes to the whole and is not shunned as pathological, to be let go of and moved on from nor idolized. We recognize each other as fellow sufferers, sister workers on this particular human difficulty. The personal ushers in the communal.

Moving out of center stage, our ego opens to neighbors with a different yet same kind of mental life. This ego-other experience calls us beyond our self: "the very ipseity of the self expresses itself . . . as openness to otherness" (Kearney 2003, 80). Kelly Oliver argues that such a sense of the social order, offering to the individual forgiveness for transgressing its laws in the name of securing one's own singularity and agency, is what establishes a society to which individuals can belong without oppressing or marginalizing one group in order to bolster a reigning group. Personal healing admits political justice and vice versa (Oliver 2004, 191).

To accept the company of others in our engagement with the weight of hate in tension with forgiveness, to realize that we are not alone, makes us see both ourselves and our community through a wider, different kind of consciousness. We wake up to different voices

in ourselves and in our communities too. There is not just one voice—
of the hurt victim of the offender's offense—but also the one in us
who could be the offender and the witness to what happened. There
is the one who would forgive and the one who would not forgive; there
is each dream character's voice. Circling around and around in inner
conversation a center builds up, sometimes unnamed, other times
showing itself in specific form.

In psychoanalytic terms our unconscious primary process thinking
wakes up to its dreaming, and our conscious secondary process thinking
relaxes into its reverie (Bion 1970, 31–33, 124; Ogden 1999, 108,
116–117, 123). Both join in a new kind of mentation that elsewhere
I have called simultaneous or synchronistic (Ulanov 1996a, 415–
420; Ulanov 2007b, 20f, 238ff). Today I call it circumambulation
thinking. One aspect of our self talks to another, each circling
around whatever is at hand, associating, fantasizing, and imagining
in images, in affects, and in words, in linear direction and circling
around a center that comes into view, not unlike the patient's dream
of the large wheel pulsating with aliveness.

Trauma shuts down all our thinking, blanks it to vacant silence
that deadens us. We cannot speak to our self nor find our voice with
others. The monstrous level of affect in response to trauma erupts
within this muteness. To engage the monster opens us to many voices;
a veritable inner conversation establishes itself, and with others we
sense a kind of speaking that feels alive and real. We no longer stay
identified with any one standpoint (Ulanov and Ulanov 1994, 57,
64, 184, 367). In the example of forgiveness we can imagine a circle
with many spokes, each voicing a different view—forgive
unconditionally, revenge, demand remorse. In the great range of human
discourse, the most advanced includes the archaic, of which
Wittgenstein says: "there is a WILD animal: *tamed*. . . . All great art
has man's primitive drives as its ground bass. They are not the *melody*
. . . but they are what gives the melody its *depth* and power" (cited in
Ulanov and Ulanov 1994, 56). Without the monstrous, the spiritual
lacks depth and originating power.

Another way to describe this change of consciousness is the
conjoining of a childlike and adult consciousness. Our childlike
consciousness opens to what is, to see what is there and not there, not
knowing things in advance, without preconceptions and with little

defense (Jung 1944, par. 48; Jung 1923, pars. 442ff). We receive the original blast of experience, immediate, present, without the protections of built-up symbols and words; we respond with our bodies, our hearts, our spirit. We connect to what is. Hence freshness, vitality, pizzazz, wonder, gladness flavor this kind of openness, along with great vulnerability, risk of terror, capacity to be wounded. I think in trauma our childlike consciousness is always the victim, sometimes smashed. Healing must include the childlike capacity, lest we "move on" and leave this part behind.

Our adult kind of consciousness includes the development of words, concepts, symbol making, links between thoughts, protective and obstructive defenses that intervene in relation to what we experience. We pause, consider, communicate with others, choose among our experiences and make something of them as they make something of us. Without childlike consciousness, we grow stale, even deadened. Without adultlike consciousness, we cannot build, assemble original experiences into meanings we rely upon and know. Healing on the personal level must include this adultlike consciousness with which we understand and speak to our self about the great wounding that happened, mourn the suffering, carry it, and learn something valuable from it.

This inner conversation with all parts of us, from slime to spirit and in all different dialects, including body-speech, increases our ability to hear the voices of other people of different races, creeds, cultures, ages, and genders and those differently abled in the world around us (Ulanov 2001a, 126; Ulanov 2007b, 234). What began as attempted conversation with monstrous hate, enabled by the witnessing of an other, grows into intersubjective converse with inner parts of our self and deepened appreciation of other people. Inner conversation builds up community within and without. It expands the range and depth of what can be experienced. We enter into and simultaneously consider, think over, connect the immediate with the remembered and the intuited not yet, able to not know while confirming what we know. This enriches and deepens human life.

I emphasize that healing comes from conjunction of childlike and adult consciousness. As I see it, integration is not the goal but rather *coniunctio*. I stress the difference to make clear the task. Here we construct and grow links between opposite forces in which we are passionately involved, to create a joint thing, an entity made of parts. They do not become absorbed, taken in and assimilated into one indistinguishable whole of us. Our enlargement is not the goal nor usually what we can accomplish. But rather this new something that comes into being is the goal. We participate in it but are not it; it transcends us.

In intersubjective terms, the goal is neither you nor me but what gets created in each of us and between us by both of us separately and together. Ogden describes this process as the intersubjective third; other authors call it a third (see Ulanov 2007a, chap. 7; and Ulanov 2007b). Alchemists symbolize it as the philosopher's stone which multiplies itself, the permanent water that penetrates everywhere, the tincture that colors everything, the food or medicine of immortality, the caelum as "the celestial . . . life-principle, which is identical with the God-image" (Edinger 1994, 18; Jung 1955–56, par. 705; see also Jung 1954c, par. 160; Ulanov 1994, 41). All these symbols indicate something that connects to something transcendent that we did not invent. We do not integrate God into ourselves, the big into the small; that would be inflation to maniacal degree, and we have known the wreckage that follows a person so inflated, such as Hitler, Stalin, or Jim Jones of Guyana. Nor do we integrate ourselves into God, the tiny into the vast. In doing so, we would be absorbed and disappear like a drop into the ocean.

Conjunction, *coniunctio,* links up parts, knits connection between them into a whole. Edinger avers, and I agree, that "the *coniunctio,* and the process that creates it . . . represent[s] the creation of consciousness" (1994, 18). Something that was not there is now there, built up over time by putting together parts of us, parts of the world and us, parts of us and other people, parts of us and something that transcends us. An interconnected web of relations is created that exceeds all our recent technological advances. For it is mysterious, this consciousness linked to something beyond itself; it multiplies into enough food for all (Mark 6:33–44), generating mutually transformative ways we feel alive and real, in exact contrast to the contagious infection of evil. To reach *coniunctio* in terms of the weight of hate and forgiveness is not to forget or condone injury; it is to become immune to trauma's power to obliterate and then deny such obliteration happened. We are rescued into a new country where recognition of our and everyone else's subjectivity and agency is secured. The knots are loosened to bring ease, gladness, and okayness, watered with the dew of forgiveness.

This first witnessing leads to establishing inner conversation, to seeing our problem (here to do with hate and forgiveness) linked with a human problem we all share and to building a conjunction of adult and childlike consciousness. These momentous experiences mark us. We may feel we will never understand them fully, but we never forget them (Ulanov and Ulanov 1975, chap. 1). This marking in our body, time, and space, living these pivotal events, is the *religio* to which we feel bound. We know something powerful transcends our knowledge and has met us, conjoined with us, linked to our life in the here and now. To move from a religious experience to sustained religious life is to remember this binding and seek its unfolding, to name who has addressed us and practice relationship with this Other.

The Second Witnessing Again

What happens then to the trauma, the offense, the offender, and the suffering? To see that our problem is not just our personal complex but is part of a collective human problem releases us from shame and quickens our sense that we contribute to a shared solution, thus restoring us to community. We also turn then to the collective, to others outside in the world and to the collective inside our psyche which meets us as objective others through our private subjectivity— our dreams, our problems, our talents. We emerge into service, serving the collective in the world and in the psyche. In what ways will we live our sense of being bound back to these primordial experiences by serving the whole?

Jung brought to a close his private active imaginings and drawings (begun as his journal while serving in World War I and published as *The Red Book*), when he saw that his problems were not his alone, but humanity's (Jung 1963, 194–199). This perception initiated his working on his problems through serving the psyche and serving others. For the remaining decades of his life, Jung researched and translated into psychological concepts and techniques the fabulous, obscure imagery of alchemy. Kristeva writes of her father's death, two weeks before the fall of the Berlin Wall, in a socialist hospital in Bulgaria at the hands of those who were experimenting on elderly patients, forbidding family to visit or interfere, and cremating the body upon death. She could only conduct her mourning through writing (Kristeva 2009, 175).

The problem of hate in response to grievous injury opens to the collective problem of the place of destructiveness in human life and leads to our task to find the form of service to the collective that fits us, is ours. This second witnessing to the psyche's objective existence yields not so much a new consciousness as our form of service to the objective, collective dimension of life, to the archetypal psyche within and to society without, and through these to what transcends both. The monstrousness of hate makes us ask what the psyche is showing us in this excess, suggesting that it is not just us who need to transform and hence desire forgiving as the recommended panacea. It is also the psyche instigating its own transformation, as if archetypal energy is caught in the personal problem that is too small to carry it (for example, see Ulanov 1996a, 404–413). When we see this archetypal energy pressing to get through to consciousness and be transformed, we understand our obsessive thoughts and gripping emotions as manifesting this energy that wants release in new forms. We need to tame "the not yet humanized part of the libido which still possesses the compulsive character of an instinct, a part still untamed by domestication" (Jung 1943, par. 133).

The new forms are not personal realizations so much as emergent channels of service to the collective. Jung recovered alchemy, which had occupied the best minds until the seventeenth century and was then discarded as hocus-pocus when chemistry took over its physical implications for experiments with matter. Jung in the twentieth century reclaims alchemy's imagery as prefiguring the operations of psychic forces reaching for transformation.

Kristeva serves the collective through her writing and her insistence that representation, symbolization, especially in words, offers a strong way to recover the abject in ourselves and in our world. To find words for suffering, to represent them in communicable forms to others, restores agency through the capacity to signify, to assert meaning, even to renew love. Capturing in words what wreaked destruction in the past opens a future. Kearney attests, "what cannot be recalled to life, because no mourning is adequate to the sense of loss or rupture, may either be repressed (and repetitively acted out), or retrieved into poetic works. This act of creative return may itself take the form of a narrative of memory . . . in the text itself" (2003, 141).

But we may object that we are not Jung with his project of alchemy or the writer with her texts or the philosopher with memory's narrative. No matter. The task of witnessing to the monsters within us falls to each of us and to all of us as the human family, the collectivity of human society. We all must reckon with transforming these monsters within and between us. Each of us thus comes in a particular personal way to the task of service to the whole. The forms of service multiply, as we saw in the outpouring of sacrificial kindness in the workers at Ground Zero in New York City after 9/11. We see service in discovery of new attitudes of combat in diplomacy that do not kill but commit to the long haul; we see it in new methods of interrogation that do not torture but establish a bond from which scheming and manipulating yield the necessary information. We see service in couples of all kinds finding new ways to deeper communication, whether parent-child, teacher-student, analyst-analysand, where new conjunctions of opposites produce livingness. We know it when it happens. We feel alive and real in ourselves, in touch with aliveness in others and in touch with creative living itself.

Our symbols of highest spiritual meaning celebrate this mystery of aliveness. When Moses asks God in the burning bush who should he say sends him to Israel, God answers, "I AM THAT I AM" (Exodus 3:14). Hebrew scholar Avivah Zornberg, drawing on Midrash, describes this announcement as God being the principle of becoming, of allowing infinite possibilities to happen (Zornberg 2001, 27–28, 32, 34). This inextinguishable energy, symbolized in the bush that burns but does not burn up, this core creative source we cannot define or capture, inhabits the livingness of the whole.

We thus come around again to spirituality and religion but this time to their conjunction. Religion binds us back to revelatory events that we have come to name and from which we develop paths of practice. We need these symbolizations because we are finite and live in the body, which means living with definite forms in time and space. We must represent the ungraspable in order to relate to it, even with the accompanying danger of reifying the symbol into the thing itself.

Then we act as if we know the thing itself, even own it, and use it as a weapon of truth to tyrannize others. We can fall into dangers of taking our projections as the real instead of as pointers to the real. Spirituality opens onto to unnamable becoming of possibilities in relation to the eternal, and there we can fall into dangers of intellectualizing and sentimentalizing. Taken together, they may balance and protect each other, bringing closer the here and now and the over there, the beyond.

To recognize the spiritual universe in which we all dwell is to see our symbols and projections pointing to the unimaginable originating mystery of aliveness itself, seemingly seeking its own transformation in us. Religion and spirituality conjoin in our facing how we are to be living in relation to this reality in ourselves and in service to others. What symbols, images, representations, and narratives will we make in attitude and action to express that which holds us in being? How to contain its many forms? Its infinite possibilities? We ourselves come into form here, specific shapes, no longer, as an analysand said, a bit of seaweed drifting on the sea but anchored to the core creative source. And this creative core comes into forms we adopt as our religions, emerging into God-images bristling with aliveness in our self and in service to the wholeness of the whole.

Chora

In keeping within my psychoanalytic location, I want to close by speaking from the spiritual place from which religious forms take shape, rather than about their differences and similarities. Chora is one name given to this source of all that exists, a spaceless space before form, before deity, antecedent to images and categories of being, before reason, symbols, or representations, in advance of language and logic. Scholars from Plato to Derrida, theologians and philosophers, ably discussed in a recent dissertation by Lamborn, find in Chora a rhythmic space whose seeming chaos destabilizes yet is generative of everything that comes to be and is linked to the feminine in contrast to manmade cultures, laws, and styles of reasoning. Yet even notions of the feminine are surpassed in this matrix of the unconscious that points beyond itself to the mysterious source of being (Lamborn 2009, 58–59 nn20–23, 190 n111, 199–203, 257–258, 260; see also p. 85).

When the work of analysis touches on what anchors a person, on what beliefs inhabit them, we dwell in the domain of Chora, for even the concrete religious idea or specific symbol, if alive in the analysand, grows from roots in this antecedent originary space. (If the roots are weak or withered, then religion becomes mostly rote, no longer quickening. If there are no roots to an embodied planting, then that which would link us remains abstract, unincarnated in actual living.) Analysands who reject religion or are unfamiliar with its forms find, if analysis goes deep enough, questions arising in them: From what do I live? To what do I belong? They express the deep human longing to connect with the what that holds the who of us in being.

In relation to trauma of offense, offender, the weight of hate, and the release of forgiveness if it comes, we experience Chora as going beneath trauma to a new childlike openness to what comes before us, as if a plumb line is dropped through our suffering all the way down to this originating space. Or we can envision this connection in yoga terms as energy originating in this core anterior space in the depths of the earth rising up through perineum, spine, back of mouth, up through the top of the head to flow down again to the earth, recalling the prayer that God's will be done in earth as well as heaven. The whole alignment now in place clicks! The unoriginated giver of infinite possibilities of becoming, that which cannot be grasped even in exalted symbols of religion, lives in our small becoming.

The spirituality that analysis entails is devoted attention, with the witnessing other of the analyst and of the psyche and to which one of infinite possibilities unfolding from Chora we shall respond. The Chora Church of Istanbul displays two mosaics that depict Chora as female, as mother of the Christ child. In one, the child is enclosed in her chest surrounded by an oval marking off the blueness of her robe. Her being, her figure, encompasses the child, holding his being within her own larger compass. She looks out with hands raised, palms open; she is host, body, to the child who manifests the source of God. Like the *Vierge ouvrante* of medieval Christian tradition, carved in wood that opens to reveal the Father-Son-Spirit Trinity inside her body, this mosaic images Chora as the unoriginating source from which the saving new eternally comes.

In the second mosaic, she and the child are together enclosed in blueness within an oval, and she is holding the child who looks out, palms open and raised to the world. In this mosaic, the child is featured, yet she is still the surround. Chora is named, "Container of the Uncontainable."

This essay was presented to the Assisi Conference in Assisi, Italy, July 20, 2009; to Jung on the Hudson, Rhinebeck, New York, July 31, 2009; and to the Dayton Ohio Friends of Jung Society, October 2009.

12

JERUSALEM

J erusalem, with its ancient, rich symbolism and pivotal place in world affairs, presents a knot that is tied, untied, tied again in a seemingly endless pattern of creation and destruction. City of David, site of Christ's crucifixion, Dome of the Rock where Mohammed ascended to heaven, it is the city that touches all of us inwardly and in our hope for the world.

The Space in Between

Jerusalem, thought to symbolize the *axis mundi*, the center of and connection to above and below, spirit and ground, divine and human, creates a space in between which is where we live. In Jungian vocabulary this is the space of individuation. We live here on the ground with all the opposites Jerusalem represents— psychological, political, religious, ethnic, historical—all mixing, muddling, competing, battling, conversing together in a liveliness that spans from the mundane to the mystical. The New Jerusalem, for example, in the book of Revelation in the New Testament, comes down from God (no longer illuminated by sun or moon), and there are now no temples or holy places in the city because the glory of God radiates throughout. This city is home to everyone, belongs to everyone. Jung says this image presents a colossal paradox, for it symbolizes both the "innermost thing, the absolutely unique thing which belongs only to oneself" and also represents a non-ego consciousness because it is a collective, a multitude of egos (Jung 1997, vol. 1, 442). He likens it to the Self which "means the inmost uniqueness and oneness of this particular being, yet that is symbolized by a city" (ibid., 442, 444).

This non-ego kind of consciousness reminds me of Erich Neumann's idea of levels of consciousness in the psyche. In the ego-centered form of knowing contents are connected with the ego and, if forgotten or repressed, can be recovered to connect with the ego and become conscious. This style of consciousness can use abstract thinking and thus adapt to different environments. We can construct images of the objective world, so we enjoy mobility. This kind of consciousness also displays binary thinking, where the field is broken into constituent parts, subject and object, differentiating into either/or opposites, for example, inner or outer. Yet this world of polarities, of ego consciousness and world, form a unity, too, with a history. We seek a single meaning. When Jung's Red Book became available, I saw that this was the world he left. His descent included not just strange encounters with personifications of other points of view but also contact with other ways of thinking, so distant from his established ego-centered consciousness that he often said he wandered ignorant, confused. He named this strange new way of thinking "magic," a mode that included comprehending the incomprehensible (Jung 2009, 314).

Neumann speaks of another level he calls extrane consciousness, an uncentered way of knowing, not originally connected to the ego complex, that yields a kind of unconscious knowing of multiple meanings. This field of knowing is related to instinctual directives and thus can be unfree, even rigid, but we humans, unlike animals, are not determined by instinct and have some measure of freedom and choice (Neumann 1956, 84). This field includes archetypal directives, too, and when this kind of consciousness is dominant we speak of an *abaissement*, even *participation mystique*. In contrast to ego-centered knowing, which stresses clarity and discrimination into opposites, this field of extrane consciousness is suffused with emotion, intuition, and oneness, experienced in the blurring of boundaries between subject and object and a multiplicity of meanings (which Jung complained about in the Red Book [2009, 270]). In this living field, I would add, intersubjective dynamics are manifest, for example, in a clinical session as a kind of knowing that emerges *between* self and other. This archetypal field also includes dynamics of the collective unconscious, for example, as analysts we feel arranged into the form of Mother either as the warm nurturer or as cold-hearted stone in relation to the analysand, who is at the moment identified with the Child (see Ulanov 2001c, 433–434).

Beneath the archetypal field is what Neumann calls a still-wider Self-ego form of consciousness that constellates the archetypal forms as images of knowing and makes cognition possible. Knowledge at this deepest level of the Self-ego axis has an a priori absolute quality that arranges a creative spontaneous ordering more flexible than order represented by archetypal structures. An ego in touch with Self, and with the extrane levels of consciousness Self undergirds, experiences synchronicity: events noncausally related appear simultaneously physically and psychically—as from far distance and with immediacy right here, as then and now—and impact us with numinosity. Inner and outer are no longer separated in these experiences nor are physical and psychical manifestations. Each appear in the other or both appear together as if from beyond the opposites. We experience in those moments a reciprocal field and a unity of all the psychic levels of knowing. In our ego we experience the Self and what is beyond the Self. The non-ego-centered knowledge appears under the definite conditions as a centered Self (Neumann 1956, 103). So our experience of the All is specific and cosmic at once, lending our lives a regulative and guiding force that paradoxically shows freedom by being spontaneous, creative, and unpredictable, that is, not rigidly determined. Creative freedom and vitality of the ego is a filiation of freedom of the Self (ibid.).

Neumann sees transformation happening in relation to all the planes of reality as they become accessible to us. For example, I would say, resurrection of a child's way of knowing, marked by absence of preconceptions and open to wonder in response to the ever new, happens to us as adults alongside ego-centered consciousness which brings reflection, communication, and consultation with others, with history. We need the child's freshness of perception, the immediacy to embrace connected oneness of our selves with others within the world and with the forms in which the wholeness of the whole communicates to us.

The Self-ego field is greater than the specific form or image or name we give to the whole, hence it keeps living, and our forms for and images of it keep getting destroyed and created. This can be seen as Jung's fugitive fourth which itself is but a name pointing to still greater depth, extension, completion of the surround. Our consciousness is central to this great unitary psyche and world that bespeaks the reality central to existence. We experience it as both luminous and numinous; we know about it and shed its light, mirror its radiance in the world, and it grasps us.

In recent work in science on complex adaptive systems interacting with their environments, they display spontaneous adaptive responses with emergent properties "meaning that interactions among the parts produce behaviors that are greater than the sum of the interactions but also manifest new, unexpected higher levels of functioning and order in the process of adapting to their surroundings" (Cambray 2009, 45). These higher orders appear in the mind as images symbolic of the Self and when experienced consciously yield a deep affective impact coinciding with a sense of purpose familiar to us from Jung's theory of synchronicity.

All this is to say that the space of individuation, symbolized as between the heavenly and earthly Jerusalems, both concretely and symbolically extends into precincts both psychological and religious, where we experience ourselves in a realm between self and other, fact and imagination, inner and outer, psyche and soma, spirit and matter, divine and human. In this space in between, the oppositions of opposites are not definitive but instead an alternating element as seen in the perception that creativity and destructiveness share a kinship. The creative intensity of living from a core of "I am" is the luminous experience that hearkens to the numinous announcement on Mount Sinai of "I am who am, I am who is with you" (see Winnicott 1964, 112; see also Ulanov 2001b, 5–7, 13–16, 30–31, 38–41).

Analysis

We do analysis in this space in between; we need our small hut of theory and its limits to ground us in the daily work spurred by emotions and intuitions that take us among the stars. Both psychological and religious themes help when conjunctions of conscious and unconscious can be collisions, monstrous and terrifying, but also yielding experiences that display the meaning of the All and Vast in this moment in a person's intensely individual life. An example: a man bought Jung's *The Red Book* and dreamed he descended into the deeps, passing African relics, religious objects, all the while thinking in the dream, "These are what are supposed to be here, but they do not move me." Only in a deeper place did he come upon his own first small-boy symbol of a beloved stuffed animal imbued with all the intensity of meeting God and of his own full heart opening to it in love. That unique individual symbol made the dream a religious experience.

The religious sense conveys that this is it: all that is real is here now in this moment of the adult man finding the alive symbol of Otherness meeting him, linking his small-boy life to his present adult life. His descent was his own "mystery play," as Jung says in the Red Book; you have your mysteries, follow those, not mine (Jung 2009, 246 n163, 247 n164). The psyche patterns these journeys, spreading out into the field between him and me, between his earthly and heaven-sent existence, between his having to descend from his life on the surface grown flat, restless, "bummed out."

Our response to what finds us in the flatness, the problem, the dream, the pattern, is essential. Without our response, the field does not constellate. What triggers our response is always some individual scrap—a coincidence, a chance happening or memory, a particular association, or, in this case, the image of a special being from the past still shining in the present, opening the heart. Our response spurs organizing images from ego and from non-ego levels of psyche into previously unimagined forms. The new appears, and we come into contact with levels of psychological organization that transcend what our ego can construct. We become the receiver and responder and shaper of this larger reality bequeathed to us through such dreams or synchronistic moments. Such moments are not about reality; they are the real and open us to interconnectedness of the whole.

Not without including the destructive, however. In the space in between heaven and earth, spirit and ground, destructiveness too must come to the table and have a place. Otherwise destructiveness stands outside and can wreck the happenings. If we can register destructiveness inside along with the creative—if we can stand the tension of their opposition, not just getting batted back and forth between them, nor repressing or acting them out, nor trying to split them, keeping one and exporting the other to elsewhere, but keenly feeling each opposite viewpoint whether they fall in a political or spiritual realm—then something emerges from the extrane level of non-ego knowing that lifts the problem to a whole new configuration. It feels like a breakthrough, a solution, new. Jung says it feels like the grace of God, but that he will keep to more modest words and call it the working of the psyche. The psyche was for Jung another channel through which God touches us. I would say from years of clinical work, the touch may be felt precisely in and through our own intractable problem and bedeviling complex that costs us so much suffering. There in the muck of that stable, or there in the still small voice, the new comes through.

Reductionist Forces 1: Destructiveness

As clinicians and as people tangled in our own individuation process, we live in the space in between our unique lives and the collective. Hence we face in our particular dreams and neighborhoods—inner and outer places we live—the general problems of humankind. Principal among them is destructiveness—where to put the bad, how to survive annihilating forces, what to do with harmful intents we lodge against others. In the twentieth century with its variety of great and small wars, every time we say "never again" to such destructiveness, yet come again it does, leaving wreckage in its wake. Jung emphasizes repeatedly in his Red Book: the brother you hate outside lives inside you; deal with violence there lest you murder outside what you cannot live with inside. Learn to live all of your life; that is your task (Jung 2009, 253, 240–250).

Individuation must include destructiveness and the dangers it presents. We get a sense of this through the problem that feels intractable, that turns up again just when we think we got rid of it. In analysis I call such efforts to quell reductionistic. For example, we reduce the problem to our projections, thereby avoiding the actual mayhem the real other causes. We use the valuable work of inner sorting of our projections as defense against dealing with outer danger. Analysis can be misused in this way.

Another example is reducing the present trauma to early object relations that no doubt figure into the genesis of the problem to some degree; but making that the only cause leaves us victims in the present without having seized the freeing insight and the verve to claim our life now. If the pain of a wound still inflicts mortal danger, then we must garner aggressive, even destructive, energy to go into that pain now, discern how psyche works with it, how it repeats in the transference/countertransference. We may have lived in spite of this wound; now we must go into it directly to revive the part of us that got killed, or nearly so, and destroy its lethal effect on us. We discover a place then for rage, even hate, as the destructive force that refuses to let one's own self be defined by another's destructive behavior toward us. We need that hateful energy that asserts our self to deal with the deeply vulnerable part of us that needs our care and protection, not to be zapped and zapped again by present rejections.

Reading again the opening chapters in the book of Deuteronomy, I was struck recently by how the Israelites in their exodus from slavery are repeatedly swamped by human needs and desires. "Meat! Cucumbers!" they cry. "We had those in Egypt. Why did you lead us from there where even though oppressed we were better off?" The Lord is repeatedly furious and punishes the Israelites' lack of trust for not seeing the Lord of Heaven and earth leading them. The Lord destroys those cities who do not show hospitality or grant permission for the Israelites to go through their lands offering the hosts due remuneration. When the hosts refuse such passage, let alone mount an attack, the Lord wipes them out for not recognizing his sovereignty.

Right there scripture confronts us: we must contend with the obliterating force of destructiveness and its link to recognizing new allegiance that is creatively summoning and building up. We cannot evade this problem within us or among us. I understand Jerusalem as embodying this problem; Jerusalem's fate is all of our fates. For me a deep religious root of anti-Semitism stems from the election of this people to know God and know that they have to know God and represent that knowing in the world (Ulanov 1989, 57ff).

Religion is not an add-on to psychic life. For Jung, religion was an instinct that drives toward meaning in and beyond us (Jung 1944, part 1; see also Ulanov and Ulanov 1975, chap. 1). Symbols of transcendent meaning live on the same borderline with symbols of the psychic drive toward wholeness, toward Self. From the psychological side, the Self assembles real symbols that anchor us in reality that transcends our selves.

The enemy of both the religious instinct and the psychic drive toward individuation is our failure to carry the tension of the opposites within and without, killing the space between. We dismiss what the symbols point to as fantasy, not real; or, in the opposite direction, we overly concretize that transcendent reality, identifying its truth with our literalization, such as our verbalization of justice, or doctrine, or equating truth with a specific territory, building, or relic. Any disagreement with our symbolic equation we experience as an attack by an enemy whom we then feel compelled to defeat. Or we place authority outside ourselves in political vision, cultural ideal, analytical theory, or religious tradition that we obey but then live by rote, not having to bear the conflict of the yea and nay inside ourselves. Or we evade the whole problem by letting symbols of the All and Vast fade, and we lose the symbolic life altogether. Symbolic life may go in us at the level of soul, but we do not connect to it.

Reductionist Forces 2: Two Dangers

Two opposite dangers must be mentioned that collapse the space in between and exert destructiveness on our ventures to become fully ourselves fully in the world. In one we seem innocent and not to be blamed, because we did not know. We stumble into something that is numinous in its authority, and we do not recognize it as such (not unlike Yahweh's wrath in Deuteronomy destroying those cities that do not recognize and honor the god authority). We do not have the right attitude toward the appearance of the sacred; we do not acknowledge it when we see it. We do not register awe, respect, even fear. We do not recognize the tremendous otherness of the other. We miss it, dismiss it as hardly noticeable.

I think of Actaeon's fate in Greek myth. Out hunting with his hounds, he blunders into the goddess Diana bathing naked in a mountain spring. In one version, he did not mean to; he did not know she was in the vicinity; he did not recognize her fast enough to prostrate himself in lavish apologies, extravagant penance. He represents our not knowing the proper distance between us and the sacred. The numinous falls on him before he wakes up to it. It is like falling into the fire we did not know was there and getting burned up. Instantly taking offense, she asserts her formidable, immortal power and turns him into a stag. His own hounds set upon him: the hunter becomes prey. The dog is Diana's theriomorphic presentation of her dark side as goddess of destruction, death (Jung 1955–56, pars. 188, 204–206). As the poet Ted Hughes writes, "His head and antlers reared from the heaving pile. . . . Only when Actaeon's life / Had been torn from his bones, to the last mouthful, / Only then / Did the remorseless anger of Diana, Goddess of the arrow, find peace" (Hughes 1997, 105–112; cited in Hederman 2001, 211).

We can identify with both sets of these emotions—those parts of us that do not know any better but later get attacked by ourselves and by others and the sacred in us, our ownmost authority that every child is born into as unique subject, which can obliterate any chance to live in relation to it because we fail to register its breath-stopping presence and the obligations it lays upon us. We live outside it, because we do not honor it. Or we may be compelled, like the goddess Diana, to punish the one who disrespects that sacred element in us—for example, the instant murders committed where the murderer explains the victim "dissed" him (or her). To disrespect because we have not woken up to the sacred evokes swift, harsh punishment. We are pushed right outside the human community, exiled to a dumb beast's life, mere food for another species, or incarcerated for murder. Subjectivity is killed when unlinked to the sacred. We do not know the sacred exists without our receiving it. It is that double extermination that so horrifies in atrocities—obliteration of persons and obliterating the limiting boundary of the sacred.

The opposite danger lurks in our extreme vulnerability to being wounded and then to experiencing ourselves as defined by the other's dismissal of us, no longer connected to the sacred Self given to each. The Nobel poet Seamus Heaney's greatest danger was his low self-esteem, which left him defenseless—exposed and helpless before his gift to take the Golden Bough and write his poems: "If fate has called you, / The bough will come away easily, of its own accord" (1991, 3; cited in Hederman 2001, 174). Against this summons he said of himself, it took "me waiting until I was nearly fifty / To credit marvels" (Heaney 1995, cited in Hederman 2001, 193). Feeling weak not strong, unworthy not able, his defenseless openness could distract him from his capacity to journey down into the earth, to the bottomless wetness, to the real his poetry embodies: "Sing yourself to where the singing comes from" (Heaney 1996, 76).

We forget that our very vulnerability is a path to wholeness, a radical openness that perceives before we interfere with knowing all about it or aiming to use it, but perceives with a gazing, a beholding connected to what is and is not. At birth and making our way to death this vulnerability asserts its unguardedness, calling us again to an open undefended heart. That heart becomes armored by layers of protections and what analysts say is the hardest to cure—our means of self-cure. Vulnerability has its special sensing of the otherness of the other, even the *tremendum* of the numinous.

Transforming 1: In the Retort

Transforming means reaching levels of consciousness, and especially the creative spontaneity of what Neumann called the Self-ego axis. Living from that perspective, we recognize the necessity of all the spokes to form a whole wheel, not just the former ones we were able to develop or selected as preferable. This means, for example, chaos along with order, our intractable problem along with enlarged space of freedom to house the complex and what it brings us instead of being driven by it.

Our specific scrap of problem and response is a small but necessary ingredient. We could even say it is essential; it is the essence of our responding that is the sine qua non of the process of transformation, as long as we understand essence not as a fixed static thing but more like an epiphany that illuminates those new patterns coming to life within us and between us.

To register the importance of our response in the transforming process paradoxically opens us to the realization that it is not I, our I-ness, our ego, that is transforming but the something else that undergoes this change. We are more like the earthly hut that contains the something. Jung says in the Red Book that we become the vessel in which the opposites undergo conversion (2009, 252 n211). In alchemy these opposites fight and come together in the retort, not in the ego. In the retort they are depicted as sun and moon, king and queen, serpent and woman, dog and man, lovers and enemies that mix, match, defeat, blend, convert into the durable stone, the permanent water, the healing medicine. The opposites transform from rivalry to "emotional realization" that can lead to "their equilibrium." Jung notes Dorn who says the opposites "become the vessel in which what was previously now one thing and now another floats vibrating, so that the painful suspension between the opposites gradually changes into the bilateral activity of the point in the centre" (Jung 1955–56, par. 296).

This process is hard to speak about but fundamental to grasp. Transforming goes on in us and changes our I-ness, rearranging our place from center to sidebar; converting our being batted back and forth between opposites—a terrible suffering that tears the flesh from our bones like Actaeon—to a consolidation that endures. But what is in the retort is what transforms.

What goes on in the retort is suffered by the It, the something else, the Self not the ego, the synchronistic event that happens to us not invented by us, the shift from symmetry in a complex adaptive system to asymmetry that, like the oft-quoted line from Leonard Cohen's song, is the "crack where the light gets in." In such jolts we glimpse the illumination of totality of which we are a tiny part, affected by the transforming but not the center of it. Denise Levertov captures the mixture of It and us in the resurrected Christ's wound where the light streams in. Jesus' disciple Thomas doubts that the figure before him is Jesus now risen as Christ. Thomas's eyes alone cannot bring him faith. Only the direct touch of his finger put right into the wound will convince him the resurrection is real: "what I felt was not / scalding pain, shame for my obstinate need, but light, light streaming into me, over me, filling the room. . . . my question not answered but given its part, in a vast unfolding design lit / by a risen sun" (Levertov 1989, 103; see also Ulanov 1992, 251).

Chief among the processes of transformation of the It is what Jung calls symbolic death (*mortificatio* in alchemy), telling us if we do not undergo this transformation, universal genocide may result (Jung 1956–57, par. 1661). In perceiving the energy behind the opposites, we lose our identification with the one we favor and we stop acting out our ferocity toward the one we fight (Edinger 1994, 68, 70, 90). It is a death in that what used to endow us with life is burned up in the retort and lies in ashes. We disidentify from what before filled us to bursting with obsessive thoughts, emotions, actions, and patterns of behavior we could not control. Like a big balloon punctured, all the air flows out of the ego which lies as if dead, as if lying in a tomb. Our I-ness thus changes, but the action of energy goes elsewhere, not to reinflate the ego, but to endow another center that we experience as non-ego which yields a different pattern of knowing, behaving, feeling.

We feel the paradox of being empty and full. Empty from having lost all that energy generated by opposites, as if nothing remains of our connection to it. We become nonattached, yet now full of spontaneous promptings toward a greater energy of a more central center, as if discovering our real rotation is around a larger planet that we can only see imaginatively, symbolically, but which feels more real than the previous fiction of ego as center. We undergo a Copernican revolution.

The It comes into more visible being, and we circumambulate around it. The mystery of Christian Eucharist describes this offering and being offered, this dance around the center. Alchemy describes it as the second phase of *coniunctio*, the conjunction where the soul returns to the body (Jung 1955–56, pars. 476, 671, 673–679, 742; see also Edinger 1994, 77–78, 92–93). We are enlisted into the service of housing the development of this It, this "not I but Christ liveth in me," this philosopher's stone to fulfill itself within us; we house it and participate in it. Poets, for example, do not write about reality; their poems are the real. The stuff of this otherness is described as imperishable divine reality, as eternal essence that shows in our small epiphanies which disclose the interconnectedness of the whole world (see Jung 1955–56, pars. 704, 786).

Transforming. 2: The Intractable Problem (The Thief)

Where do we know of this, work on it? Our intractable problem, small and persistent, keeps us engaged in transforming. Our problem contributes to the process going on in the retort because we circle round it (*circumambulatio* in alchemy), no linear going ahead and leaving problems behind. Being caught again in our complex, tossed back and forth between opposites, means working still on what catches us and registering the It that undergoes alteration, both in us and not us, changing us radically but at cost of disidentifying, which feels like a death.

We take into ourselves the experience of nothingness: we are both unique and zero, freed from unconscious compulsive identification with bits and pieces of our personality and world, self-image or addiction, or our plan for peace. In this stripping we recognize our poor state (Ulanov and Ulanov 1975, 188–190, 218–219, 231–232). From the disidentified ego we can move into the free-associating ego able to receive what is at hand, not force it into what we wish it to be or think it should be, especially into our children. Held firmly to a point of view and simultaneously standing aside from it, we are reached by what comes through the unconscious and through our neighbor, views different from our conscious ones. We can accept psychic levels of consciousness beyond our ego-centered ways of knowing and be filled because we are empty.

A recurrent problem typical of many of us is the thief, the one who attracts our libido and usurps it; the one who swindles, defrauds, gets away; the outlier who does not belong; the betrayer as in sexual theft; the murderer as in stealing a life (see Jung 1955–56, pars. 194, 202–203). Here is a typical dream of an analysand, presenting a motif that can reappear years after working a complex through, not to extinction but now to a deeper level of confrontation. I include the analysand's associations as she tells me the dream:

> I am staying with women on my way home [being in a context of the feminine is a weak place in her]. I am showering and discover half my stuff has been taken, stolen [cleansed of

> defenses, she then faces this theft]: all my money [her way to
> get around in the world], my cosmetics bag, with medicines I
> take [feminine beauty and self care] and two pairs of my glasses
> [ability to see up close and far away], and my clothes too
> [covering and presenting myself to others as a feminine person].
> I tell the women of this theft! I tell the man driving me to the
> airport. No one even notices or responds [repeating theme of
> early trauma]. I am deposited somewhere [the complex repeats
> delivering her to a nowhere place], but how to get home [to a
> place of belonging]?

This dream displays her repeated experience of being transgressed by
an archetypal field of abandonment complex, her losing her sense of
existing, recognized by others and validated as a feminine woman with
her own agency.

Looking into the thief, she discovers this is an anonymous person
just not making enough of his life or having been given enough so
stealing life from others, a taker. The thief is poor, unable to support
himself and soon places the dream-ego into the same position—
helpless and impotent—by stealing her ability to get around in the
world, to care for her feminine self and for her health, or even clothing
herself with suitable complimentary protection.

That the thief fastens on such uniquely personal items as her
clothes (which were attractive and newly feminine in style), cosmetics,
medicine, and eyeglasses makes her exclaim: this thief is female! She
wants to dress up, look beautiful, see clearly! This thief connects directly
to what she called her weak, unconfident place as a woman—a life
issue going all the way back to interferences in her mother that resulted
in leaving the daughter unmothered.

She saw the thief now as a part of herself still stuck, not yet in her
life but stealing it. Individuation is a process, not finished, not a
completion. The dream shows her precisely where to work again and
more, seemingly a beginning dream until she realizes it confronts her
with foundational issues. She connects this thief with the part of her
that nearly died from lack of nurture and still needs rescue from the
nowhere place. The thief lies in wait for her in the place of the feminine,
the context of being with women. Her lack of secure roots in the
feminine she experiences as the threat of evil itself that can annihilate
her (see Jung 1955–56, par. 187).

In Neumann's terms her ego-centered knowing opens to the determination of an archetypal field of abandonment and opens further to the Self-ego axis that moves her to spontaneous creative response. She sees this female thief is willing to steal in order to live and live as an attractive, femininely dressed woman. And it is as if the Self supports this aggressive invasion as the thief gets way with it. The dreamer finally, on waking, receives the thief's communication that she insists on living.

The usual meaning of thief as a narrow-minded exploiter of another for self-gain who dismisses anything that cannot be turned into self-profit is here. But added is the thief as wanting her own feminine beauty in attractive clothing and makeup. Through the dream scrap—the detail of feminine clothing, medicine, and unguents—the thief wants to show herself as feminine and with the means (money) to sustain that life. The destructiveness of stealing wants to fill in the weak place of the feminine in the dreamer's personality. The thief is part of her, not dominated by the abandonment complex but instead urged toward living the feminine. The dreamer must respond, and she does when awake, discovering this part is her missing femininity. Then the lack of response from others that she usually experiences as annihilating loss (a repeat of a child who loses her mother) changes into excitement that this lost part of her has not given up; she is showing herself and wants to belong in the dreamer's life. Thievery transforms into announcement: Here I am! I am going to live!

Reflection

To the space in between heaven and earth we bring our accumulated ego ability to reflect on problems and breakthroughs that occur through the scraps of our individual life prompted by our unpredictable, spontaneous, creative responses. For when we respond to a synchronistic moment with an intense sense of meaningful interconnection of all the world or when we experience the emergence of the amazing new—image, release of energy, solution—as if there is a higher order of Self addressing our ego, we need to reflect on these happenings.

They are amazing; they are ephemeral; they are powerful. We may try to concretize them in order to repeat them, and then they become dead things, idols once again put into beliefs or behaviors that we ordain as correct. We reify the infinite in order to hold on to it. And we thus lose it; it is not a commodity that we can store. Or when we experience the marvelous coming into contact with levels of organizing within our small selves a sense of the beyond, of forces transcendent to our ego capacities, we may try to capture the archetypal constellations congruent with this new field of experience, but this exceeds our psychological abilities. We can experience this beyond organizing us, so to speak, in the numinous moment. But we cannot possess it as though we plugged into a higher intelligence and found ourselves elected to be its spokesperson. This is madness (see Ulanov 2013, chap. 3).

The wonder of our child consciousness ever to see afresh needs adult capacities of discernment, reflection, consultation, and communication with others. Reflection on what comes into view and what limits our abilities to house it is integral to finding the place of destructiveness in life. For otherwise we fall into identification with these forces and want to tell others how to think, believe, and act. We wreak violence once again, on our neighbor, on parts of ourselves, on our children whom we love.

In religious terms, when we respond to the gap separating heaven and earth and to the moments when their connection displays itself to us, the gap changes into a space in between heaven and earth where, so to speak, we converse with both dimensions. Then we become citizens of Jerusalem. In that space still more is required, namely, our ethical reflection, because increased contact with reality that comes through archetypal resonances can be used for good or ill purposes. Empathy as a means of perceiving the other's viewpoint can be used to hurt them as well as to endorse their growing. This process of responding, reflecting, brings what has been separated and differentiated together again.

How does such reflecting happen? From the scraps through which we create. We can learn from artists. Paul Klee, the painter, writes movingly of his trust in letting things grow within him in response to what he observes around him. The creative image grows of its own accord, "a something not from here shines, not from here, not from me, but of God" (Haftmann 1967, 68), recalling the poet Heaney's words, "let the shine come up" and the space in between becomes the place that "spelled promise / And newness in the backyard of our life" (cited in Hederman 2001, 200, 189, respectively). The creative bits grow of their own accord, as Klee waited "patiently until the creative image ripened within him, gave him . . . his secure feeling of being in the hands of a superior being" (Haftmann 1967, 34). He was trying "to make visible as form something which is in the process of forming"; "even evil shall no longer be a triumphant or shaming enemy but a force co-operating towards a Whole"; this unity "must have common roots in the earth below and . . . meet in the cosmos above" (ibid., 86, 89, 90).

We wait on the creative image or some other scrap that will show the way to underlying abundance that Neumann calls ego-Self axis—which Klee portrays in his painting *Monument to the Land of Plenty*. Our personal scrap is also a fragment of the whole, maybe like the Higgs boson particle, called the God particle, which joins with force to create mass—visible, tangible incarnation (Randall 2011, 287 and chap. 16).

Our ethical response is to give a name to this process—call it being creative, doing a painting, believing in God, achieving a genius for cooking. The name is evidence that something transferred itself from the region of the unknown into that of the familiar and known. We live it. But what transforms in the jar, the retort, the sacrament, is the It, and we all benefit. Individuation is not a solipsistic venture. The philosopher's stone, the blood and wine, multiply. Others catch it from us, or we find it in seeing another's journey. It begets among us, augments, generates, propagates, reproduces. Thus each of us, separately and together, add to the storehouse of currency of the whole. We add our small bit from work with our intractable problems to good of the whole. Scraps.

This essay was presented at a meeting of the Jerusalem Jung Society, January 2013, in Jerusalem, Israel.

13

REFERENCES

Anderson, F. S., ed. 2008. *Bodies in Treatment, the Unspoken Dimension.* Hillsdale, NJ: Analytic Press.

Anderson, W. T. 1990. *Reality Isn't What It Used to Be.* San Francisco: Harper.

Arendt, H. 1958. *The Human Condition.* Chicago: Chicago University Press.

Atwood, G., and R. Stolorow. 1992. "Three Realms of the Unconscious." In *Relational Psychoanalysis*, edited by Stephen A. Mitchell and Lewis Aron. Hillsdale, NJ: Analytic Press, 1999.

Babinsky, E. L., trans. 1993. *Marguerite of Porete: The Mirror of Simple Souls.* Mahwah, NJ: Paulist Press.

Balint, E. 1993. *Before I Was I: Psychoanalysis and the Imagination.* Edited by Juliet Mitchell and Michael Parsons. London: Free Association Press.

Bion, W. R. 1970. *Attention and Interpretation.* London: Tavistock.

———. 1991. *Transformations.* London: Karnac.

———. 1993. *Second Thoughts.* London: Karnac.

Blass, R. B. 2006. "Beyond Illusion: Psychoanalysis and the Question of Religious Truth." In *Psychoanalysis and Religion in the 21st Century*, edited by David M. Black. New York: Routledge.

Bléandonu, G. 2000. *Wilfred Bion: His Life and Works 1897–1979*. Translated by Claire Pajaczkowska. New York: Other Press.

Boechat, W., and P. Pantoja. 2007 (August 14). "Race, Racism, and Inter-racialism in Brazil: Clinical and Cultural Perspectives." Seventeenth International Congress for Analytical Psychology, Cape Town, South Africa.

Bollas, C. 1991. *Forces of Destiny*. London: Free Association Books.

The Book of Common Prayer. 1944. New York: Oxford University Press.

Borges, J. L. 1957. "Borges and I." In *Labyrinths: Selected Stories and Other Writings*, edited by D. Yates and J. Irby. New York: New Directions, 1962.

Boss, M. 1963. *Psychoanalysis and Daseinanalysis*. Translated by L. B. LeFebre. New York: Basic Books.

Brenman, E. 2006. *Recovery of the Lost Good Object*. Edited by Gigliola Fornari Spoto. New York: Routledge.

Briggs, K. 2008. *The Power of Forgiveness*. Minneapolis: Fortress Press.

Bright, G. 1997. "Synchroncity as a Basis of Analytic Attitude." *Journal of Analytical Psychology* 42 (4): 613–636.

Bromberg, P. M. 1993. "Shadow and Substance: A Relational Perspective on Clinical Process." In *Relational Psychoanalysis: The Emergence of a Tradition*, edited by Stephen A. Mitchell and Lewis Aron. Hillsdale, NJ: Analytic Press, 1999.

———. 2006. *Awakening the Dreamer*. Mahwah, NJ: Analytic Press.

Capps, D. 1995. *Agents of Hope*. Minneapolis: Fortress Press.

Cambray, J. 2009. *Synchronicity, Nature, and Psyche in an Interconnected Universe*. College Station: Texas A&M University Press.

Cassirer, E. 1946. *Language and Myth*. Translated by Suzanne K. Langer. New York: Dover Publications.

Celan, P. 1986. *Collected Prose*. Translated by Rosemarie Waldrop. Manchester, England: Carcanet.

Conforti, M. 2007 (February 4). Presentation to the Jungian Psychoanalytic Association, New York.

Cooper, J. C. 1982. *An Illustrated Encyclopedia of Traditional Symbols*. London: Thames and Hudson.

Digeser, P. E. 2001. *Political Forgiveness*. Ithaca, NY: Cornell University Press.

Dobbs, T. M. 2007. *Faith, Theology, and Psychoanalysis*. Eugene, OR: Pickwick Publications.

Doniger, W. 2007. "Magic Rings and the Return of the Repressed." In *Spirituality and Religion: Psychoanalytic Perspectives*. Edited by Jerome A. Winer and James William Anderson. Catskill, NY: Mental Health Perspectives.

Drewery, B. 1975. "Deification." In *Christian Spirituality: Essays in Honour of Gordon Rupp*. Edited by Peter Brooks. London: SCM Press.

Edinger, E. F. 1985. *The Anatomy of the Psyche*. La Salle, IL: Open Court.

———. 1994. *The Mystery of the Coniunctio: Alchemical Image of Individuation*. Edited by Joan Dexter Blackmer. Toronto: Inner City Books.

———. 1995. *The Mysterium Lectures: A Journey through Jung's "Mysterium Coniunctionis."* Transcribed and edited by Joan Dexter Blackmer. Toronto: Inner City Books.

———. 2004. *The Sacred Psyche: A Psychological Approach to the Psalms*. Edited and transcribed by Joan Dexter Blackmer. Toronto: Inner City Books.

Eisold, K. 1994. "Intolerance of Diversity in Psycho-Analytic Institutes." *International Journal of Psycho-Analysis* 75:785–800.

Eliot, T. S. 1943. "Little Gidding." In *The Four Quartets*. New York: Harcourt, Brace.

———. 1963. "The Wasteland." In *Collected Poems 1909–1962*. New York: Harcourt, Brace and World.

Fairfield, S. 2002. "Analyzing Multiplicity." In *Bringing in the Plague*, edited by Susan Fairfield, Lynne Layton, and Carolynn Stock. New York: Other Press.

Felstiner, John. 1995. *Paul Celan: Poet, Survivor, Jew*. New Haven, CT: Yale University Press.

Ferro, A. 2005. *Seeds of Illness, Seeds of Recovery*. Translated by Philip Slotkin. New York: Routledge.

———. 2008 (May 6). "Forgetting Freud, Rediscovering Freud." Lecture delivered to the Association for Psychoanalytic Medicine, Academy of Medicine, New York, NY.

Flax, J. 1987. "Remembering the Selves: Is the Repressed Gendered?" *Michigan Quarterly Review* 16:92–110.

Forge, A. 2007. *Paintings and Works on Paper*. New York: Betty Cunningham Gallery.

Freud, S. 1900. *The Interpretation of Dreams*, vol. 4, *The Standard Edition of the Complete Psychological Works of Sigmund Freud*. Translated by James Strachey. London: Hogarth Press, 1973.

———. 1921. *Group Psychology and the Analysis of the Ego*, vol. 18, *The Standard Edition of the Complete Psychological Works of Sigmund Freud*. Translated by James Strachey. London: Hogarth Press, 1973.

———. 1923. "Mysticism Is the Obscure Self-Perception of the Realm Outside the Ego, of the Id." In *The Standard Edition of the Complete Psychological Works of Sigmund Freud*, vol. 23. Translated by James Strachey. London: Hogarth Press, 1973.

Friedman, T. L. 2005. "A Poverty of Dignity and a Wealth of Rage." *New York Times*, July 15.

Gadamer, H.-G. 1975. *Truth and Method*. New York: Seabury Press.

Gobodo-Madikizela, P. 2003. *A Human Being Died That Night*. New York: Houghton Mifflin.

———. 2007 (August 13). "Trauma, Forgiveness, and the Witnessing Dance: Making Public Spaces Intimate." Seventeenth International Congress for Analytical Psychology IAAP, Cape Town, South Africa.

Gourevitch, P. 2009. "The Life After." *New Yorker*, May 4, pp. 36–49.

Grand, S. 2000. *The Reproduction of Evil: A Clinical and Cultural Perspective*. Hillsdale, NJ: Analytic Press.

Grimm. 2011. *The Fairy Tales of the Brothers Grimm*. Edited by Noel Daniel. Translated by Matthew B. Price. Koln, Germany: Taschen.

Grotstein, J. S. 2000. *Who Is the Dreamer Who Dreams the Dream?* Hillsdale, NJ: Analytic Press.

———. 2007. *A Beam of Intense Darkness*. London: Karnac.

Haftmann, W. 1967. *The Mind and Work of Paul Klee*. London: Faber and Faber.

Hamburger, M. 1988. *The Poems of Paul Celan*. New York: Persea Books.

Heaney, S. 1987. *The Haw Lantern*. London: Faber and Faber.

———. 1991. *Seeing Things*. London: Faber and Faber.

———. 1995. *Crediting Poetry: The Nobel Lecture*. Dublin: Gallery Press.

————. 1996. *The Spirit Level.* New York: Farrar, Straus, and Giroux.

Hederman, M. P. 2001. *The Haunted Inkwell.* Dublin, Ireland: Columba Press.

The Herder Symbol Dictionary. 1986. Translated by Boris Matthews. Wilmette, IL: Chiron Publications.

Hind, R. 2004. *One Thousand Faces of God.* New York: Barnes and Noble Books.

Hughes, T. 1997. *Tales from Ovid.* London: Faber and Faber.

Jones, L. G. 1995. *Embodying Forgiveness: A Theological Analysis.* Grand Rapids, MI: William B. Eerdmans.

Jung, C. G. 1923. *Psychological Types*, vol. 6, *The Collected Works of C. G. Jung.* Translated by R. F. C. Hull. Princeton, NJ: Princeton University Press, 1971.

————. 1928. "The Relations between the Ego and the Unconscious." In *Two Essays on Analytical Psychology*, vol. 7, *The Collected Works of C. G. Jung.* Translated by R. F. C. Hull. Princeton, NJ: Princeton University Press, 1953.

————. 1931. "Freud and Jung: Contrasts." In *Freud and Psychoanalysis*, vol. 4, *The Collected Works of C. G. Jung.* Translated by R. F. C. Hull. Princeton, NJ: Princeton University Press, 1961.

————. 1933a. "Psychotherapist or Clergy." In *Modern Man in Search of a Soul.* New York: Harcourt, Brace.

————. 1933b. "The Spiritual Problem of Modern Man." In *Modern Man in Search of a Soul.* Translated by W. S. Dell and Cary F. Baynes. New York: Harcourt, Brace and World.

————. 1934. "The Development of the Personality." In *The Development of Personality*, vol. 17, *The Collected Works of C. G. Jung.* Translated by R. F. C. Hull. Princeton, NJ: Princeton University Press, 1954.

————. 1935. "The Tavistock Lectures." In *The Symbolic Life*, vol. 18, *The Collected Works of C. G. Jung.* Translated by R. F. C. Hull. Princeton, NJ: Princeton University Press, 1976.

————. 1939a. "Foreword to Suzuki's *Introduction to Zen Buddhism.*" In *Psychology and Religion*, vol. 11, *The Collected Works of C. G. Jung.* Translated by R. F. C. Hull. Princeton, NJ: Princeton University Press, 1958, 1969.

————. 1939b. "Conscious, Unconscious, and Individuation." In *The Archetypes and the Collective Unconscious*, vol. 9i, *The Collected Works of C. G. Jung*. Translated by R. F. C. Hull. Princeton, NJ: Princeton University Press, 1959, 1968.

———. 1939c. "The Symbolic Life." In *The Symbolic Life*, vol. 18, *The Collected Works of C. G. Jung*. Translated by R. F. C. Hull. Princeton, NJ: Princeton University Press, 1976.

———. 1940. "Psychology and Religion." In *Psychology and Religion*, vol. 11, *The Collected Works of C. G. Jung*. Translated by R. F. C. Hull. Princeton, NJ: Princeton University Press, 1958, 1969.

———. 1943. "On the Psychology of the Unconscious." In *Two Essays in Analytical Psychology*, vol. 7, *The Collected Works of C. G. Jung*. Translated by R. F. C. Hull. Princeton, NJ: Princeton University Press, 1953, 1966.

———. 1944. *Psychology and Alchemy*, vol. 12, *The Collected Works of C. G. Jung*. Princeton, NJ: Princeton University Press, 1953, 1968.

———. 1946. "Psychology of the Transference." In *The Practice of Psychotherapy*, vol. 16, *The Collected Works of C. G. Jung*. Translated by R. F. C. Hull. Princeton, NJ: Princeton University Press, 1954, 1966.

———. 1948a. "A Psychological Approach to the Trinity." In *Psychology and Religion*, vol. 11, *The Collected Works of C. G. Jung*. Translated by R. F. C. Hull. Princeton, NJ: Princeton University Press, 1958, 1969.

———. 1948b. "General Aspects of Dream Psychology." In *The Structure and Dynamics of the Psyche*, vol. 8, *The Collected Works of C. G. Jung*. Translated by R. F. C. Hull. Princeton, NJ: Princeton University Press, 1960, 1969.

———. 1950. "A Study in the Process of Individuation" In *The Archetypes and the Collective Unconscious*, vol. 9i, *The Collected Works of C. G. Jung*. Translated by R. F. C. Hull. Princeton, NJ: Princeton University Press, 1959, 1968.

———. 1952a. "Answer to Job." In *Psychology and Religion*, vol. 11, *The Collected Works of C. G. Jung*. Translated by R. F. C. Hull. Princeton, NJ: Princeton University Press, 1958, 1969.

———. 1952b. "Synchronicity: An Acausal Connecting Principle." In *The Structure and Dynamics of the Psyche*, vol. 8, *The Collected Works of C. G. Jung*. Translated by R. F. C. Hull. Princeton, NJ: Princeton University Press, 1960, 1969.

————. 1954a. "Archetypes of the Collective Unconscious." In *The Archetypes and the Collective Unconscious*, vol. 9i, *The Collected Works of C. G. Jung*. Translated by R. F. C. Hull. Princeton, NJ: Princeton University Press, 1959, 1968.

————. 1954b. "On the Nature of the Psyche." In *The Structure and Dynamics of the Psyche*, vol. 8, *The Collected Works of C. G. Jung*. Translated by R. F. C. Hull. Princeton, NJ: Princeton University Press, 1960, 1969.

————. 1954c. "Transformation Symbolism in the Mass." In *Psychology and Religion*, vol. 11, *The Collected Works of C. G. Jung*. Translated by R. F. C. Hull. Princeton, NJ: Princeton University Press, 1958, 1969.

————. 1955–56. *Mysterium Coniunctionis*, vol. 14, *The Collected Works of C. G. Jung*. Translated by R. F. C. Hull. Princeton, NJ: Princeton University Press, 1963, 1970.

————. 1956–57. "Jung and Religious Belief." In *The Symbolic Life*, vol. 18, *The Collected Works of C. G. Jung*. Translated by R. F. C. Hull. Princeton, NJ: Princeton University Press, 1976.

————. 1957. "Commentary on 'The Secret of the Golden Flower.'" In *Alchemical Studies*, vol. 13, *The Collected Works of C. G. Jung*. Translated by R. F. C. Hull. Princeton, NJ: Princeton University Press, 1967.

————. 1958a. "Flying Saucers: A Modern Myth of Things Seen in the Skies." In *Civilization in Transition*, vol. 10, *The Collected Works of C. G. Jung*. Translated by R. F. C. Hull. Princeton, NJ: Princeton University Press, 1964.

————. 1958b. "The Transcendent Function." In *The Structure and Dynamics of the Psyche*, vol. 8, *The Collected Works of C. G. Jung*. Translated by R. F. C. Hull. Princeton, NJ: Princeton University Press, 1960, 1969.

————. 1959. "Good and Evil in Analytical Psychology." In *Civilization in Transition*, vol. 10, *The Collected Works of C. G. Jung*. Translated by R. F. C. Hull. Princeton, NJ: Princeton University Press, 1964.

————. 1963. *Memories, Dreams, Reflections*. Edited by Aniela Jaffé. Translated by Richard and Clara Winston. New York: Pantheon.

————. 1976. *Letters, Vol. II, 1951–1961*. Edited by Gerhard Adler. Translated by J. Hulen. Princeton, NJ: Princeton University Press.

————. 1988. *Nietzsche's Zarathustra.* 2 vols. Edited by James L. Jarrett. Princeton, NJ: Princeton University Press.

————. 1992. *Letters, Vol. 1, 1906–1950.* Edited by Gerhard Adler with Aniela Jaffé. Translated by R. F. C. Hull. Princeton, NJ: Princeton University Press.

————. 1997. *Visions: Notes of the Seminar Given in 1930–1934.* 2 vols. Edited by Claire Douglas. Princeton, NJ: Princeton University Press.

————. 2009. *The Red Book: Liber Novus.* Edited by Sonu Shamdasani. New York: W. W. Norton.

Kakar, S. 1991. *The Analyst and the Mystic.* Chicago: University of Chicago Press.

Kearney, R. 2003. *Strangers, Gods, and Monsters: Interpreting Otherness.* New York: Routledge.

Khan, M. M. R. 1963. "The Concept of Cumulative Trauma." In *The Privacy of the Self,* by M. M. R. Khan. New York: International Universities Press, 1974.

Kierkegaard, S. 1941. *Concluding Unscientific Postscript.* Translated by David F. Swenson. Princeton, NJ: Princeton University Press.

Klein, M. 1957. *Envy and Gratitude and Other Works 1946–1968.* New York: Delacorte Press/Seymour Lawrence, 1975.

————. 1975. *Psychoanalysis of Children.* Translated by Alix Strachey. New York: Delacorte Press/Seymour Lawrence.

Kohut, H. 1981. "On Empathy." In *The Search for the Self,* vol. 4. Edited by Paul H. Ornstein. Madison, CT: International Universities Press, 1991.

Kraybill, D. B., S. M. Nolt, and D. L. Weaver-Zercher. 2007. *Amish Grace: How Forgiveness Transcended Tragedy.* San Francisco: Jossey-Bass.

Kristeva, J. 1989. *Black Sun: Depression and Melancholia.* Translated by Leon S. Roudiez. New York: Columbia University Press.

————. 1995. *New Maladies of the Soul.* New York: Columbia University Press.

————. 2009. "A Father Is Being." In *The Dead Father,* edited by Lila J. Kalinich and Stuart W. Taylor. New York: Routledge.

Krog, A. 2006. *Body Bereft.* Roggebaai, South Africa: Umuzi/ Random House.

————. 2007 (August 15). "My Heart Is on My Tongue: The Untranslated Self in a Translated World." Seventeenth International Congress for Analytical Psychology, Cape Town, South Africa.

Laing, R. 1967. *The Politics of Experience.* Hammondsworth, England: Penguin Books.

Lamborn, A. B. 2009. "Figuring the Self, Figuring the Sacred: Imagining Unity and Multiplicity in Depth Psychology and Theology." Diss., Program of Psychiatry and Religion, Union Theological Seminary, New York.

Langendorf, U. 2007 (August 14). "The Stranger in the Therapy Room." Seventeenth International Congress for Analytical Psychology, Cape Town, South Africa.

Layton, L. 2004. *Who's That Girl? Who's That Boy? Clinical Practice Meets Postmodern Gender Theory.* Hillsdale, NJ: Analytic Press.

Lear, J. 1990. *Love and Its Place in Nature.* New York: Farrar, Straus, and Giroux.

Levertov, D. 1989. *A Door in the Hive.* New York: New Directions.

Loewald, H. W. 1970. "Psychoanalytic Theory and Psychoanalytic Process." In *Papers on Psychoanalysis.* New Haven, CT: Yale University Press, 1980.

————. 1978. *Psychoanalysis and the History of the Individual.* New Haven, CT: Yale University Press.

Martyn, D. W. 2007. *Beyond Deserving.* Grand Rapids, MI: Eerdmans.

Matisse, H. 1983. *Jazz.* New York: George Brazillier.

McGuire, W., ed. 1974. *The Freud/Jung Letters.* Translated by R. Manheim and R. F. C. Hull. Princeton, NJ: Princeton University Press.

Miller, Alice. 1981. *The Drama of the Gifted Child.* Translated by Ruth Miller. New York: Basic Books.

Miller, Barbara Stoler, trans. 1986. *The Bhagavad-Gita.* New York: Bantam.

Milner, M. 1937. *An Experiment in Leisure.* London: Routledge, 2011.

————. 1978. "D. W. Winnicott and the Two-Way Journey." In *Between Fantasy and Reality,* edited by S. A. Grolnick and L. Barkin. New York: Jason Aronson.

Milosz, C. 2004. *Second Space.* Translated by C. Milosz and Robert Hass. New York: Ecco.

Murakami, H. 2002. "Thailand." In *After the Quake,* translated by Jay Rubin. New York: Vintage International.

Neumann, E. 1956. "The Psyche and the Transformation of the Reality Planes." In *Spring*. Translated by Hildegard Nagel. New York: New York Analytical Psychological Club.

———. 1969. *Depth Psychology and the New Ethic*. Translated by Eugene Rolfe. New York: Putnam's.

Ogden, T. H. 1992. *The Primitive Edge of Experience*. Lanham, MD: Rowman and Littlefield.

———. 1994. *Subjects of Analysis*. London: Karnac.

———. 1999. *Interpretation and Reverie*. London: Karnac.

———. 2001. *Conversations at the Frontier of Dreaming*. Northvale, NJ: Jason Aronson.

———. 2009. *Rediscovering Psychoanalysis, Thinking and Dreaming, Learning and Forgetting*. New York: Routledge.

Oliver, K. 2004. *The Colonization of Psychic Space*. Minneapolis: University of Minnesota Press.

Parsons, M. 2006. "Ways of Transformation." In *Psychoanalysis and Religion in the 21st Century*, edited by David M. Black. London: Routledge.

Peck, J. 2008. "Nitemares, Useful Monsters, and Spiritual Responsibility: Facing Jung's Psychology toward Structural Violence." Presentation given at Symposium: Spirituality and Depth Psychology, Wasan Island, Ontario, Canada.

Randall, L. 2011. *Knocking on Heaven's Door*. New York: HarperCollins.

Rank, O. 1941. *Beyond Psychology*. New York: Dover Publications.

Ricoeur, P. 1970. *Freud and Philosophy: An Essay on Interpretation*. Translated by Denis Savage. New Haven, CT: Yale University Press.

———. 2004. *Memory, History, Forgetting*. Translated by Kathleen Blamey and David Pellauer. Chicago: Chicago University Press.

Rilke, R. M. 1922. "To Nike." In *Rainer Maria Rilke: Selected Works*, vol. 2. Translated by J. B. Leischman. Norfolk, CT: New Directions Books, 1960.

Rivera, M. 2002. "Linking the Psychological and the Social." In *Gender in Psychoanalytic Space*, edited by Muriel Dimen and Virginia Goldner. New York: Other Press.

Rizzuto, A.-M., 2007. "God in the Mind: The Psychodynamics of an Unusual Relationship." In *Spirituality and Religion: Psychoanalytic Perspectives*, edited by Jerome A. Winer and James William Anderson. Catskill, NY: Mental Health Resources.

Rothko, M. 2009. *Rothko: The Late Series*. Edited by Achim Borchardt-Hume. Millbank, London: Tate Enterprises Ltd.

Sacks, O. 1985. *The Man Who Mistook His Wife for a Hat*. New York: Summit Books.

Sieff, Daniela. 2009. "Confronting the Death Mother: An Interview with Marion Woodman." In *Spring*, vol. 81, *The Psychology of Violence*. New Orleans: Spring Journal Books.

Singer, T., and S. L. Kimbles. 2004. "The Emerging Theory of Cultural Complexes." In *Analytical Psychology: Contemporary Perspectives in Jungian Analysis*, edited by Joseph Cambray and Linda Carter. New York: Brunner-Routledge.

Spurling, H. 1998. *The Unknown Matisse*, vol. 1. New York: Knopf.

Stein, M. 2002. "Psychoanalysis and Spirituality." *Quadrant* 32(2): 7–20.

Stern, D. 1983. "Unformulated Experience: From Familiar Chaos to Creative Disorder." In *Relational Analysis*, edited by Stephen Mitchell and Lewis Aron. Hillsdale, NJ: Analytic Press, 1999.

Stevens, W. 1935. "The Idea of Order at Key West." *The Idea of Order* cited in Frank Kermode, *Wallace Stevens*. New York: Grove Press, 1960.

Stocks, K. 1988. *Emily Dickinson and the Modern Consciousness*. New York: St. Martin's Press.

Sutherland, J. D. 1989. *Fairbairn's Journey into the Interior*. London: Free Association Books.

Symington, N. 2001. *The Spirit of Sanity*. London: Karnac.

Teresa of Ávila. 1957. *Complete Works*. 3 vols. Translated by E. Allison Peers. New York: Sheed and Ward.

Tomkins, C. 2005. *The New Yorker*. May 23.

Tutu, D. 1999. *No Future without Forgiveness*. New York: Doubleday.

Ulanov, A. B. 1971. *The Feminine in Jungian Psychology and in Christian Theology*. Evanston, IL: Northwestern University Press.

———. 1986a. "Aging: On the Way to One's End." In *Picturing God*, by A. B. Ulanov. Einsiedeln, Switzerland: Daimon, 2002.

———. 1986b. *Picturing God*. Einsiedeln, Switzerland: Daimon, 2002.

———. 1988. *The Wisdom of the Psyche*. Einsiedeln, Switzerland: Daimon, 2000.

———. 1989. "Scapegoating: The Double Cross." In *Spirit in Jung*. Einsiedeln, Switzerland: Daimon, 2005.

————. 1992. "Unseen Boundaries, Dangerous Crossings." In *Spiritual Aspects of Clinical Work*. Einsiedeln, Switzerland: Daimon, 2004.

————. 1993a. *The Female Ancestors of Christ*. Einsiedeln, Switzerland: Daimon, 1998.

————. 1993b. "The Perverse and the Transcendent." In *The Transcendent Function: Individual and Collective Aspects*. Proceedings of the Twelfth International Congress for Analytical Psychology, Chicago, 1992. Edited by Mary Ann Matoon. Einsiedeln, Switzerland: Daimon, 1996.

————. 1994. *The Wizards' Gate: Picturing Consciousness*. Einsiedeln, Switzerland: Daimon.

————. 1996a. "Ritual, Repetition, and Psychic Reality." In *Spiritual Aspects of Clinical Work*. Einsiedeln, Switzerland: Daimon, 2004.

————. 1996b. *The Functioning Transcendent*. Wilmette, IL: Chiron Publications.

————. 1998. "The Gift of Consciousness." In *Spiritual Aspects of Clinical Work*. Einsiedeln, Switzerland: Daimon, 2004.

————. 2001a. *Attacked by Poison Ivy: A Psychological Study*. York Beach, ME: Nicolas-Hayes.

————. 2001b. *Finding Space: Winnicott, God, and Psychic Reality*. Louisville, KY: Westminster John Knox.

————. 2001c. "Hate in the Analyst." In *Spiritual Aspects of Clinical Work*. Einsiedeln, Switzerland: Daimon, 2004.

————. 2007a. "The Third in the Shadow of the Fourth." *Journal of Analytical Psychology* 52 (5):585–607.

————. 2007b. *The Unshuttered Heart: Opening to Aliveness and Deadness in the Self*. Nashville, TN: Abingdon.

————. 2010 (June 19). "Encountering Jung Being Encountered," Presentation on C. G. Jung, *The Red Book*, Library of Congress, Washington, DC. Published in *Jung Journal: Culture and Psyche* 5, no. 3 (August 2011).

————. 2013. *Madness and Creativity*. College Station: Texas A&M University Press.

Ulanov, A., and B. Ulanov. 1975. *Religion and the Unconscious*. Louisville, KY: Westminster John Knox.

———. 1982. *Primary Speech: A Psychology of Prayer*. Louisville, KY: Westminster John Knox.

———. 1987. *The Witch and the Clown: Two Archetypes of Human Sexuality*. Wilmette, IL: Chiron Publications.

———. 1991. *The Healing Imagination*. Einsiedeln, Switzerland: Daimon, 1999.

———. 1994. *Transforming Sexuality: The Archetypal World of Anima and Animus*. Boston: Shambhala.

———. 1995. "Looking: Subjectivity and the True Self." *Powers of Being: David Holbrook and His Work*. Edited by Edwin Webb. Madison, NJ: Farleigh Dickinson Press.

von Franz, M.-L. 1971. *The Inferior Function*. New York: Spring.

———. 1972. *The Feminine in Fairy Tales*. New York: Spring Publications.

———. 1974. *Number and Time*. Translated by Andrea Dykes. Evanston, IL: Northwestern University Press.

———. 1980a. *On Divination and Synchronicity*. Toronto: Inner City Books.

———. 1980b. *The Psychological Meaning of Redemption Motifs in Fairy Tales*. Toronto: Inner City Books.

———. 1992. *Psyche and Matter*. Boston: Shambhala.

———. 2002. *Anima and Animus in Fairy Tales*. Toronto: Inner City Books.

Wilhelm, R., trans. 1950. *The I Ching*. Translated into English by Cary F. Baynes. New York: Pantheon.

Winnicott, C. 1978. "D. W. W.: A Reflection." In *Between Reality and Fantasy*, edited by Simon A. Grolnick and Leonard Barkin in collaboration with Werner Muensterberger. New York: Jason Aronson.

Winnicott, D. W. 1947. "Hate in the Countertransference." In *Through Paediatrics to Psycho-Analysis*. New York: Basic Books, 1975.

———. 1963. *The Maturational Processes and the Facilitating Environment*. New York: International Universities Press, 1965.

———. 1964. "Psycho-Somatic Disorder." In *Psychoanalytic Explorations*, edited by Clare Winnicott, Ray Shepherd, and Madeline Davis. London: Karnac, 1989.

———. 1971a. *Playing and Reality*. London: Tavistock.

————. 1971b. *Therapeutic Consultations in Child Psychiatry*. New York: Basic Books.

Worthington, E. L. 2003. *Forgiving and Reconciling: Bridges to Wholeness and Hope*. Downers Grove, IL: InterVarsity Press.

Zornberg, A. G. 1996. *Genesis: The Beginning of Desire*. Philadelphia: The Jewish Publication Society.

————. 2001. *The Particulars of Rapture: Reflections on Exodus*. New York: Doubleday.

————. 2009. *The Murmuring: Deep Reflections on the Biblical Unconscious*. New York: Schocken Books.

Index

CPSIA information can be obtained at www.ICGtesting.com
Printed in the USA
BVOW08s0836170714

359476BV00007B/73/P